About the Author

Jane Gilmore is an author, feminist and ex-journalist from Melbourne, Australia. She has been studying and writing about the causes and effects of violence and poverty for almost two decades. In 2015, she created the Fixed It campaign to correct misleading and misogynist headlines about men's violence against women.

In 2025, Jane started a PhD at Monash University's Faculty of Education, in which she will be interviewing perpetrators of sexual violence to find out what they think about masculinity and shame and whether this knowledge could be used to make prevention education more effective.

Her previous books, *Fixed It: violence and the representation of women in the media* and *Fairy Tale Princesses Will Kill Your Children* are available direct from the author's website or from any book retailer.

Scan the QR code or go to www.JaneGilmore.com where you can sign up to Jane Gilmore's monthly e-newsletter and receive a 20% discount and free postage on any book purchase.

It Takes a Village to Teach Your Children About Consent

Jane Gilmore

www.JaneGilmore.com

I acknowledge that Aboriginal and Torres Strait Islander peoples are the Traditional Custodians and the first storytellers of the lands on which I live and work. I honour Aboriginal and Torres Strait Islander peoples' continuous connection to Country, waters, skies and communities. I celebrate Aboriginal and Torres Strait Islander stories, traditions and living cultures; and I pay my respects to Elders past and present.

Published by Jane Gilmore 2025

Copyright ©Jane Gilmore 2025

The moral rights of the author have been asserted.

All rights reserved. No part of this book may be reproduced or transmitted in any form or by any means, electronic or mechanical, including photocopying, recording or by any information storage and retrieval system, without prior permission in writing from the publisher. The Australian *Copyright Act 1968* (the Act) allows a maximum of one chapter or 10 per cent of this book, whichever is the greater, to be photocopied by any educational institution for its educational purposes provided that the educational institution (or body that administers it) has given a remuneration notice to the Copyright Agency (Australia) under the Act.

Cover design by Christa Moffitt of Christabell Designs

 A catalogue record for this book is available from the National Library of Australia

'If it takes a village to raise a child, it takes a village to abuse one.'
- Spotlight, *Open Road Films, 2015*

Content note: This book is about preventing child sexual abuse, sexual violence, and domestic and family violence. Much of the content is about those topics. While there are no graphic descriptions of violence in this book, readers should be aware that there are descriptions of grooming, discussions of child sexual abuse, sexual assault, image based abuse and sexual harassment. Please skip over or stop reading if anything causes you pain. Helplines are listed in Appendix 1 if you need to talk to someone and your GP can help with finding counselling if you need it. Genuine self-care is not always easy, but you deserve to be cared for when you are troubled or hurt.

Contents

Glossary	4
Children's stories and confidentiality	8
Introduction	10
Teaching the end of violence	20
The consent and respectful relationships curriculum	26
An imperfect system	30
Managing backlash from other parents	38
Protecting kids from sexual abuse	44
How to protect children from sexual harm	46
Responding to disclosures	65
Where to find help	68
Safety, secrets and emotional literacy	72
Creating a safe classroom	73
Recognising emotions	77
'Keep' secrets and 'tell' secrets	80
Helping children ask for help	83
Bodies, reproduction and sexuality	87
Naming body parts	88
Puberty	90
Sex and reproduction	92
Gender and sexuality	96
Gender myths	104
The opposite sex	107
Warrior kings and fairytale princesses	110
Shame and violence	118
How does shame lead to violence?	119
How to help your kids build self-worth	125

Why non-violent kids need to learn about violence	127
Respect in all relationships	132
Understanding consent	138
Defining Consent	143
Understanding choices	146
Understanding power	148
Recognising power imbalances	154
Consent and the law	155
Safety and consent online	162
Online communities: the good, the bad and the dangerously ugly	167
The rapid rise of technology facilitated abuse	171
CSAM and 'child porn'	179
AI and abuse in the virtual world	182
Consent and porn	195
Young children and exposure to porn	197
Porn and teens	200
How to talk to your kids about porn	202
The Manosphere	209
Understanding the manosphere	210
The rise and fall of Andrew Tate	218
The manosphere in our algorithms	222
How to raise our children to be safe adults	230
Afterword	232
Appendix 1: Helplines	234
Appendix 2: Data and statistics	242
Acknowledgements	246
Endnotes	248

Glossary

Child Sexual Abuse: Any act with a person under eighteen that exposes them to or involves them in sexual activity when they do not or cannot give consent.

Child sexual abuse may include (but is not limited to):

- Sexual touching of any part of the body, either clothed or unclothed
- Preparing, encouraging, persuading, coercing or forcing a child to engage in sexual activity, including viewing explicit content or watching other people engage in sexual activity.
- Any sexual acts done by an adult to or in front of a child.

Child Sexual Abuse Material (CSAM)/Child Sexual Exploitation Material (CSEM): Sometimes inaccurately labelled 'child porn' CSAM/CSEM is any content that depicts a person who is (or appears to be) under eighteen involved in any sexual activity or pose, or is in the presence of someone involved in any sexual activity or pose. It also includes any images or content of private body parts of a person who is or appears to be a child.

Deep fakes: A photo or video that has been manipulated with photo altering programs or apps to make it look like someone or something that it's not.

- **AI (Artificial Intelligence) Deep fakes:** colloquial expression to describe tools that can create fake images and videos of a person.

Doomscrolling: Spending a lot of time looking at your smart phone or device to skim through bad or negative content.

Family and domestic violence: Threatening, coercive, dominating, controlling or abusive behaviour towards a partner or family member.

- **Intimate partner violence** usually refers to this behaviour being perpetrated against a spouse, cohabiting partner, non-cohabiting partner, boyfriend, girlfriend or date.
- **Family violence** is a broader term that includes abuse by relatives, carers, people within a kinship group, or anyone else who has a family-like relationship with the victim.
- **Coercive control:** An ongoing and repeated pattern of behaviour used to control or dominate another person by humiliating, destabilising, undermining, intimidating, monitoring, and/or isolating them.
- **Financial abuse:** Withholding or controlling a person's access to money or ability to earn, save, manage or spend money.
- **Physical abuse:** Any behaviour that causes physical harm or injury to a victim or their pet.
- **Reproductive abuse:** Manipulating, coercing, forcing or tricking someone to use or not use birth control, become pregnant or terminate a pregnancy.
- **Sexual abuse:** Any form of abuse that involves sexual activity

Gaslighting: Psychological manipulation of a person, usually over an extended period, to make the victim question the validity of their own thoughts, judgement, independence, perception of reality, or memories. The term comes from the name of a 1938 play and 1944 film, *Gaslight*, in which a husband manipulates his wife into thinking she has a mental illness.

Gender-based violence: Any form of violence committed against or by someone because of their gender.

Image-based abuse: 'Non-consensual creation, distribution, and/or threats to distribute, nude or sexual images'.[1]

Manfluencer: A person (usually a man) with a strong online profile who targets content at men and can influence their ideas, thoughts, attitudes and purchasing choices.

Manosphere: A diverse collection of websites, blogs, and online forums promoting masculinity, misogyny, and opposition to feminism. While there are many subgroups and variations, many members of the manosphere self-identify into four main groups, although they can (and do) move around various groups over time.

- **Men's Rights Activists (MRAs)** tend to concentrate on what they believe are structural and legal issues that disadvantage men, such as domestic violence and rape law reform, child support regulation, family law, and mandatory reporting of gender pay gaps and gender balance in organisations and public structures such as parliaments and government agencies.

- **Involuntary Celibates (incels)** believe they are forced to be celibate because women refuse to allow small, weak or unattractive men to have sex. They are often bound up in rage, self-loathing and revenge fantasies.

- **Men Going Their Own Way (MGTOW)** believe women and feminism is so damaging to men that they cannot accept any relationships with women and girls. They therefore choose to remain celibate.

- **Pick-Up Artists (PUAs)** believe women are targets and acquisitions. They share tips on how to find women for sex (for example, negging, which is deliberately directing negative comments at a woman with the intention that she will have sex with the man putting her down to change his opinion of her).

Sexting: Sending sexual messages or texts with or without photos, video and/or audio. Sharing naked or semi-naked selfies is the most common form of sexting.

Sexual violence: Legal definitions for each of the following terms can differ across states and territories in Australia. The following explanations are therefore broad and not intended to apply to criminal cases.

- **Rape:** Non-consensual penetration of the mouth, vagina or anus by a penis, object, part of a body or mouth
- **Sexual assault:** An act of a sexual nature carried out against a person's will through physical force, intimidation or coercion, including any attempts to do this.
- **Sexual harassment:** unwelcome sexual behaviour that could make a person feel offended, humiliated or intimidated.
- **Stealthing:** deliberately removing a condom or lying about using a condom without the knowledge and consent of a sexual partner.

Technology facilitated abuse: 'A wide-ranging term that encompasses many subtypes of interpersonal violence and abuse using mobile, online and other digital technologies. These include harassing behaviours, sexual violence and image-based sexual abuse, monitoring and controlling behaviours, and emotional abuse and threats.'[2]

Children's stories and confidentiality

It's very rare that we get to hear children's stories in their own words. Not because no one cares about children – they do, deeply – but because the ethics of telling children's stories are so complicated.

Children, even teenagers on the edge of adulthood, cannot understand how having their stories published might affect their present or future. Books are around for a very long time and children cannot comprehend the effect being identified in a book like this might have on their adult lives. Keeping children's confidences is always crucial – even more so in matters of violence or abuse. Even if it's just sharing a passing conversation or an anecdote about one of their schoolmates, protecting children's privacy and safety is paramount.

Stories, though, are how we have learned to understand each other since prehistoric times. How do we understand the lives children and teens are living if we can't hear their stories?

We can make children's stories anonymous – up to a point. But there is a fine line between including enough truth to tell the real story and holding back anything that could identify someone. A step too far in either direction can have unpredictable consequences. It's hardly ever a risk worth taking, so children's stories are rarely told and too often children become forgotten and invisible victims and perpetrators in our understanding of violence and abuse.

This book is my answer to that dilemma. All the stories I've written are true, but none of them are fact.

I've taken threads, phrases, descriptions and observations from hundreds of interactions and woven them together to produce composites that cannot be recognised but are all real people in real moments.

If you think you recognise a person or an experience in this book, you are mistaken. Every story has been very carefully blended to make sure that no one could ever identify any child, teacher, parent or teen. Even if you saw me in your classroom and noticed me talking to a kid with red hair or the girl who was good at maths, that child's life is not a story in this book.

Adults are so terribly worried about children that we sometimes shield them (and ourselves) from knowledge that could help keep them safe. The very thought that children are being abused (or are abusers themselves) is so horrifying that we want to hide the fact that it could happen — that it is happening — behind a belief it could *never* happen. But the undeniable truth is that too many children know too much about violence, trauma, coercion, unbearable pressure and powerlessness — both as victims and perpetrators. Telling true stories that are not about real people is one way to face these frightening facts and find a way through to the other side, where we all know how to keep our children safe and we can teach them what they need to know to maintain that safety into adulthood.

Introduction

It takes a village...

I've been writing for publication for almost twenty years. And, while I have wandered in and out of other topics, my fascination with the intersection between gender, power, poverty and violence started very early and has never wavered. It has become the dominant feature of my professional life, tracing through my career as a journalist, an author, a researcher and an activist.

Some purists claim that no one can be both an activist and a journalist.[3] Journalism, they say, requires objectivity and verification, while activism is a single minded devotion to a cause. Journalists try to inform debate whereas activists want to influence it.[4] I agree with these statements, but I don't agree they are in conflict. Much of my writing could only be described as journalism and my aim has always been to influence debate about gender-based violence by sharing verified, objectively assessed information.

I've always believed that the best way to understand and verify information is to see it from the frontline, watching and working with the people who deal with violence every day. I've worked in domestic violence crisis services and prevention education classrooms. I've sat in courtrooms, police stations, refuges, rape crisis centres, psychologists' offices and school staffrooms to see how the people who work in those rooms use what they know about gendered violence to reduce its effect (or, sometimes, exacerbate its effect – the world is not a perfect place).

None of this makes me an expert on policing, psychology or teaching. But it has given me a wide perspective on gendered violence. I believe we know what we need to do to give support to people who have been victims of violence. Usually, when support services fail it's not because they didn't know what to do, it's because the people involved (police, teachers, courts, child protection etc.) chose to not do what they were supposed to do. Or the services are structurally underfunded and *cannot* do what they are supposed to do (rape and domestic violence services, child protection, housing, mental health services etc.).

What we don't really understand yet is how to prevent violence. We're still trying to understand what drives some men and boys to violence. We're also still trying to work out how we can get men and boys who are not violent to be part of the solution.

Education in schools seems the logical place to start. It's easier to teach young and flexible children new lessons than to get adults to unlearn the lessons of a lifetime. Schools, which are so often the centre of community for people with children, provide a pathway to reach entire families, not just a scattered few.

Violence prevention education is not just about respectful relationships and consent lessons. It also includes sex, sexuality, gender roles, critical thinking, media literacy, empathy, anti-bullying, and body safety. It's also about the whole community – from policy at the state and federal level, to standards of behaviour in each school, campus, classroom and schoolyard. In other words, it takes a village to raise a child who will be safe from experiencing or committing violence.

This book cannot answer every question about violence prevention education in Australia. Most importantly, I cannot tell you definitively whether it works or how well it works. Anyone who tells you they can answer those questions is lying. This education is too new, still too imperfect in its implementation to evaluate properly.

What I can do in this book is answer some of the most common questions about what kids learn in consent and respectful relationships classes and why those lessons might help prevent violence. The evidence says that there are some things that work well, some things that might help, and a few more things that probably won't do any harm.

Just over a third of this book is about the online world, which has grown at breathtaking speed and shot tentacles into almost every aspect of our kids' lives. No one knows exactly how much this is impacting their risk of enacting or experiencing violence, but I suspect that some parts of it are terribly dangerous, other parts are enormously helpful and the rest of it has little or no impact at all. I also know how difficult it is for some parents to tell the difference between the dangerous stuff and the helpful stuff – or even to know what content their kids are consuming. Hopefully, this book will make that a bit easier.

Many of the dangers are structural, in that they are built into the digital infrastructure of our lives and it's almost impossible to fully participate in modern life without them. Online identity, friends they never meet in the physical world and being constantly contactable can both harm and help kids, but learning to manage these issues are likely to be essential skills by the time they're adults.

As you'll read throughout this book, I believe very strongly that structural problems require structural responses. When governments and other public institutions push all the responsibility for keeping children safe back to individual parents, the result is a world that is inherently dangerous for our kids.

Fortunately, the state and federal governments around Australia have largely supported one of the most important structural protections for children and teens – prevention education delivered to every child every year through the education system. It's new, uneven, imperfect and, in large part, untested. But I believe it is a huge step forward in the structural changes we need to permanently reduce sexual abuse and violence.

Prevention through education

In October 1924, *The Age* newspaper published an article about sex education. The article praised the 'frank and sensible' advocacy of the National Council of Women of Australia, who were promoting sex education classes for parents so they could pass accurate and useful information on to their children. This common sense approach, the article said, would help children 'made awkward and morbidly curious with foolish mysteries' by giving them simple, practical information.[5]

Many people and organisations have continued that advocacy over the hundred years since that article was published. Basic education about human reproduction was introduced in most government schools in the middle of the 20th century, but it was limited to eggs, sperm and fertilisation, no intercourse or orgasm talk allowed. Masturbation was mentioned but only to nail it down as degenerate behaviour that needed a stern disciplinary cure. Babies magically appeared out of thin air because no teacher could say 'vagina' to school children in the 1950s.[6]

Contraception and the sexual revolution in the 1960s and 1970s tore apart the puritanism of the 1950s and education for children and teens kept expanding through to the early 2000s. Vaginas, oral sex, and orgasms (well... kind of... clitoral orgasms that are mostly for women's pleasure are still a challenging topic) made their way into the curriculum and are now covered in the health syllabus in government schools and most independent schools around Australia.

Education specifically to reduce or prevent sexual violence grew alongside sex education. Several programs in Victoria during the 1990s and early 2000s showed promise in improving understanding and attitudes to sexual violence, but most of them were delivered in schools by external organisations and depended on parents, school leadership and teachers not just acquiescing but enthusiastically supporting (and paying for) the programs.[7] This could only happen *if* school leaders understood the importance of violence prevention education and *if* they had the support of the teachers and parents and *if* they have the courage to overcome any backlash and *if* there were any expert organisations available in their area that could deliver the programs and *if* the school have the budget to pay for it. That's a whole lot of ifs. Many of them insurmountable for schools with high proportions of children from families living in poverty and violence.

Imperfect and patchy as they were, however, those programs laid the foundation for the first mandatory consent and respectful relationships education program developed for the Victorian state curriculum which were implemented across the state in 2016.[8] [9]

Moving violence and abuse prevention education away from outside organisations and into the mandatory curriculum was a huge step in making the kind of structural change we need to reduce structural violence. With prevention education in the state and federal curriculum it's no longer dependent on luck, money or the presence of deeply engaged individual teachers or principals. As of 2024, all schools will have to at least make an attempt to deliver prevention education to all their students.

There are, of course, problems with forcing this education into structures that were not designed to hold it. There wasn't really a natural fit in the curriculum, so a somewhat awkward hole was made in the physical education syllabus, expanding it to include 'health' topics such as sex, violence prevention and child abuse prevention, along with mental health protections, online safety and substance abuse education.

In the same way that maths or English teachers typically study maths or English at university along with their bachelor or post grad certification in education, physical education teachers study sports science, biomechanics, motor learning, health and nutrition. They do not study most of the complex issues about power, violence and gender in the consent and respectful relationships curriculum. This is a huge problem for the teachers now responsible for these subjects. Even if they have the best of intentions, they do not always have the expertise to recognise the subtle interactions of gender roles playing out in their classrooms. They may not have the skills to untangle the myths about gender, sex, power and relationships that teens can breathe in from their online and physical worlds and exhale into a consent class. Many teachers may not even recognise their own susceptibility to the gender myths they've been inculcated with through a lifetime of playing gendered sport and just being a person in the world.

In Victoria, health and physical education teachers have had some help from the state education department but anecdotal evidence says that even after all this time, some teachers still finding parts of the curriculum intimidating, difficult and uncomfortable.[10] It's not a failing in the teachers, it's just a natural consequence of creating such a huge change in a very short time. No one can wave a magic wand and have a national cohort of trained and experienced experts ready to teach an entirely new and emotionally complex curriculum to a generation of kids still reeling from the effects of Covid lock-downs.

Hopefully, the education system will adjust so well to the new curriculum content that schools will be viewed as the natural place to start preventing violence in the same way we now think of them as the natural place to prevent illiteracy. By the time that happens, violence prevention will be its own area of expertise and the people who teach it will be as common in schools as maths and science teachers. They may not be the same people who teach kids how to play netball and manage their sleep and nutrition, but they will have the subject expertise we would expect in any specialist teacher. It may take years for the education system to reach that point, but I think it's the inevitable outcome of the progress we've made in violence prevention education over the last 50 years.

In the meantime, teachers, parents, families and communities will have to keep finding their own ways to learn the skills they need to keep kids safe. That will get easier as we continue to build and strengthen the state and federal curriculum, academic research and institutions such as the eSafety commissioner, the Children's Commissioner, the Australian Institutes of Family Affairs and Health and Welfare. All these organisations work extremely well together and separately to provide hugely useful information in formats that are easy to understand and share.

In 2012, then Prime Minister Julia Gillard initiated the Royal Commission into Institutional Responses to Child Sexual Abuse, which handed down its final report in 2017. This followed years of activism by journalists and people who had been abused by priests and teachers. It was the first time Australia had applied a national spotlight to the institutions that provided systemic protection for the men (and a few women) who sexually abused children.

The Royal Commission proved that those men were not just a problem of few bad apples.

People who want to hurt children need structural support. They need systems that isolate vulnerable children by removing them from their communities and putting them in institutions such as churches, orphanages, out-of-home care and juvenile detention facilities. The public need to believe that abused and marginalised children are delinquents in need of discipline, born 'bad' and destined for trouble. Large and powerful organisations (such as the Catholic Church or the private companies that manage children's prisons) need to know they have assistance protecting secrets so they don't lose money, power and status. Parents and children need to be ignorant about what child abuse looks like. They must be conditioned to believe that the acts of abuse are minimal, unimportant and, at least partly, instigated by the child. They cannot know the abuse is widespread and protected. They must also believe they are powerless to act and that no one will help them, that instead they will be blamed, vilified and punished if they speak up.

All the people who contribute to building and maintaining those structures are participating in the abuse. There are no clean hands.

Equally, all the people who participate in destroying those structures are preventing abuse, even if they never (knowingly) speak to a victim or a perpetrator. Everyone in the village raising a child must be part of preventing harm to that child, which means everyone needs the skills and knowledge that makes them invulnerable to structural gaslighting.

The village that abuses a child can be destroyed by something like the 2013 Royal Commission or the Spotlight investigation that revealed the Catholic Church's cover up of the hundreds of paedophile priests in Boston.[11] They changed the structures that enabled institutions to turn responsibility for the abuse back onto the children and families targeted by abusers.

The 2013 Royal Commission made hundreds of recommendations on how to prevent and respond to child sexual abuse. Almost all of them were about altering existing structures or creating new ones that would prevent institutions covering up systemic abuse of children.

This resulted in the creation of the Child Safe Standards, the National Office for Child Safety, and strengthened mandatory reporting requirements, among many other measures.

The Commissioners also recommended that prevention education be embedded in the early childhood, primary and secondary school curriculum. They were also very clear that parents, families and communities needed to be part of that education so they could learn how to prevent, recognise and respond to anyone sexually abusing a child.

Almost all the recommendations from the Royal Commissions have been implemented now, and while they don't apply to families or private homes (where most sexual abuse occurs), the changes in schools and other institutions because of the Royal Commission make systemic cover up of sexual abuse all but impossible. The recent Australian Childhood Maltreatment study suggests all this work was fundamental to a significant reduction in child sexual abuse facilitated by institutions. Accountability, as it turns out, is fundamental to prevention.

Systems that work to protect men who sexually abused children did not stop at the church gates. The Royal Commission heard how abusers and their enablers were protected by police who refused to investigate, politicians who reinforced perpetrators and accomplices' veneer of moral rectitude, journalists who refused to report abuses and lawyers who silenced victims and protected paedophiles. The beliefs that for so long enabled those protections are also woven into the structures that ignore, dismiss and sneer at adult women, men and non-binary people who were (and are) subjected to sexual violence by men who know they will never be held accountable. Less than 2 per cent of men who commit sexual violence against adults are currently held accountable by the criminal system (see Appendix 2). The myths that make this possible are remarkably similar to the myths that enabled paedophile priests, which I'll explore in much more detail in Chapter 2. For now, it's enough to make the connection between the structures that support men who sexually abuse children and the ones that support men who sexually abuse adults. They all rest on beliefs about gender, sex and rape. *Men can't control their need for sex. Reputations of good men and public institutions are more important than the hysterical lies of delinquent children and vengeful women. Only monsters commit these crimes so anyone who accuses a good man must be a liar.*

As long as those myths have any traction in public consciousness, we will never stop the increasing rates of sexual violence that do so much harm. We are all part of the village raising children and one of the ways we can contribute to keeping them safe is to increase the entire village's knowledge and skills about how to prevent sexual violence. This book is my small contribution to that effort. I hope you find it helpful.

1

Teaching the end of violence

Many people may not make the immediate connection between sex education and consent education. It can be complex, but in the simplest terms, kids need to understand what sex is if they're going to learn how to give, receive and ask for consent.

When I was a child our local primary school taught kids up to Year 8. Many primary schools did back then. I think it was because the selective entry high schools often started in Year 9 and lots of parents wanted their kids to have the opportunity to get into those elite (but free) schools.

Undiagnosed dyslexia meant I was never going to get into the selective entry schools, so my mother sent me to a Catholic girl's school, because, she said, it had lovely gardens, nice teachers and the girls (mostly) did their shrieking and swearing out of the public eye.

In primary school I think we did some very basic lessons on reproduction. Our teacher read us some of the Peter Mayle book, *Where did I Come From?* which was first published in 1973. I'm pretty sure she skipped over the parts that describe (in a delightfully age appropriate way) orgasm and sexual pleasure because I remember being very surprised to find them there when I revisited the book a few years later. But I learned about periods, orgasms and contraception from my friends, one of whom was convinced that she couldn't get pregnant if she smoked menthol cigarettes. The 1980s were a magical time.

Sex education was mandatory by the time I went to high school. The biology teacher was the only man in our entire school and it was his job to explain sex and reproduction to the Year 9 girls. Although he just seemed like another boring adult to us at the time, he was probably only in his twenties and was desperately embarrassed. Fourteen and fifteens-year-olds can be *awful*, particularly when they sense weakness. We put so much effort into making him stutter and blush that we didn't really learn anything – which might have contributed to my menthol-smoking friend's unplanned teen pregnancy.

The closest we got to violence prevention education was one of the last remaining teaching nuns exhorting us to keep our skirts long, our knees together, our voices low and our opinions to ourselves. A slovenly appearance (socks falling down, sleeves rolled up, tie and hair askew) she told us in doom-laden tones, would give the impression of 'easy virtue' and boys would not hesitate to 'take advantage'. Despite her antiquated ideas, she was a very kind woman, so when we laughed at her warnings, we didn't do it with contempt.

From there to university and hospitality work, where barmaids who couldn't fend off groping customers were 'simply not cut out' for that kind of work.

It's astounding how much had changed by the time my daughter went to school, where she received detailed lessons about what to expect in puberty before she finished primary school and even more detailed lessons about contraception and reproduction in secondary school (not Catholic). She also had teachers and guest speakers talk to her and her classmates about bullying, sexual harassment, sexual violence, drugs, alcohol, consent and what we now call image-based abuse. She and her friends debated the relative merits of contraceptive pills, implants and IUDs. None of them relied on menthol cigarettes – none of them smoked cigarettes at all, although quite a few of them used vapes.

In the couple of years since she left school, education designed to prevent violence has become even more detailed and firmly embedded in school life.

Change has been rapid, intense and difficult to track, but one thing we know for sure is that no matter how young or old you were when you first had children, the education they will get on sex, violence and consent is *nothing* like what you had when you were at school.

Structural prevention of violence

This book is not going to be all dry information and lists, but a few details (yes, OK, it's dry) about the structures Australia now has to understand, prevent and respond to violence will help the rest of the book make sense. I'll get through it as quickly as possible.

One of the greatest structural advantages Australia has in the fight against gender-based violence is the National Plan to End Violence Against Women and Children. It was initiated by the Gillard government in 2010 and updated under Anthony Albanese in 2022. The plan is not perfect. The implementation is patchy, some of its adherents are deeply resistant to review or change and all of it is shockingly underfunded. None of this diminishes the power of a national, government-endorsed roadmap to a safer and less violent society. It gives public and institutional response some level of accountability and measurement, as well as helping to keep everyone working towards the same goal.

People in what we call 'the sector' (anyone working to reduce the causes and effects of gender-based violence) often get caught up in passionate arguments about the National Plan. We defend some parts and decry others. All of us need more time, more people, more expertise, more research, and most of all, more money. Crucially, we need much more support to work with all the worried parents and adults in children's villages to make sure they have the knowledge and support they need. There are many ways to do this and we don't all agree on the best way. But even when it might look and feel like these disagreements are just destructive infighting, I believe they are a necessary part of making sure the National Plan is working. Having these arguments is how we know we're not getting complacent or lazy in the way we think about preventing violence.

The National Plan broadly separates activities to end violence into four domains:

- **Prevention:** stopping violence before it starts.
- **Early Intervention:** stopping violence escalating and preventing it recurring
- **Response:** efforts and programs used to address existing violence
- **Recovery and Healing:** helping to break the cycle of violence and reduce the risk of re-traumatisation

Prevention (also known as primary prevention). Most of the education programs discussed in this book would be labelled prevention, because they are designed to give people the knowledge and skills to help prevent children becoming victims or perpetrators of violence. Part of this is aimed at attitudes (instilling values of respect for self and others, based on empathy and inclusion) and part of it is aimed at behaviour (teaching adults the behavioural tools they need to protect children from violence and model respectful and consensual interactions so children and teens learn to replicate the safe behaviours and reject the unsafe ones).

Prevention takes a whole of community approach, meaning that everyone needs to understand the signs, causes and effects of violence.

Every sports coach, faith leader, music teacher, game designer, police officer and politician in a community needs to know how to recognise the lead up to violent behaviour and how to help someone who might be at risk of being violent or having someone else be violent to them.[12] In other words, it takes a village to teach consent.

Prevention education also includes aspects of attitudinal inoculation, which is about making sure children are prepared and therefore less susceptible to misinformation and disinformation. For example, explaining the profit motives and deceptions in misogynistic online content so children are less likely to be taken in by grifters and algorithms (covered in detail in Chapter 11).

Outside prevention, these education programs also lay the groundwork for more effective early intervention, response and recovery programs.

Early Intervention (also known as secondary prevention) in an education setting, this involves recognising early signs that a child might be at risk of or is already engaging in violent behaviour or is being subjected to violent behaviour by peers. Addressing this is usually done in targeted, in-depth programs for small groups, covering topics from the prevention programs that are directly relevant to their behaviour. For example, girls who talk about hating their bodies or being afraid to eat in case they put on weight can be directed to eating-disorder prevention programs. Children who struggle with assertiveness and might therefore be vulnerable to manipulation or coercion can be helped with targeted work on resilience and boldness. Boys who believe they should hide fear, anxiety or empathy behind a 'tough guy' veneer can be taught to be proud of the courage it takes to reveal their vulnerabilities and strengths. Children of any age who display problematic sexual or violent behaviours are often identified in primary prevention work and, where possible, can be moved into targeted intervention programs designed to teach them safer ways to respond to fear, shame, lack of self-worth, or rejection.

Response is usually centred on frontline organisations such as domestic violence or sexual crisis response services, helplines, police, courts, housing services, emergency medical care, men's behaviour change programs, family law services, and community legal services. A lot of the work involved in frontline response starts with unpicking myths about gender-based violence, such as minimising the abuse ('he didn't really mean it'), mistrust of women ('she's lying to get back at him'), victim blaming attitudes ('she was asking for it' or 'she drove him to it'), or gender myths ('real men always want sex'). People of all genders can be susceptible to these myths and sometimes even believe them without knowing it. Frontline response is much faster and more effective if juries, workers, witnesses, victims and perpetrators understand the facts that refute these myths and don't expect police and courts to support them.

Recovery and healing work is also more effective when people who have been abused can believe the abuse was not their fault. Understanding this is how they free themselves of the shame taken on by so many people who have been hurt by shamelessly violent men. If they grow up with these concepts and understand them from childhood, it is much easier for recovery support to help them make the connection between the theory of holding perpetrators accountable and their own feelings about the abuse they've suffered.

Breaking something down into manageable pieces is a logical and effective way to approach any huge problem. The danger, however, is that problems and solutions become siloed rather than being designed (and funded) to work cohesively together.

As you can see, these four domains are all connected and each of them is easier and more effective if all of them are done properly. Prevention is about laying the groundwork for and identifying the people who need early intervention, which in turn is often dealing with people who have not recovered from the abuse they've been subjected to, usually by violent, angry or predatory men. Crisis response is the ideal time to start prevention, intervention and recovery with adults and children who need immediate help to deal with the violent person in their life. Recovery and healing are faster and much more effective when comprehensive prevention work has already undermined abusers' attempts to blame and shame their victims. Schools, where children and teens are soaking up new concepts and ideas, can be the perfect places for this education to start. Parents and families are the ones who will help kids learn to ask questions, embed ideas into behaviour and understand how this is part of their values and beliefs about themselves.

This book is (mostly) about primary prevention education, so while I'm doling out all the dry background information, it's helpful to understand how the curriculum is structured.

The consent and respectful relationships curriculum

The Australian national curriculum is set by the federal department of education and provides an overview of the topics each subject must cover. Each state and territory also has its own curriculum, which lays out the detailed syllabus designed to achieve the goals of the national curriculum. The state curriculum includes classroom material and resources for teachers to use in the lesson plans. While all students at a particular year level need to reach a minimum standard, teachers are expected to use or create resources that will work best for the individual needs of their students.

The national curriculum for consent and respectful relationships doesn't have enough detail to be useful in a book like this, and it would be far too confusing and messy to try to explain the nuances and variations of every state program. I've based the book on the Victorian curriculum. Partly because it's the one I know best and also because Victoria was the first state to develop its own consent and respectful relationships education program. While there was a long slow movement towards this development well before the 2010s, the Royal Commission into Family Violence, which handed down its report in 2016, gave the movement strength and impetus by recommending that the 'Victorian Government mandate the introduction of respectful relationships education into every government school in Victoria from prep to year 12'.[13]

The main resources for violence prevention education in Victoria are the 'Resilience, Rights and Respectful Relationships: teaching for social and emotional learning curriculum' documents (RRRR resources). They lay out a detailed syllabus and classroom activities to help kids understand themselves and each other, covering every year from Foundation to Year 12. The latest version was updated in 2024 and is based on recent and very robust evidence.

The RRRR resources separate learning into eight broad categories:
- Topic 1 Emotional literacy: learning how to recognise understand, manage and respond to a range of emotions.
- Topic 2 Personal and cultural strengths: understanding and valuing strength in self and others.
- Topic 3 Positive coping: resilience, self-worth and recovery skills.
- Topic 4 Problem solving: assertiveness, critical thinking and strategic decision making.
- Topic 5 Stress management: learning how to cope positively with difficult situations or people.
- Topic 6 Help seeking: learning when, where and how to ask for help on various issues.

- Topic 7 Gender norms and stereotypes.
- Topic 8 Positive gender relations.

Topics 1 through 5 rarely present significant challenges for most teachers. They start with games and basic lessons in primary school, where they are taught by the classroom teacher and work up to more complex lessons and classroom discussions in secondary school in the health and physical exercise subject. Each topic develops skills to help children understand their emotional and physiological responses to various situations and build empathy for the way other people feel and act. These skills might help reduce the risk they will one day be the victim or perpetrator of violence, but even if that were never going to happen, they're still very useful life skills for any child to learn.

Most of this book, however, will concentrate on Topics 6, 7 and 8. These are the ones that teachers sometimes find more difficult to teach and where backlash from angry students and fearful parents can cause significant disruption (which I will come back to in a moment).

The Victorian Education Department is aware of the challenges posed by these topics and has provided additional resources to help with lesson plans and classroom activities. 'Catching on Early' is the primary school resource for sexuality lessons that cover sex, reproduction, consent and puberty. 'Catching on Later' expands on those lessons for secondary school kids. The 'Catching On' resources were written in 2011 and 2013 respectively. Updates are in the works but as of the middle of 2025, are still waiting on approval from the Department of Education before they can be released to teachers. Teachers who want to cover more challenging topics related to gender based violence also have access to 'Building Respectful Relationships: Stepping out against gender-based violence', which was published in 2018.[14] It provides lesson ideas and activities to help middle and senior secondary school students understand how power and gender interact in violent behaviour.

Victoria may have had a head start on the other states in developing and implementing education, but, as you can tell, it's still a bit fragmented and struggling to stay up to date.

Despite prevention education being concentrated on children and teens, the intent is not (or at least should not) be to teach children to protect themselves from adult abuse and violence. Children can't do this, no matter how much they've been taught. They're too small and too dependent on adults to be able to defend themselves from someone who has so much power over them and means them harm.[15]

Education for children, particularly little children, is about teaching them to recognise the signs that someone is hurting them and making sure they know where and how to ask for help. It's also designed to teach them to understand the use and abuse of power and show them that gender should never confine anyone to a rigid narrow expectation of the life they can have or the future they might want.

As they get older, they can learn how to manage conflict and even dangerous interactions with people their own age but even older teens still don't have the capacity to manage really frightening problems alone. When prevention education is done properly, the safe adults in a child's life are the ones who learn how to protect children from abuse and from the beliefs and behaviour that create and endorse violence.

To do this, every adult in a child's village needs to learn to recognise signs a child is being abused. They need to understand the grooming process and how predators manipulate children into believing they are not only to blame for the abuse, but that they wanted it and love the person abusing them *because* of the abuse, not in spite of it. Adults also need to know how their ideas about gender can connect to fear and shame and they need to be able to see the connecting line between shame and violence (see Chapter 6). They need to have the skills and support to overcome their own lifetime of lessons on shame and gender so they can show kids what it looks like to have the robust sense of self-worth that never needs to control or abuse others.

Safe adults need to know how to hear a disclosure, how to respond, where to get help, how to spot trauma responses in children and teens, what to do when they're acting out and how to support kids who have been abused as they recover.

When adults are given these tools and children know how to speak up, what to say and who to say it to, the whole community prevents people who want to abuse others from accessing the structural support they need to perpetuate their crimes. All of which is just another way of repeating the old African proverb that it takes a village to raise a child.

An imperfect system

The Victorian Resilience, Rights and Respectful Relationship curriculum and the 'Catching On' resources are, of course, far more detailed than my outlines in this book. They include lots of games and exercises, details on research and underlying theories, as well as outlines for some of the simpler topics that I have not covered.

The curriculum – and my explanation of it – are the ideal. The teachers I was fortunate enough to watch and interview were all willing to be involved in this book because they care deeply for their students and worry about children, parents and families trying to manage so many complications with so little support. All the teachers I talked to regularly give far more time, energy, money and devotion to their classes than they can sustain in the long term. As one of them told me, 'The only future I can see is to either burn out or stop caring and I cannot decide which one would be worse.'

They know, I know, you know, and your children know that some teachers still working in schools have already made that choice. Or they simply never cared enough to have to face it. Those teachers work with the curriculum, but they skim over the difficult topics and skim past challenging behaviour. They are not teaching the lessons I've outlined in this book. There are schools where toxic behaviour is so normalised that the lessons on consent and respect are perceived as oppression. And others where one or two people in leadership positions impose such a lack of respect on their staff that they cannot effectively teach children how to respect each other.[16]

Research shows that schools are often so hidebound by outdated notions (boys will be boys, girls should be 'nice' and keep quiet, 'real violence' isn't happening in our school) that not only do they refuse to acknowledge the violence being committed by and against their students, they actively create and then ignore the systems that encourage boys to believe they are entitled to use violence against women and girls.[17]

As much as we want to believe schools are safe havens for children, we need to remember that the Australian school system is a descendent of 19th century English schooling. That system was purposefully designed to segregate students by class, gender and religion – it was supposed to reinforce not reduce those differences.[18]

We're retrofitting a patriarchal class-based system to deliver prevention education, that depends on understanding power imbalances created by gender, race and wealth (among other things). It's akin to trying to repurpose a coal-fired power station into a renewable energy resource while it's still operating and employing all the workers hired and trained under the coal-fired approach.

Despite this, I've written this book to describe what your children would learn in the best of circumstances, not the worst. Sometimes this approach might seem absurdly Pollyannaish. I understand anyone who has that reaction but I'm writing this for people – like you – who are so engaged in your children's education that you have the interest and capacity to read a book like this. You are part of the collective movement towards ensuring all schools have the resources and support to deliver this education effectively, and you are the reason I can take an aspirational approach to this topic.

Resistance to sex, consent, and prevention education, however, existed long before it was mandated in schools. One of the favourite arguments of conservatives and nay-sayers is that parents should be the ones to teach their children about these topics, not teachers.[19]

The argument both creates and plays on parents' fears about malignant outside influences taking advantage of their children's innocence to drag them into a dangerously sexual ideology. It has, however, no basis in fact. All the people who have done decades of work on the curriculum were very focused on making sure the lessons are safe and useful for each age group. There is nothing dangerous in the curriculum but there is absolutely danger in depriving children of vital information when they need it.[20]

Most parents want their children's schools and teachers involved in giving kids information on sex and relationships. Even parents who are comfortable talking to their kids about sex, masturbation and porn still support formal education on these topics. Very few of us have time to become experts in sex education, sexuality development, gender stereotypes, consent, respectful relationships, the cause and effects of violence, profit-motive influences on online content and pornography, shame, self-worth, identity, power imbalances, bystander behaviour and the warning signs of harmful relationships.

It would be as unfair to expect this expertise in parents as it would to expect expertise in trigonometry, physics and ancient history. That's why we send our kids to school – so they can learn from teachers who are experts in their subject matter and in how to help young minds absorb that knowledge.

We also need to teach kids the topics that can help them grow up to reject violence because, sadly, there are some parents who are dangerous to their partners and children. Sometimes these parents are directly abusing the children themselves or they're being violent to the child's other parent (which is also child abuse and happens to around 40 per cent of Australians).[21]

Many children of abusive parents will learn to reject any form of violence and aggression and decide (successfully) that they will never replicate their parent's destructive behaviour. Others, however, learn to emulate toxic beliefs and actions. Some of them will one day become violent partners and parents themselves. Those children go to school like everyone else. They interact with their classmates and teachers. They sit in classrooms, share their thoughts and opinions. They hurt themselves and the people around them. Sometimes they find the support they need (and often want) to unlearn the lessons they were taught at home. Sometimes they don't. But their beliefs and behaviours do not occur in an isolated world sealed off from the rest of us. They're part of our lives and our children's lives.

Prevention education may not reach all those troubled children, but it does help the children around them understand the context and reject the behaviour they see in some of their classmates. And even if our own kids are not the ones who have problematic attitudes or behaviour, they are almost certainly sharing a classroom with someone who does.

Since 2009, the National Community Attitudes Survey has been measuring Australian's attitudes to violence, gender and relationships. It's a robust, world-leading study that in 2021 surveyed just under 20,000 people. The results are mostly encouraging. The majority of Australians say they have good knowledge of gender-based violence and positive attitudes to women and safe relationships. There is, however, a significant minority of boys and young men (25 to 30 per cent) who hold attitudes and beliefs that support or even encourage violence.[22]

This means that in a standard co-ed classroom of 26 kids, three of four boys will have some really awful attitudes to women and violence (assume half the 26 kids are boys = 13 boys in total, 13 x 0.25 = 3.25). Most of the time they don't try to hide it, in fact, they're often proud of it. They perform aggressively for each other, displaying contempt and even threats for the perceived enemy – girls and women. But these are not adult men, they're children. They don't know anything about adult relationships with women. I remember watching one rather sweet freckly little twelve-year-old loudly proclaiming that women are all gold diggers and men need to be 'stern' to protect themselves. This was not an idea he'd come up with on his own. He'd never even been on a date. And it's not like there are hordes of twelve-year-old girls roaming the playground scheming to do him out of his pocket money.

When the teacher asked Freckly Boy to explain what he meant by 'gold digger', he said that most women just marry men for their money. Then she asked if that's why his mum married his dad. He was outraged. 'Don't you say things like that about my mum,' he said. 'She's a nurse. She got *heaps* of money!'

When he talked about his parents, who he clearly adored, he described a loving mother and father who were both deeply involved in their son's life and were doing everything to raise him to be a kind, thoughtful, hard-working man. He said his dad 'really loves' his mum and 'even when they have a fight, he's never scary or mean'. His fear of gold diggers didn't come from his home life. At a guess I would say that he may have heard the idea from online sources, from one of his friends or, more likely, a combination of the two.

Freckly Boy at twelve years old was not dangerous. His proclaimed ideas about women might make the classroom a bit tense but he was clearly not violent. If, however, the source of his fears about women becomes a pervasive influence in his life, he could become dangerous later. It's an easy fix when he's twelve, but changing those attitudes (and the behaviour they can create) is much more difficult if they persist into adulthood.

If his teacher and parents haven't had access to any information about how these ideas about women are pushed onto young boys and how to disrupt them, the next step can start a domino effect of misunderstandings.

If Freckly Boy's teacher, as she should, takes this problem to his parents – the lovely nurse and a father who sounded like Bluey's dad – they need to believe her. But their sweet freckly boy does not behave at home the way he behaves in the classroom. He doesn't have any of his mates to perform for and he loves his mum, so he's never even slightly aggressive or contemptuous of her. Of course, his parents think the teacher must be wrong about his behaviour at school – or worse, she's lying. And then things can really start to fall apart. If this situation keeps spiralling out of control, Lovely Nurse and Bluey's Dad stop trusting the teacher because she says things about their son that couldn't possibly be true. The teacher stops trusting the parents because when she tries to tell them her concerns about their son, they just get angry with her. Lovely Nurse and Bluey's Dad are upset and confused, so they talk to their friends and family about what the teacher said and, inevitably, someone will tell them it's just woke feminists trying to make out that all men are evil. Sweet little Freckly Boy overhears this conversation and it confirms everything the pernicious outside influence tells him about women. So he returns to that influence, eager to hear more.

If that pattern continues uninterrupted, by the time he's fourteen, he and his mates are saying things to their female teachers that would be sexual harassment if it were said by adults. By sixteen he's starting to treat girls he's dating with contempt, by twenty he's beginning to show signs of controlling and abusive behaviour and by twenty-five, that sweet little boy has become at real risk of turning into a dangerous man who believes he needs to be aggressively powerful and in control of every woman in every relationship he ever has for the rest of his life.

If that happened, there's no doubt that someone would say it was because his parents or teachers failed him. But the failure was not in any individual people. It was structural.

The strongest, most motivated and effective violence prevention workforce in the country is parents, teachers, and families – the key people in the villages raising our children. But every workforce needs knowledge, skills and training to do its job well.

Lovely Nurse and Bluey's Dad needed help to understand the online world their son lives in, and why his behaviour at school might be different to what they see at home. How are they supposed to find that information if they don't even know that they don't know it?

The teacher needed support from her school's leaders to deal with Freckly Boy's behaviour in the classroom and to talk to his parents. That takes training, time, practice and expert guidance. Accessing such things is difficult because there just are not enough people who have that expertise and there is no funding to pay for the few who do exist. These are all structural barriers – and they exist for Lovely Nurse and Bluey's Dad, a household that sounded so wholesome I'd expect it to spontaneously spawn golden retriever puppies in the backyard.

What if that family, instead of their comfortable happy existence, is living in poverty, where every day is a struggle to find enough food and pay the rent – I've lived that. It's all-consuming. In poverty, that family has no time or space to fix a problem they don't know exists, and little capacity to access protection and help even if they did know.

What if someone in the family has a disability? Or they don't speak English very well? What if one of them has a mental illness or substance-abuse issue? What if dad isn't Bluey's Dad, instead he's violent and controlling and Lovely Nurse knows that if she tries to get help for her son, not only will she be punished but so will her little boy? She'll protect him by keeping him away from that help. If she knows that leaving her abusive partner means she and her son will be sleeping in a car, she might well believe that he's safer where he has food and shelter and can go to school. If they were a First Nations family, even without any of those other barriers, the overwhelming one is knowing that asking for help carries a risk of someone turning up to say, 'oh, are you not looking after your children properly, we'd better take them away from you'.

Those barriers are structural and sometimes insurmountable, but they're the ones I think of when I hear people talking about problematic boys or violent men and asking, 'Why didn't his parents do something?'

There are two ways to address those structural problems. The first is to help parents find the knowledge and skills they need (for example, by writing a book about helping children understand violence and abuse). The second is to advocate for more public investment in prevention. It won't come cheaply, but that doesn't mean it's an expense. Ten years ago, KPMG estimated the national cost of men's violence against women and children was about $22 billion *each year*.[23] If we took even half of what it was back then and invested it into upskilling all the prevention workforces in the villages raising our children, we would make a huge difference in children's lives and futures.

Governments rarely lead change, but they almost always follow it. In the 2023/24 budget the federal government made a small investment in consent and respectful relationships education ($77.8M[24] over four years across roughly 9600 schools[25] or about $2000 per school per year). Ask your child's school how much of that money they will get and whether it will be enough to give the teachers the training and support they need to deliver violence prevention education properly. I doubt you'll be surprised by the answer.

You, the parents and families of children who will get this education, have a great deal of power to push for change. Writing to your local MP and the relevant state and federal ministers can be surprisingly effective, particularly if you organise other parents in your network to do the same. Time is always a problem for parents, so it's totally fine to have one message and the email address that all the parents at your local school can copy and paste. It's the collective effort that matters as much, maybe even more than the content.

Consent advocate Chanel Contos made a huge impact with an Instagram poll and a single petition in 2021, which contributed so much support to the national demand for mandated consent education that the Morrison government agreed to put it on the National Curriculum. This wasn't the start of the work to get comprehensive violence prevention education delivered to every child in Australia and it's by no means the end of it either. There is more work to be done, and it involves people like you, who care enough about these issues to read this book (thank you!). Your advocacy can be part of the change we need for all our children.

Managing backlash from other parents

Most parents are like you. They want their children to have all the knowledge and support they need to be safe, and they know this includes giving children trustworthy information about sex, sexuality, consent and respect. Parents want information too, to help them understand all the people and pressures that influence their children and how they can help put those influences in context. Research in 2022 found that 90 per cent of parents in Australia support school-based sex, consent and respectful relationships education because they trust teachers and schools to give their children the information they need.[26]

Unfortunately, there is a small but vocal minority of parents who are afraid of these lessons, which can lead them to enraged protests and disproportionate power over how (or even if) schools deliver comprehensive consent and respectful relationships education. Independent schools, who must treat their parent community as clients rather than service recipients, can have great difficulty resisting persistent or vocal backlash. Regardless of where they get their funding however, all schools find it difficult, if not impossible, to ignore angry parents who believe their children (or other people's children) are being harmed at school.

This backlash is often sparked or exacerbated by deliberate online misinformation campaigns designed to whip up fear and anger for profit and political gain (more on that in a moment). This can be challenging and upsetting for parents who want their children to learn the skills that can help them stay safe, so it's worth taking some time to consider why this backlash occurs and how to manage an effective response.

Broadly, backlash is based on one or more of the following fears:[27]
- The class will portray all boys and men as rapists and wife beaters or teach boys to hate themselves and their gender.
- The educator will teach children to be gay or convince perfectly contented cisgender children to 'surgically mutilate' themselves.

- Teachers and class resources will provide graphic details of sex and violence, which will 'destroy children's innocence', encourage very young children to have sex or anticipate sexual violence.

Backlash often starts with one parent who doesn't understand the program and is furious that their child is being 'forced' to participate in 'dangerous' education. They're angry, but mostly they are frightened for their child, which makes it difficult for them to listen to anyone who tells them there is nothing to fear from consent education. Parents in this state have an alarming habit of whipping up fear in other parents or even sending their complaints to eagerly receptive tabloid news outlets. Schools are risk averse and often find it safer and easier to cancel or amend violence prevention lessons than to stare down outraged parents or a sensationalised tabloid hit piece.

A common source of this misinformation (apart from deliberately deceptive online disinformation) is confusing the lessons designed for junior primary school with the lessons for senior secondary students. This is often exacerbated when people assume that consent education is always about sex – they see the curriculum for consent starting in the first year of primary school and think their six-year-old is being taught how to say yes or no to sexual intercourse.[28]

Chapter 8 contains much more detail about what children are taught about consent at various ages, but to be clear, consent education in primary school is about hugs and sharing toys. The curriculum and supporting resources all provide tips for teachers on how to quickly answer or turn aside questions that might be sexually explicit.[29] Anyone who works with young children should immediately recognise children showing familiarity with sexual acts as a warning sign for abuse (see Chapter 2).

Right wing ideologues have a long history of weaponising parents' fears of sexual harm being done to their children. They portray 'lefty governments', 'progressives' and the 'woke agenda' as dangerous enemies and 'sensible' conservatives as the natural protectors of innocent children.[30]

In 2017, for example, then One Nation Queensland leader Steve Dickson, in response to the Safe Schools program, unleashed this alarmist bollocks into the world: 'We are having little kids in grade four at school, young girls being taught by teachers how to masturbate, how to strap on dildos, how to do this sort of stuff – that is the real problem in this country.'[31]

Safe Schools was a voluntary program, written at the request of teachers who wanted help explaining LGBTIQA+ issues to their students. It aimed to reduce homophobic and transphobic bullying and increase empathy for LGBTIQA+ kids by providing students and teachers with accurate information. The Coalition government commissioned a review of the program in 2016, which found the program was effective and the resources it provided were 'suitable, robust, age-appropriate, educationally sound and aligned with the Australian Curriculum'.[32]

Dickson was forced to retract his statement.[33] This didn't stop right-wing tabloids and politicians demonising the Safe Schools program. They tied it to the marriage equality plebiscite with propaganda claiming, 'If same-sex marriage is legalised, Safe Schools and others like it will be mandatory in schools.'[34]

By 2024, cost-of-living pressures were drowning out almost everything else and parents were far more worried about making rent and mortgage payments than whether their children learn empathy for gay and trans people. Unfortunately, however, those seeds fears are deeply sown and myths about 'the gay agenda transing our kids' still worm their way into online parent groups and social media feeds.[35]

In Australia, this issue is almost entirely manufactured by right-wing conservatives and political operatives. They encouraged a loud but very small minority of parents to complain and ensured those complaints were amplified by partisan media. Most parents, as I've already said, support sexuality education. Children and teens not only support it, but most of them also want it to go further, be more explicit and more inclusive. They are frequently 'teaching up' – explaining and correcting teachers' and parents' binary understanding of gender, sexuality and language – and challenging gender stereotyping in school traditions.[36]

For some parents, this can be difficult even frightening. Sex, sexuality, gender, and identity are highly sensitised topics for anyone, but never more so than when it comes to our children. The purveyors of misinformation know that nothing will grab people's attention more than telling them someone is going to hurt their kids. Particularly if that harm is sexual. It's only a very small step from there to making them hate the people they think will hurt their kids. Once that level of emotion is engaged, it's very difficult to get people to change their mind and no one is more vulnerable to sensationalised misinformation than harried parents of young children.

It would be easy to dismiss those parents as gullible and foolish, but I think that's ungenerous. I clearly remember how little time I had when my kids were in those early childhood and primary years. I was working, studying and raising two children. I barely had time to shower, let alone spend hours researching entirely unfamiliar ideas about something as complex as sexuality and gender. While consent, respectful relationships and sex ed are all separate components of the health curriculum, they're all based on the same principles and it's easy for misinformation to conflate them into a single amorphous mass of flashing red danger. Particularly when they are so new that most parents had almost none of these lessons when they were at school. Add to that the complexity of the concepts – I had to write a whole book to explain them – and I can easily understand how vulnerable parents are to misinformation.

The counters to misinformation are facts and empathy – anger and scorn only make people cling to their beliefs even more tightly. Parents who face backlash in their school community can sometimes change minds by providing kindly delivered facts that disprove misinformation. But this can take a lot of time and energy, which is not easy to find when we're so busy with our own family needs. And, of course, it doesn't always work. The simplest thing you can do is to make sure the school knows how much you value sex, sexuality and consent education and the teachers who deliver it. Ask other parents to join you in supporting those teachers. If the backlash is growing, ask the school to organise parent workshops and provide written information for parents who can't or won't attend. You could even ask them to put copies of this book in the library!

Your knowledge and support are the most effective tools for reducing backlash and protecting your children from ignorance and misinformation.

2

Protecting kids from sexual abuse

The most important thing to know about preventing child sexual abuse is that we cannot teach little children to protect themselves from predatory adults. Children can't do that. They are physically, emotionally, intellectually and psychologically incapable of defending themselves against a fully grown adult, or even against an adolescent or older child. Telling little children that they could or should defend themselves is cruel and unfair. Protecting children is an adult responsibility.[37]

What we can, and must, teach children is how to tell a safe adult when someone is doing something that makes them uncomfortable, scared or ashamed. This is rarely as simple as it sounds and kids need to learn specific techniques to do it effectively:

- They need to be able to recognise the physical and mental signs that they're in danger.
- They must have the language to explain their feelings.
- They have to understand how to identify safe adults, and know that those adults will hear them, believe them and help them.[38]

The adults in their lives must learn skills too.
- They need to know how to recognise and interpret inarticulate or confused disclosures.
- They must recognise grooming and identify signs a child is being abused.
- They need to be confident they can safely and effectively respond to disclosures.
- They need to know where and how to report abuse.[39]

Adults and children cannot learn these skills by themselves. They can be complicated, challenging and sometimes run counter to many of the myths we've absorbed over a lifetime of misinformation. The Royal Commission into Institutional Responses to Child Sexual Abuse (announced in 2012 and completed in 2017) said these lessons should be embedded in the curriculum for all 'preschool, school and other community institutional settings' along with 'prevention education for parents delivered through day care, preschool, school, sport and recreational settings'.[40]

A survey of just over 1000 Australian adults in 2021 found that while 85 per cent agreed that children would be harmed if someone did not believe their disclosure of abuse, around one third believe children sometimes make up stories about being abused.[41] Another third was not sure whether they should believe children who disclose abuse (this includes any kind of abuse, not just sexual abuse). If this research is accurate, this means a child who tells an adult that they are being abused has a two in three chance that adult might not believe them.

These adults are not malicious or uncaring, they simply can't comprehend the reality of child sexual abuse and have probably heard too many stories from little children about fighting dragons or flying cars. They're right that small children have very active imaginations and frequently mix fact and fantasy in their games. But children's imaginations are limited to what they know. They've been in cars and seen planes in the sky and watched animated movies about dragons. Imagination can put all these things together for a game in the backyard, but a five-year-old who has never seen a car or a plane or an image of a dragon cannot describe the shape of a steering wheel, the sound of a jet engine or gigantic, winged lizards that breathe fire. They need to get those details from somewhere. Equally, children cannot imagine the details of sexual acts without some external input. It might be that they've seen something online or been told about something by an older child, or the reason might be even more dangerous. Any demonstration of sexual knowledge by a small child cannot be dismissed as imagination, it's always based in some reality.[42]

The statistics on child sexual abuse are gut-wrenching. Just under 40 per cent of girls and 20 per cent of boys experience some form of sexual abuse before they turn eighteen and almost 80 per cent of those people said it happened more than one time. It typically starts between the ages of five and nine for girls and ten to fourteen for boys. The person most likely to abuse a child is someone the child and their family knows and trusts. Often the abuser is an adolescent, barely out of childhood themselves. Sexual abuse is almost always committed by men and boys, although women can and do perpetrate other kinds of abuse (see Appendix 2 for more detail on statistics).

How to protect children from sexual harm

Predatory men do not start by grooming children. They start by grooming adults. They join the CFA, fundraise for community sports clubs and organise Easter egg hunts for the local primary school. They cheerfully take on organising community events, help struggling families with shopping, and tending overgrown lawns. They're friendly but distant with children at first, careful to pose no threat or set off alarm bells until they're firmly established as 'a great bloke' and a pillar of the community. Then they start searching through the available children for vulnerabilities. They will give a rejected child acceptance, a lonely child companionship or a neglected child love. They make them feel special, important, different to other children and more loved because of this difference. They make themselves so essential to the vulnerable child that the child will do *anything* to protect their relationship. They will keep their abuser's secrets, lie for him, collude with him to hide the abuse and believe him when he tells them it's what they must do to ensure he can continue to love them and stand between them and the loneliness he makes sure they never forget. This is how men who sexually abuse children manipulate their victims into believing the abuse was something the child wanted. When those children become adults, that lie stays with them, turns to shame and self-blame, and reinforces their ongoing silence.[43]

Once he has coerced the child into believing he is essential to their happiness, a groomer starts testing the child's boundaries. What will they do in response to a dirty joke? A pat on the bottom? A tight hug with hands that do not stay on the back or waist? Will they object? Tell an adult? Will the adult believe them? Will they do anything? Those seemingly innocent interactions can be easily explained away if no one knows how to listen to children explaining their discomfort.[44]

This is why children need to learn to understand and describe their feelings as well as their body parts – and adults need to learn how to hear and understand those descriptions.

A five-year-old child's claim that Uncle Bob touched her bottom when he picked her up to reach something on a high shelf is easy to laugh off – *'Haha! Did I? She's such a big girl now. I almost dropped her!'* How could you not dismiss this as nothing more than a trivial mistake? But if that little girl says 'Mummy, it made my tummy feel all squiggly' and her mother knows this is her daughter's way of saying she feels scared and threatened, the incident is much less likely to be dismissed. It's unlikely anyone will call the police at this point, but parents who understand grooming and children's explanation of feelings will keep an eye on Uncle Bob's interactions with their children and know who to contact if they see further signs of harmful behaviour from Uncle Bob.[45]

One of the most difficult issues for parents is knowing the difference between the safe, loving, protective relationships their children have with adult men, and associations predatory men create to groom children.[46] Too many mothers carry memories of being abused when they were small and helpless. They're determined to never let the same thing happen to their own children and it can make them deeply afraid of leaving them alone with anyone.

One woman who had been abused as a child told me that she wouldn't let her father (who had never abused her) bath her kids. 'I didn't even like my husband being alone with them when they were in the bath. I mean, I trust him, but my mother trusted my uncle and she shouldn't have.' She had very good reasons for her fears, but this common and justifiable fear is also a huge barrier for men who want to be bathing their kids, reading them stories, tucking them in at night and comforting them when they're sad or having scary dreams – and it's so important that they do these things. Apart from the benefits of parents sharing equally in the work and joys of raising kids, preventing fathers from providing this care can do real harm to children. Australian researchers produce one of the only large scale longitudinal studies of men who commit violence, and their most recent findings showed that boys who grow up having a loving, affectionate relationship with a father or father figure are much less likely to ever abuse their partners as adults.[47]

The village we need to raise our children is full of loving dads, granddads, uncles and stepfathers. Children are safest when all those men are deeply involved in their lives and that starts with sharing the basic care of babies and little children.

Those relationships are so important in a child's life. Not just because they bring joy and fun, but also because they provide safety and protection from people who might mean harm.

A few years ago, a six-year-old boy told me about his regular fishing trips with his granddad. They would take some lunch and fishing gear out on the weekends and sit together for hours. Sometimes they'd sit in silence; other times they would talk about football, or Fisher Boy would tell Granddad about the books he was reading, and Granddad would talk about the books he read when he was a child, the characters he loved and how one of them made him want to be a soldier. 'Granddad wasn't a soldier though,' Fisher Boy told me, 'he was a plumber, and he said that was lots of fun because he got to look at people's poo.' Cue uproarious laughter, because when you're six, the only thing funnier than poo is farts.

Fisher Boy was relaxed and unguarded when he was telling me about Granddad. He wasn't worried about what I heard or whether he was giving anything away. He felt no need to protect secrets about Granddad or stop me knowing about their time together. All the conversations he told me about were exactly right for a six-year-old – books, football, soldiers, and poo. Granddad didn't try to drag him into adult conversations about failed ambitions or adult responsibilities that may have forced him away from his military dreams and into an apprenticeship. Fisher Boy knew Granddad was sad when Grandma died but he was not responsible for healing Granddad's grief or loneliness. Red flags would be raised if Granddad had been telling him about adult worries – money, sex, marriages – or asking him to keep secrets that made him careful or cagey when he talked about the things they did together. The relationship Fisher Boy had with Granddad was wonderfully protective and I'd bet that Granddad would have been one of the first people he'd tell if someone did hurt or frighten him. That loving, honest, close relationship with Granddad was also its own protection from abuse. Anyone attempting to groom Fisher Boy would find it difficult because his need for acceptance, love and companionship was already fulfilled by a safe, protective adult.

Children and adults are not equals. In safe, caring relationships, we don't talk to little children the same way we talk to other adults. I might tell a six-year-old that I left my headlights on last night and when I went to start my car that morning my battery was flat and the car wouldn't start – 'Ergh, so annoying, but someone came to fix it for me so it was all OK.' But I wouldn't tell them that I was late to work because of the flat battery and this made me worry that I might lose my job or that the cost of getting the car started meant I would struggle to pay the gas bill or that I'm sure my asshole neighbours saw the headlights on when they got home and chose to not tell me because we're arguing over the cost of fixing the fence. Such things would be signs I was trying to create a relationship that's not appropriate for an adult and a six-year-old. The other adults in that child's life, if they knew the signs to look for, would stand between me and any time alone with that child. Or they might talk to me about what I say to the child and warn me away from further inappropriate conversations. An abuser will understand this as evidence their grooming isn't working. They might keep trying but if they see more signs of awareness and protection, they'll know that abusing that child will lead to being caught and will usually keep away.

The danger, of course, is that this doesn't stop them, they may simply move away from the protected child and find a child who does not have those informed and aware adults in their life. This is why we need to keep pumping out a steady flow of information about grooming and warning signs, so all parents, families and communities know what to look for and how to hear children when they're trying to tell us that someone is hurting them, making them uncomfortable or simply that they feel alone and vulnerable.

Abusers who see their initial touches or inappropriate stories being ignored will start pushing the boundaries much further. They'll share overtly sexual stories and adult woes as if the child were an equal. They'll start showing the child sexual images and videos or telling them stories about adult sexual experiences. Then they'll move to touching that moves from 'accidental' to directly sexual. When the boundaries are already broken and secret keeping is established, an abused child is rendered powerless before the abuse even begins.[48]

Most of the adults in children's lives want to keep them safe. But precisely because they are protective and well-intentioned, they don't know the grooming script and they don't recognise vulnerabilities in the same way predators do. Loneliness, isolation, sadness, even feeling like they're a bit weird or different can be painful for a child. That alone should be enough reason for the adults around them to find ways to connect and help them feel heard and understood. Knowing that those feelings also make children vulnerable to predators makes this not just important, it's essential to keeping them safe.

The villages raising our children are much better at protecting children from predatory adults than they were a few decades ago. Mandatory reporting and widespread education for schools and parents has put significant limits on the adults who want to sexually abuse children and the result of this is showing up in decreasing rates of child sexual abuse by adults (see Appendix 2).

Tragically, however, we have not been able to keep up with the increasing abuses committed by other children and teens.

When children and teens commit abuse

Like most people, I have a few friends I know well enough to text but not well enough to call without prearrangement. When I get a call from one of those friends without warning, it's usually because they, or someone they know, needs help dealing with a violent man. I carry all the services around in my head and I know why they want to get a recommendation from a person not a screen, so I'm happy to be the first voice on a phone telling someone that what happened was not their fault and help is available. I just need to be sure I'm not the only person who tells them that.

One of my Text Friends called me a few years back with disturbing variation in this pattern. I knew her through other friends, and I'd met her clever, quiet husband and their six-year-old son a few times. Their little boy was a lot of fun. Full of smartarsery and mischief, never stuck for a comeback, even if he was too often graphically scatological. Charm was often the only thing that kept him on the right side of the line between resilient and obnoxious.

Text Friend told me that a friend of hers had accused Charming Boy of sexually abusing her six-year-old daughter and reported him to the police. She wanted me to come with her to the interview because her husband wanted to stay home with their son. She said Charming Boy didn't know about the police interview but when I went to pick her up, he was there, watching us with a pale, pinched look.

The detective turned out to be a lovely man who only wanted to see Text Friend because he was worried about her son. 'Six year olds are not criminals,' he told us. 'I just want to make sure he's not a victim of someone who *is* a criminal.'

The detective came to talk to my friend's son and, in the gentlest, kindest way, managed to get to the truth of what happened. A kid at school had been showing the other kids a picture of adults having oral sex. My friend's son didn't understand why a woman would want to put a penis in her mouth and slid straight around the parental blocks on the home wi-fi to find more images of oral sex. They confirmed for him that fellatio is a real thing but didn't explain it, so he had tried to understand it by recreating it with the six-year-old girl. He told the detective that the kids at school said they would get in trouble if adults found out about the image and he knew he might get in trouble for what he did with the little girl, but he didn't understand that what he'd asked her to do could hurt her because 'the lady in the video liked it a lot'.

Everyone involved spent at least a year in therapy afterwards. All the children (and parents) needed help to understand what happened and make sure it didn't turn into the kind of secret trauma that can ruin lives. They were all very lucky that they had the means to find that support and stay with it for as long as they did.

No one involved faced any criminal charges, because, as the detective said, no one had committed a crime. But something went very wrong for all the children in this story. None of them were to blame but who was responsible for protecting all of them from the expanding ricochets of one confusing image in a playground?

There are no grey areas, no complexities involved when a mature adult involves a child in sexual activity. Adults have far too much power over children for there to be any ambiguity – adults who sexually abuse children are entirely responsible for the abuse. Children cannot consent, cannot defend themselves from adult manipulation and abuses of power. It's a very clear distinction.

When the abuser is also a child that distinction is not nearly so clear. 'Perpetrator' is the wrong word to use about children who sexually abuse other children. The official term is 'children who exhibit problematic and harmful sexual behaviour' but parents and families of a child who's been sexually abused by an older child or teen are rarely concerned about appropriate language.

In their 2021 survey of over 8500 people, the Australian Child Maltreatment Study found that when they were children, 12 per cent of people born between 1997 and 2005 were sexually abused by adults and 18 per cent were sexually abused by adolescents. But for people born before 1976, these figures were reversed, with 21 per cent reporting adult perpetrators and 12 per cent reporting adolescent perpetrators.[49]

We know enough to know that it *is* happening but not enough about *why* it's happening. However, the increase in children and teens perpetrating sexual abuse over the last twenty years tracks smoothly alongside the increase in free online porn and it seems impossible to believe there is no connection. Graphic, often violent, sexual images are free and easily accessible online, and we know children, like my friend's son and all his classmates, are seeing them.

We don't have the smoking gun that proves a direct link between children and teens seeing porn and sexually abusing each other. But we do have common sense, which tells us that graphic sexual images could easily confuse and upset young children. We have a sound evidence base that says children will try to process problems and confusion in their play with other children.[50] We have good reason to believe there is a risk of serious harm when children are exposed to graphic or violent pornography, and we have the skills and knowledge we need to reduce that risk.

What might have kept my Text Friend's son and all those other children safe? Ideally, no six-year-old would ever see graphic images of oral sex. If there was a way to guarantee that could never happen, then slam that bolt home and let's move on to solving the next problem. Sadly, that's not possible (more on this in Chapter 10), so the only thing we can do is prepare children, even very little children, for the content they might see online and make sure all the adults around them know how to have conversations that will help kids bring their questions and fears and curiosity to safe adults instead of the unregulated, profit-driven online world – or each other.

There are simple lessons children can learn that can help them to know how and when to tell adults what is happening before everything escalates to the point that children are being so terribly wounded. The following pointers are all taken from the Victorian Department of Education's curriculum materials for Foundation to Level Two.[51]

It's important to remember that while your child should be learning these lessons at school, the curriculum is very crowded, and some teachers find these topics difficult to teach (more on this in Chapter 1). Even when teachers are doing their best and covering these topics in detail, kids might be home sick during those lessons. Or they're just not paying attention that day. They might even be there and have great fun in the class, but don't retain the details because they didn't seem relevant or important at the time. If parents and families reinforce these ideas at home, routinely and casually, in the same way you remind them about manners, clean socks and looking both ways when they cross a road, your children are much more likely to remember what they've been taught and be able to act on it in emotionally charged moments.

What do your kids need to know?

- Genitals are private parts, which means we keep them covered in public places and people don't touch them unless they are helping us stay clean or managing our health. Even then, if we feel yuky or scared, we tell an adult about it.
- We use the proper words for our private parts – penis, scrotum, testicles, vulva, vagina and anus. If we have cute little euphemism for our genitals, doctors or teachers might not understand us when we say that something hurts or feels weird.

- There isn't anything embarrassing or shameful about our genitals so it's OK to talk about them and it's always OK to ask questions about them. But they are private, so we don't need to tell the lady we met at the shops about our genitals.
- Sometimes adults take pictures of their private parts and put them online. This is something for grown-ups and it is not meant for children.
- If you see those pictures by accident or because someone shows them to you, you have not done anything wrong and you will not get in trouble. But you should tell an adult that it happened so they can make sure you're OK.
- If the person who showed you is another child they will not get in trouble either. But someone needs to help them understand what the picture means and make sure they are OK, so we need to tell a teacher or their parents what happened.
- If it was an adult who showed you the picture, the adult (not the child) did the wrong thing, and they need to know they shouldn't show those pictures to children. So we have to tell someone who can make sure they understand and don't do it again.
- Sometimes those pictures can be confusing and upsetting for kids, so we don't show them to each other, we tell a grown-up about it.
- If we see pictures online that don't make sense, it's OK to have questions about them. Even if you think it might be rude or private, you are never doing the wrong thing when you ask a safe adult a question about things you don't understand.
- It's never OK to touch someone else's private parts, especially someone who is smaller or younger than you. It might hurt

them or scare them, but they might not be able to tell you that they're hurt or scared.

- If you do touch another child, or if someone touches your private parts, or if someone shows you a picture or video that makes you feel uncomfortable, you never have to keep that secret.
- It's great that you tell your dog or your big sister about the things that upset you, but an adult is someone who has finished growing and could take you to a doctor if needed. Who are the adults you would go to if you had a question that was a bit rude or embarrassing or scary?[52]

Children also need to know that it is never their fault if someone older, bigger or more powerful did something to hurt or frighten them. It's also not their fault if another child was hurt or frightened. Even if they were naughty or rude or had bad thoughts about someone, nothing they did or could ever do would make it their fault or mean they deserved to be hurt. No child ever deserves to be hurt.[53]

You and your child need to have a clear understanding of the safe adults in their life. Sometimes it will be you but if they're lucky, they will have other adults in their life as well. It's very difficult for one person to be in charge of consequences ('you were sending rude messages to a kid at school, so you have to put your phone in a drawer when you get home each day') and confidences ('it's OK to tell me if you've done something you regret'). We need the village.

All state and national curriculum include lessons on help-seeking, which usually starts with asking kids to think about the safe adults in their life as well as the more official resources such as police and helplines. It's still important for you to have that conversation with your kids because if they choose a family member or friend as one of their safe adults, you'll need to talk to that person too.

What do their safe adults need to know?

When I was a child, one of my mother's close friends was my father's cousin. She would disagree, but at the time, I thought she looked a bit like Madonna - a different aesthetic but the same vibes of glamour and excitement. Cousin Madonna took a shine to me, and she would often take me on outings when I was in my tweens. By the time I was in my mid-teens, Cousin Madonna and I were firm friends. I talked to her about most of the things I was either too embarrassed or too cagey to tell my mother – periods, sex, pregnancy scares, depression, falling in love, experimenting with drugs, cutting school. All the usual dumb teenage stuff.

Years later, I found out my mother had told Cousin Madonna that if I asked her to keep something confidential, she could promise to do so and mean it. Mum worried about me, but she said it was more important that I had someone she trusted to help me if I was in trouble than it was for her to know everything about my life. It was a brave call – I didn't realise how brave until I had teens of my own and had to make same promises to them. But I'm grateful she had that courage and showed me how much it mattered. Not only did Cousin Madonna do an enormous amount to keep me safe, just by being someone to talk to, I can see now that it made my relationship with my mother much stronger.

If your child tells you that Cousin Harry is the adult they would go to with a 'rude' question and you trust Cousin Harry to answer their questions safely, then make sure your child knows they can call or message him whenever they want.

Your child's Cousin Harry could be a friend, family member, teacher, sports coach, faith leader or neighbour. They can be any (adult) age or gender. The only thing that matters is that they are someone you and your child both trust and someone who has a relationship with your child that you can see is safe and age appropriate.

Cousin Harry also needs to know that he's been chosen as a safe adult. He needs to understand what that means and agree to be that person for your child. He needs to know the boundaries you set, and you need to know that he can work with them when necessary or work around them if he must. You also need to trust his judgement. It's not a small thing for either of you.

He also needs to be an adult, which means he probably didn't grow up with influencers and strangers reaching out through online games or social media. He likely didn't have adults watching his every move in the physical world and seeing almost nothing of his online world. He won't have any experience of navigating the blended online and physical worlds that are so real for children who can't imagine life existing any other way.

He may not have solutions to these complex problems (who does?) but if he is a good listener, he will be a solid support for your child. He does need to know when something is serious enough that they both need expert help and where to find that help (maybe take a photo of the helplines in Appendix 1 to send him).

At minimum, you should both agree that if Cousin Harry thinks your child is being hurt or is at risk of hurting himself or someone else, he must talk to someone about what to do next. If not you, then a teacher, doctor or counsellor who can give some objective expert advice.

Warning signs

The following is adapted from the National Office for Child Safety's guide on signs and indicators of child sexual abuse.[54] Their website is full of helpful information and resources if you're looking for more detailed information.

Children and teens can have a very wide range of reactions to being abused. Some may show no signs at all, others can have huge and sudden changes to their behaviour and personality.

While it is useful to know some of the signs to look for, the most effective way to know if something is happening to your child is to make sure they are comfortable talking to you about difficult subjects and that they know to talk to a safe adult if anyone does or says something that makes them feel sad, ashamed or scared – especially if that person tells them to keep it a secret.

Physical signs might include:
- Persistent or recurring headaches and stomach aches.
- Bedwetting.
- Unexplained change in appetite or weight.
- Nightmares and sleep disturbances.
- Bruises on thighs or buttocks.
- Changes to genitals, such as redness, swelling or discharge.
- Pain or burning when they pee.

Emotional and behavioural changes might include:
- Depression, anxiety, social withdrawal.
- Poor hygiene.
- Alcohol and drug abuse.
- Over-compliance and eagerness to please.
- Aggression and anger.
- Running away.
- Using baggy clothes to hide gender and body parts.
- Disordered eating.
- Unexplained fear of particular people or places.

Appropriate and inappropriate touch

Any touch between an adult and a child that is at all sexual or for the purpose of sexual gratification is not just inappropriate touch, it is criminal sexual abuse.

Other forms of touching can be appropriate in some cultures or families and not in others. Some people, for example, habitually kiss family members on the lips in greeting or farewell, while other families might find kissing children on the lips odd or incongruous. Some cultures deem bared skin to be inappropriate; others might be entirely comfortable with nudity or near nudity in the home or at the beach. There's not a definitive right or wrong in this, it's about how your child feels and helping them learn what is appropriate in different contexts. They need to know they can safely say 'I don't want to kiss Nana', they cannot go to school naked or touch other people's private parts, and they can have a splendid time getting all soapy and wriggly in a splashy bath at home.

Young children of similar ages where there is no threat, coercion or power imbalance will often show a natural curiosity about their own and other people's bodies. As resources published by the Royal Children's Hospital in Melbourne explain, three and four-year-olds peering or poking at each other's genitals is not unusual or anything to worry about.[55]

You might have reason to be concerned if it is persistent, compulsive or displaying signs of unexpected sexual knowledge, such as simulating adult sexual positions or oral sex.

Behaviours that might give parents reason for concern are often so specific to their child and circumstance that it's not possible to address all of them in a book like this – and I am not a therapist or a doctor.

If your child is doing something you think might not be appropriate for their age, it's best to talk to someone who knows them and has some expertise in child development. If your child goes to preschool or school, you could ask a teacher (who will be very accustomed to all the weird and wonderful vagaries of children's behaviour) or talk to your GP.

If you want to look for information online, make sure it comes from a reputable site, such as the Royal Children's Hospital resource I cited above. It can be frighteningly easy to fall down a conspiracy theory rabbit hole of misinformation pushed online by people who benefit financially or politically by frightening parents. If people are peddling theories about child sexual abuse from out on the fringe of reality, they're not there because they're more visionary or dedicated or knowledgeable than the doctors and specialists who've spent years proving themselves and their expertise.

If you're worried that your children or other children in your community are not safe, you could ask your child's school or your local council to organise sexual abuse prevention workshops for parents, families and community workers. There are many experts and organisations that offer these workshops around Australia. Several of the Centres Against Sexual Assault in Victoria, for example, have community workshops and parent education programs.[56] Knowledge is a powerful defence against abuse, especially when it is shared across the entire community.

Risks and protective factors

We might feel like watching over our children's every move and interaction is the only thing we can do to protect them, but this rarely works.

Firstly, it's just not possible – our children need to go out into the world and learn how to interact with other people on their own. It's how they grow and get ready for an independent adult life.

Secondly, feeling that they are being constantly monitored is more likely to lead to secretive behaviour than to open communication about fears and threats.

Finally, and perhaps even more importantly, kids who grow up thinking it's normal, even protective to have someone monitoring their every move can create its own danger.

Research by the eSafety Commission in 2025 found that 20 – 30 per cent of men and people aged 18 – 24 see tracking, monitoring and controlling romantic partners online as a sign of care in a relationship rather than recognising this as dangerous coercive control. It's possible that growing up with parental surveillance portrayed as loving and protective contributes to normalising this kind of monitoring for younger people.[57]

This is not to say that using tracking and location apps will prime your kids up for abuse when they're older. But what might be appropriate for an eight-year-old is not OK when that kid is seventeen. Slowly withdrawing your access to their digital world as they get older shows your kids that trust and respect are more important in adult relationships than monitoring and control.

Research shows that the strongest protective factors against sexual abuse are:[58]

- Supportive and trustworthy adults who know how to recognise warning signs, listen to disclosures and where to find help for children in danger: this means making sure all the adults in your children's life know what to look for and how to respond. Reach out to other parents in your street, your children's school or preschool, your family and friends, make sure you're all talking about what your kids are telling you and each other.
- Language skills to communicate their feelings or explain what is happening to them: make sure you check in with your kids regularly about how they're feeling in mind and body.

- Clear understanding of appropriate touch and inappropriate sexual behaviour: your child's school and preschool will have access to resources for teaching these topics. Make sure the lessons are being delivered comprehensively, and your child is participating and understanding everything. If you have any concerns about the information your child is getting, talk to the school leaders. There are still several organisations that can come to your child's school and provide more detailed or intensive information for students, teachers and parents. Safe4Kids and KidsROAR are both long-standing organisations with proven track records, but there are many others.
- Strong community or cultural connections.

Sometimes we have these connections because they were there before we were born and will still be there long after we're gone. Other families might be new to the city or country and have no connections. They can be difficult to build if you're starting from nothing but schools, preschools and parent groups (typically organised for new parents by child and family health services) are very good places to start. If your kids have made friends at school or preschool, try suggesting play dates or park trips together. Community sport is another great way to connect with other parents. If your kids play any kind of sport, there will always be other parents struggling to manage all the driving around. Volunteering to join car pooling is a great way to start those connections. Make sure all the adults in your children's lives know what to look for and how to respond. Keep talking to each other about what your kids are telling you and make sure all the children know they will never get in trouble for asking for help when they're scared or confused.

Responding to disclosures

People who work with children: If you or your organisation works for or with children you are probably included in mandatory reporting requirements, which means you must report any reasonable suspicion that a child is in danger.

All the states and territories have slightly different laws, regulations and reporting bodies. If you are unsure about your obligations, check with your organisation or the child protection organisation in your state (see Appendix 1).

Parents, family members and other adults might also be covered by mandatory reporting requirements in some states. But kids don't come with an instruction manual and most of us don't get any training on how to respond to a child telling us that someone is sexually abusing them.

It can often come as a terrible shock, especially if the person committing the abuse is someone you know, or worse, someone you love. This is why it is so important to know what to do *before* it happens, so you can, in the moment, take a breath and feel confident about what to do next.

These suggestions are adapted from the Australian Institute of Family Studies guides on responding to disclosures:[59]

- **Your job is only to listen.** You don't have to be a therapist, and it is not your job to investigate the claim or clarify any details. Just listen and give the child your full attention. It's common for children to start a disclosure at inconvenient times, partly out of uncertainty and possibly to give both of you an excuse to ignore what they're saying. It's OK to say you need to move to a quiet or private place or even a later time if that is the only way you'll be able to listen to what they want to tell you.

- **Don't ask questions about the abuse or the abuser.** Don't ask for any details or timelines. Don't suggest words or phrases to articulate the abuse. Just let them tell you what they want to say in their own words. Give them time to get those words out. The only question you need to ask is whether there is anything else they want to tell you.

- **Stay as calm as possible.** If you are angry or grief-stricken the child might believe they are the cause and may even change the disclosure to protect you, themselves or the person abusing them. If you (understandably) can't hold back how you feel, make sure you tell the child you are not upset with them. Explain you are upset because adults are meant to keep kids safe and you are sad that some adults don't do that.

- **Tell the child that you believe them.** Their story might be confused, and the details might not make sense, but they are telling you something important about what someone has done to them. Even if you haven't fully understood what they were saying, the child needs to know that you believe they're trying to tell you about something serious and you will do something about it.

- **Reassure the child** that they did the right thing in telling you and recognise the courage and strength they needed to do that.

- **Tell the child the abuse was not their fault.** They did not cause it or ask for it or deserve it. Some children might have been groomed to believe they instigated or wanted the abuse. Creating these beliefs is part of the grooming process and unravelling them is a significant part of healing and recovery.

- **Don't make promises you can't keep.** You may not be able to keep them safe. You cannot keep their secret. You don't know if everything is going to be OK.

- **Tell the child you are going to do your best to help.** If you don't know who you are going to go to for help, don't speculate about organisations they might find frightening or unfamiliar. Just tell them you will have to ask someone what to do next. Don't keep them waiting or guessing. If you're going to make a phone call the next day, tell them that and ask if they want you to let them know what you found out in the call. Let them know how they can contact you if they want to ask about what is happening.

- **Do not confront the person who abused the child.** You cannot predict what they might do – you might give them warning to erase evidence or intimidate the child into silence. This is a job for police or child protection workers.

- **Keep the child's confidences as much as you can.** While you do have to report the abuse to someone who can help, you don't have to tell anyone else. The child chose you to trust with their disclosure and you may not know all the reasons they chose to not tell other people in their family or community. If you think other children might be at risk from the person committing the abuse, you must include this information when you ask for help. If you believe any children are in immediate danger, keep the child who disclosed with you and call the police on 000.

- **Look after yourself.** It's perfectly normal to feel shock, rage, grief, exhaustion or even numbness after hearing a disclosure. Those feelings can come and go for weeks even months afterwards, particularly if you have your own experiences of abuse. Therapists, helplines, GPs, friends and family are all resources you can and should lean on as you deal with this (for a full list of support services see Appendix 1). It's likely that the investigation and response will take a long time and you will need help along the way. You are never being a bother or being unreasonable when you ask for help in this situation.

Where to find help

If you or someone you know is in immediate danger, call the police on 000.

Helplines for a wide range of concerns are listed in Appendix 1 of this book, including state-based child protection services, which is where most cases of child sexual abuse will be reported.

If you've seen something that concerns you but you're unsure whether it's significant, you can call the parent helplines (also listed in Appendix 1). Trusted GPs are also a good resource, as are teachers and well-being officers at your child's school or psychiatrists, psychologists and social workers. Keep in mind that all those people are covered by mandatory reporting requirements and they may have no choice about reporting what you tell them.

Helplines such as Lifeline, 1800 Respect and Kidshelpline all allow callers to be anonymous, but they might be limited in what help they can offer without identifying details.

The eSafety commissioner is an excellent resource and the eSafety website www.esafety.gov.au has a wide range of very helpful information and guides for parents.

The Australian Institute of Health and Welfare www.aihw.gov.au the Australian Institute of Family Studies www.aifs.gov.au and the National Office for Child Safety www.childsafety.gov.au all provide excellent plain language summaries of research, advice, information and explanations about child sexual abuse, as well as other forms of violence and abuse.

Sexual abuse in childcare centres

I know many parents were horrified and frightened after reports in July 2025 that police charged a man with more than 70 counts of child sexual abuse after he had been working in dozens of childcare centres around Melbourne since 2017. Like so many other parents, I felt sick when I read those reports. I sent my son to childcare when he was a baby and I still remember how it felt knowing that he couldn't tell me what happened when I wasn't there. I think I was more concerned about him feeling sad or abandoned than that he might be abused, but even that was enough to have me changing work arrangements and accepting a much reduced income so I could work from home until both my kids had learned to talk. I know that is just not an option for most parents now. Even if it was, accepting a massive reduction in economic safety (the burden of which will fall almost entirely on women) because the childcare system is unsafe for children is a terrible outcome for everyone.

Unfortunately, there is no quick fix. The childcare system has been structurally underfunded and under-resourced for decades. No one says it explicitly anymore, but the attitude that childcare centres are nothing more than glorified babysitting services for ambitious (i.e. 'bad') mothers hasn't been truly eradicated yet and it does terrible damage to everyone involved. Childcare is an essential service and the starting point of the national education system. People who work in childcare deserve the same respect, employment conditions (including salary!) and responsibilities as any other staff or teachers in schools. They don't get that respect or salary so the people who work in childcare struggle to manage the most basic living costs and are sometimes forced out of the sector in search of liveable wages.

Low wages and the strong profit motive built into the childcare system (around 70 per cent of childcare centres are owned by for-profit providers) builds structural risks into the childcare and early childhood education system. The pressure to cut expenses can push some centres to reduce their highly experienced and qualified staff in favour of cheaper, less knowledgeable workers. This in turn can cause burnout, lots of people calling in sick, high staff turnover and an increasing reliance on casual and agency staff. Not having trained long-term staff makes it much more difficult for little children to tell someone that they're scared or uncomfortable with a new staff member because they haven't learned to know and trust the workers and the workers haven't learned the child's language and ability to explain abuse. High staff turnover and top-down pressure to reduce expenses also means young, inexperienced or casual workers are less able and confident to see and report disturbing changes in the behaviour of children or other staff. A 2023 report by the Australian Competition and Consumer Commission found that on average the large organisations pay lower wages, use more casual staff and have higher staff turnover than the not-for-profit centres. This is not to say that every private childcare centre is a hotbed of abuse and negligence (they're absolutely not) but it is worth noting that childcare is the only section of the education system that doesn't refuse funding for profit-driven organisations. Even private schools in our two-tier education system must be not-for-profit to access government funding.

If men who want to sexually abuse children know that mandatory reporting, trained staff and all the other regulations that prevent sexual abuse are far more robust in schools than in early childhood centres, they will naturally take the path of least resistance.

The charges against the Melbourne man working in childcare centres were shocking and deeply disturbing, but this is not the first time it's happened. As Dr Michael Salter wrote on his website*, there are records going back to the 1980s of people working in childcare being reported for sexually abusing the children in their care. These

---

* www.organisedabuse.com/blog

cases almost never result in structural change because after the initial shock wears off, the impetus for that change dissipates in the face of the huge amount of work that needs to be done.

Reform needs long-term, structural investment in early childhood education. It probably needs a slow and painful transition away from profit-based childcare and into the education system that will only provide funding to not-for-profit organisations. This will take an enormous amount of work, political will and funding. I can't imagine any government taking this on without a great deal of pushing from voters. Which is where parents have real power to demand change, but unlike the parents of the 1980s, you don't have to do it on your own. We have technology, knowledge and leadership now that gives us options for collective action and informed advocacy that has never before been possible.

Sign up to support organisations such as The Parenthood, where CEO Georgie Dent leads an incredible team of people to advocate on behalf of a community of more than 80,000 parents and carers. Follow Children's Commissioners in your state as well as the National Children's Commissioner. Check petitions and social media posts to make sure they're saying the things you want said, then sign and share. Pull in everyone you know who is (or should be) part of the village raising our children and ask them to help. Even liking and sharing social media posts can help. It's about making sure the people who have the power to enforce systemic change can't avoid seeing how many people care about an issue and how much they care about it.

3

Safety, secrets and emotional literacy

Starting school is a huge change in a child's life. Some kids will come from full time childcare or part time pre-school, and others will have never seen the inside of a classroom. Regardless of their experience, all of them must adjust to each other, their teachers, the school rules, their classmates and the older children they see tumbling around the schoolyard.

In addition to all these adjustments, they're also starting (or continuing) their academic education and learning to navigate relationships outside their homes. That's a lot of learning for a five or six-year-old.

As I outlined in Chapter 1, the curriculum for consent and respectful relationships starts in the first year of primary school. Some early childhood centres and preschools provide early consent and child abuse prevention lessons for children under five, but only about half the children in Australia attend formal childcare or preschool.[60] So, for many children, primary school is the first time they've been exposed to these concepts outside the conversations they may have had with their parents.

Parents and family members who continue and extend this knowledge at home will make a big difference to how much their children remember, understand and benefit from the lessons that can help your village raise your children.

They're not learning about having sex in the first years of primary school. They learn about private and public body parts, health and respectful behaviour. But if they have questions about where babies come from or sexual acts they've heard about, it is far better that they have their natural curiosity satisfied by a parent or teacher who will give them accurate, age-appropriate information than an unfiltered Google search that could have awful consequences, as it did for my Text Friend in Chapter 2.

Anyone who's ever met a small child knows how curious they can be. *How did the sky get there? Why is that cup blue? Can you guess what I'm thinking about - it's not a shop.* They have questions about everything – and rightly so, most of the world doesn't make any sense at all, and no one has a good explanation for why a cup is blue.

Children can – and do – ask endless unanswerable questions of their parents but in a class of 26 curious children, a teacher must set some rules to make sure everyone gets a chance to ask questions and, even more importantly, understand the answer.

Creating a safe classroom

Teachers know how important it is for children to feel safe when they're trying to explain how they feel and what they think. It's in all their resources and documents and they're very well trained on how to work with the kids to make the classroom feel like a safe and trustworthy place.[61]

Several primary school teachers told me this is much easier in the early years of primary school, when children are often much more responsive to each other's needs and feelings. It can get more difficult as they get older. They're more aware of outside influences, the power dynamics in the school and the various ways they need to perform for each other. As they get older, boys who've been taught that they must be 'hard' will sometimes aggressively reject any hint of empathy or kindness for people they see as weak. Girls will sometimes try to please or placate at the expense of their own learning. By secondary school, if those gendered expectations have been allowed to embed themselves in school culture, they can impose real limits on teens' ability to learn, listen and discuss ideas with each other.[62]

Despite this, teachers persist in working with their students to establish rules that will keep everyone safe and ensure everyone can participate. This is almost always a collective exercise. In the first year of school, they play games like the Bubble Game, where all the kids pretend they're encased in a big bubble and they try to move around the classroom without bursting each other's bubbles. The lessons they learn in this game – looking around, noticing each other, moving carefully when they're near each other, become part of the class rules.[63]

From there the teachers move on to a class conversation about making the classroom a happy place for everyone. The typical responses from kids include things like letting each other finish before speaking, encouraging each other to join in, listening to each other, being kind to each other if even they don't agree, and letting the teacher know if they're not feeling OK.[64]

This technique follows the children from their first year in primary school to their final year of secondary school. Obviously, it becomes more sophisticated as they get older but the underlying principle of collectively deciding how to help everyone feel safe and able to participate remain constant.

A Year 10 teacher once told me her health students spent an entire class talking about how they should manage discussions about religions that banned homosexuality when there might be some gay kids in the class who shouldn't be hurt or shamed by their classmates. Eventually they decided to make a class rule that said 'hateful slurs about someone's religion, race, gender or sexuality are never OK' because, regardless of their differences, if everyone abided by that rule then no-one could get hurt.

Once the class has agreed on the rules the teacher will usually write them on the board or a piece of paper and keep them permanently on display. They serve as a reminder and a reference point, as well as being a living document that can be revised and updated if necessary.

You could easily adapt this approach to creating family or household rules for discussions, managing housework, or setting rules for online habits and behaviour. Say, for example, your family is getting into too many arguments at the dinner table, and you want to make it easier and safer for everyone to discuss things as a group. You could adapt the teaching resources like this:

- Make a time for everyone in the house to meet and work out rules for household discussions.
- All suggestions need to be framed as positive actions: 'We always let each other finish' rather than 'don't interrupt'.
- Everyone makes at least one suggestion about what ground rules will make it easy and safe for everyone to explain what they think and feel.
- Keep the rules simple and general: 'It's OK to disagree if we do it respectfully' rather than 'Uncle Charlie is only allowed to talk about religion if he doesn't say X or Y'.
- When you've all agreed on around five simple rules, put them up where everyone can see them in a common area, such as near the kitchen table or next to the TV.

- Review how the rules are working every few months, giving everyone a chance to be heard. Change the ones that aren't working and recognise how well everyone has done with the ones that are working.

The other discussion teachers will have with older teens is about the difference between feeling uncomfortable and feeling distressed. Most people find it uncomfortable when their beliefs are challenged. That's OK, sometimes we learn our best lessons from discomfort, but feeling uncomfortable is different to feeling scared or hurt. Teachers will always be very clear that any students who are distressed by anything in the lessons can leave the class, ask for help, or simply tune out for a while if they needed a break.[65] Teachers rarely tell students they can leave a classroom or tune out in lessons (any more than authors tell readers to stop reading or key skip sections in a book). But sometimes these topics can be painful to read or think about. No one should force themselves to do it if it causes pain. Anyone who teaches kids (or indeed adults) about violence must never forget that they do not know what other people are hiding.

Statistically, in a typical classroom of 25 – 30 students, around ten of those kids, and possibly more, have been abused themselves or are living in a family where they have seen someone they love being harmed – which is also abuse. Around seven of them will have experienced some form of sexual abuse and two or three are neglected (see Appendix 2). The rest of the students in the class might not know about their classmates' experiences and wouldn't understand it if they did know. This makes for a tricky balancing act. Teachers need to make sure that any child who needs help will hear enough to know they can ask for help and that they're given time in private to explain what they need. At the same time, they don't want the children who are growing up in safe happy homes to suddenly start having nightmares about abuse they've never experienced. Managing these competing, sometimes opposing needs requires a very delicate touch and constant monitoring for even signs in the kids' body language and facial expressions. Noticing who speaks and who stays silent and being aware of changing dynamics in the silence. Teachers need to be constantly observing patterns, trusting their instincts and if they're worried about any child, making time to ask if they're OK.

This approach is also something for parents to keep in mind. I know parents often help each other out with ferrying kids around and hosting sleepovers. They're all part of the village raising children and they will sometimes see or hear things about other people's children that raise red flags. This can be very challenging and is not something you should handle on your own unless you have specific training. If you see something that worries you, you could try talking to the teacher or well-being officer at the child's school or contact one of the services listed in Appendix 1.

Recognising emotions

As I outlined in Chapter 2, children and their adults need to understand how to talk to each other about feelings. The very young child who can say 'Mummy, my tummy feelings all squiggly' is much safer if his mother understands this means he is scared and wants help than if she thinks it might mean her son ate something weird from the garden and might be about to throw up.

As they get older, children also need help to recognise the physical signs of fear. Shaky legs, rumbling tummies, freezing up, feeling sick, overwhelming giggles, racing thoughts or no thoughts at all are very common physiological responses to fear.[66] Children and teens don't always recognise the connection between their legs getting wobbly and feeling afraid, they might just remember that they wanted to run away but didn't.

Fear is not always about abuse. Almost all kids know the feeling of being afraid. Some will feel terror if they have to stand up in front of the class and read out loud. Others might have been in car accidents or fallen out of trees or off bikes. They might have had bad dreams or been confronted by an angry dog at the park. And of course, sadly, some of them might be living with a violent, frightening person at home.

Regardless of the reason for their fear, they need to know that it is a totally normal response to freeze, struggle, run or desperately try to please or appease someone who feels threatening.[67]

Teachers also talk to kids about how our brains and bodies can have all kinds of reactions to strong feelings. We can cry in happiness or sadness, scream in joy or fear, yell in celebration or recrimination. There is no right or wrong way to express feelings – as long as no one gets hurt. It's also important that children know that if they couldn't understand or talk about how they felt as something was happening, they can tell someone about it afterwards and know they didn't do anything wrong if they couldn't recognise their feelings at the time.

In the later primary school and early secondary school years, teachers help kids recognise and explain nuances in their feelings. Scared is an umbrella term. Anxious, worried, uncomfortable, afraid, intimidated, frightened, terrified, panic-stricken or alarmed are all nuanced words that describe different states of fear. There are no right or wrong words for feelings, but it's helpful for children to understand that being nervous can make them a bit sweaty and agitated, while being terrified can make them forget their own name or feel so frozen they can't move.

Kids also need to learn the difference between fear responses that they *cannot* control (fight, flight, freeze, fawn) and anger responses they *can* control (hitting, hurting, humiliating).

One of the greatest myths about violence is that it only happens because people cannot control their anger – the 'he just snapped' cliché, but the truth is he doesn't 'snap', he makes a choice. Kids don't hit each other when a teacher is in the room to see them. Abusive men rarely beat their partners and children when police are in the house. Soldiers almost never commit war crimes when officers are present. In fact, all those people will almost always cease their violent behaviour as soon as they are aware of the witnesses and transform themselves from aggressor to victim within seconds – 'I wasn't doing anything to her, she started it' is a cry commonly heard by both teachers and police. No one who was truly unable to control their emotions could make that rapid change, so we need to understand that violence is almost always something we can choose to do or choose to *not* do.

Children are entirely able to appreciate that violence is a choice. They might not always understand that the choice is driven by fear, shame, opportunism or entitlement (see Chapter 6), but they can understand that they always have a choice to do something else when very strong feelings of anger or fear overwhelm them.

Some things you can suggest (and model yourself) to manage strong emotions:
- Walking away and doing five minutes of slow breathing exercises (slowly count to three as they breathe in, hold for a slow count of two, then slowly count to three as they breathe out and repeat until they feel better).
- A sprint around the playground, dancing or rapid star jumps can help release the physical build-up of feelings.
- Yelling into the wind or loud singing (if there is somewhere appropriate for that kind of noise).

- Stretching and relaxing each muscle in the body, starting with the toes and working all the way up to the top of the head is a very effective calming exercise.
- Art, music, writing and storytelling through acting or dance can be very cathartic.
- Knowing where to find a calm, quiet room or corner to escape when they're feeling overwhelmed can be very important for some children.

'Keep' secrets and 'tell' secrets

Abuse of any kind depends on secrecy. One of the first things any abusive person does is test potential victims to see whether they will resist shame, put-downs and secret keeping. Even between adults, the abuser needs to make sure the person they're abusing won't tell anyone or ask for help. Children and teens who knowingly manipulate or abuse other children are often not sophisticated in their demand for secrecy. Whether the threat is overt ('if you tell anyone I did this, I'll hurt you'), implied ('I hope your mum never finds out about this, she'd be really upset') or manipulative ('if you tell someone about this they will make the police put me in jail or even shoot me'). Secrecy is almost always part of abuse.[68]

Kids understand secrets. Most of them have eaten their brother's Easter egg, broken a plate, made a new baby cry or had ferocious thoughts about a parent who gave them Vegemite instead of jam on their toast. And they almost all share the fear of 'getting into trouble' for various transgressions. There's nothing sinister about any of this, but they do need to know the difference between secrets they can keep and secrets they should tell.

All preschool and primary school curriculum resources include topics such as safe and unsafe secrets.[69] These lessons are not about teaching children to betray confidences or tell tales. They're about helping them recognise a secret that can hurt them or someone else and a secret that will make someone happy.

For the first year of primary school, the curriculum suggests some scenarios for the teacher to give to the kids and ask them to decide whether it's a safe or an unsafe secret. *Lee knows what his big sister is getting for her birthday, but his parents told him to keep it a secret. Ollie's older cousin showed him a picture of adults who were naked and touching each other's private parts, he feels yuky about it, but his cousin said he couldn't tell anyone. Ali is making a special card and present for his mum, and he has to stop himself telling her about it. Trent used the family iPad when he wasn't supposed to, and he saw something that scared him. He wants to keep it secret because he doesn't want to get in trouble, but he can't stop thinking about the scary thing he saw.* The teacher presents each of these to the class and helps them clarify the safe and the unsafe secrets. Teachers help children understand that safe secrets are the ones they will tell their adults about after a short time and when they do tell it will make people happy – a birthday present or special surprise. Unsafe secrets are where they are never supposed to tell anyone or keeping the secret makes them feel scared, worried or 'wobbly' inside.[70]

The same principles apply to older children and teens, although we use more sophisticated language to talk to them about keeping secrets that make them feel shame, fear or self-loathing.

Every adult in a child's life needs to reinforce the idea that safe secrets are OK, but they should always take unsafe secrets to an adult they trust. If they're not sure whether a secret is safe or unsafe, ask someone. They might need a guarantee that they won't be punished for something naughty (such as using the iPad without permission) but no discipline is more important than ensuring they have an adult they can trust with their scary feelings and secrets.

Identity

As children begin to understand themselves and their place in the world, they start to recognise the characteristics that make them unique and how they are both different and similar to other kids in their class. Little kids start with obvious characteristics, 'I have brown eyes', 'I like carrots', 'I play football', and as they get older, they explore more complexities. 'I'm an introvert', 'I'm funny', 'I have legs that work differently', 'I'm not neurotypical', 'I'm a Muslim', 'I'm Italian and Australian'.

The curriculum includes many lessons, games and activities designed to help kids understand how their gender is woven into their sense of identity – their own and other people's.

Gender is one of the most defining characteristics of our identity. It's so fundamental to our understanding of who we are that, counter-intuitively, children often don't even think to mention it in their description of themselves. Despite this, children will usually frame most other core characteristics around their understanding of gender. This understanding can change, fluctuate or become entwined in other parts of our identity and move over time or even between circumstances. A black Muslim girl might have a very different sense of herself than a white Christian girl, as would a gay Aboriginal boy, a non-binary Hindu child, an athletic Indian girl and a white boy with disabilities. That white Christian and the black Muslim girl might also have shared experience in feeling they are different people when they are in their faith communities, in their school communities or out with friends from their sports club. While there are shifts and nuances in how gender frames our identity, it remains the most central and fixed characteristic in how children understand themselves and their place in the world.[71]

Identity is also about all our strengths and weaknesses, which includes characteristics we can't change (height) and physical characteristics we can change with a lot of work (physical strength). It's also the things we've learned or can learn (vocabulary, second languages, art and music). Certain aspects of us are innate – some kids might be naturally more assertive and others quite shy. A naturally shy person can learn to be more assertive, but they must learn and practice and concentrate on it, while other kids might need to learn to tone done their natural assertiveness to give others a chance to participate.

Helping children ask for help

For all ages, classes, and programs, in every curriculum, teachers talk to children and teens about asking for help when they feel scared, worried or sad. They also make sure the kids think about who they can talk to and how to contact them. Most of us want to believe our kids will tell us straight away if someone was threatening or hurting them. But all the evidence says that many children don't ever tell someone when they're being abused. Often, this is because abusers groom their victims to believe they must keep secrets or that other adults will be angry with them if they tell anyone (see Chapter 2). Children might also not ask for help because they don't have the language and knowledge to describe how they feel or what is happening. Or they may not know where they can go for help. And, of course, many children are worried about 'getting into trouble' or getting someone else in trouble.

There are many reasons and often this silence can cause as much harm to the silent child as the cause of the anxiety. This is why teachers put so much emphasis on the variety of ways children can find help and support. Equally, all the protective adults in a child's life need to know how to be supportive confidants for children. These are skills we need to learn in the same way that we needed to learn how to change nappies and bath babies. It doesn't always come naturally, and no one should assume that someone has all the knowledge and skills they need just because they survived childhood themselves.

Knowing how to respond to disclosures of abuse, pick up on warning signs and where to find help (see Chapter 2) are not things adults know unless they're told. Children often have no idea what to do or how to explain complex problems, particularly if they've been made to feel shame or fear about anyone finding out about their secret. The key task for adults is making sure kids know they can talk to someone when they're upset or scared, and they never have to worry about being in trouble when they ask for help – even if they think they've done something wrong. This is not just a set and forget statement. It needs regular reinforcement (at minimum once a month – you want them rolling their eyes and sighing 'yes, I *know*' at you every time you say it). They also need you to prove that you're telling the truth. If they smashed a plate, broke the TV or lied to a teacher and they tell you to ask you for help, you must follow through on your promise. Sometimes things just get broken, but kids will also occasionally break something deliberately to test a promise. If you take a deep breath and say, 'I'm glad you told me, now what do we need to do to fix it?' they can trust you with much more difficult problems.

Teachers delivering prevention education will also talk through all the various options available to children who need help – parents, family members, family friends, school nurse or counsellor, teachers, doctors, and parents of the child's friends. Hopefully, they will also make sure children know about all the helplines listed in Appendix 1. One of my friend's children showed me her school diary, which had all the helplines and webchat sites listed inside the front cover – such a practical and useful idea. Maybe something you could suggest to the school if they don't already do it?

Teens also need to know that while they might be old enough to solve some problems on their own, no one expects them to be able to solve huge or frightening problems alone. That's what adults are for. Talking to friends and siblings and dogs can be comforting, but it's not enough when something serious happens. An eight-year-old boy once told me that his dog was twenty in dog years and 'he's much wiser than anyone else I know'. I get it. I've had old and wise dogs too, I know how consoling they can be in the tough times. But when children (or their friends) are being hurt or are in trouble they can't escape on their own, they need a safe and knowledgeable adult to help them.

Involving police and mandatory reporting

Everyone who works with children and, in some states, even parents and family members are required to report any reasonable belief that a child is being abused (see Appendix 1 for reporting lines). Mandatory reporting was recommended by the Royal Commission into Institutional Responses to Child Sexual Abuse and can be very effective in preventing systemic cover up of child abuse. It's not, however, a perfect system. Myths about who does and does not commit child abuse can skew our perspective. Over-reporting of First Nations mothers, for example, perpetuates intergenerational systemic violence against First Nations people and might offer more harm than protection to First Nations children.[72]

Reporting abuse to police can save lives. It can also destroy them. Untrained or biased police can misidentify perpetrators or feed children into a court system that forces the child to live with a parent who sexually abuses them because fathers have 'rights'.[73]

Children's view of police is always very telling. Some are scared, thinking police officers are waiting on every corner, ready to pounce on innocent children and hurl them into prison for the slightest infraction. Others talk about them as heroes, the shining knights who will save them from any danger. 'My neighbour, he once told me that every time I jump there's an earthquake. That's a horrible thing to say. I should have called the police on him.'

Others have a much bleaker view. 'Police take your mum to jail if she's being hurt.' 'Police take you away from your family if you tell them about anything bad.' This is the reality of too many lives in First Nations and refugee communities, which means we often have to be cautious about suggesting police stations as safe places to find help. The compromise is helping them identify adults in their lives who can decide whether to call the police.

We make sure they know about all the support services available in their community, doctors, faith leaders, sports coaches and school counsellors and well-being officers (it never fails to surprise me how many kids don't know that their school has those people available to them). We talk them through naming the five safe adults in their life and make sure they know all the support lines (see Appendix 1) and that they can call those helplines anonymously or chat online if they don't want to say something out loud. I couldn't count the number of times I've heard children say something like, 'oh yeah, I forgot about kids helpline' so it's always worth taking the time to remind them about those services.

Help is available for children who need it but sometimes they need help to find it. All the adults in a child's life are responsible for making sure the child knows who, where and how to find help if they're feeling scared, under pressure or just need someone to talk to about their feelings.

4

Bodies, reproduction and sexuality

Violence prevention education teaches kids (and adults) about minds and bodies. They need to understand feelings, thoughts, develop empathy and habits of respect (which I'll cover in later chapters) but they also need to understand their own and other people's bodies.

They start school as little children who need to know the names and functions of all the different parts of their bodies. As they get older, they need to be prepared for the physical and emotional changes puberty will bring. By secondary school they need to know about the mechanics of sex, reproduction, contraception and sexually transmitted infections (STIs). In the later years of secondary school they should have a thorough understanding of what their bodies need to get physical, emotional, psychological and sexual pleasure. It's very rare that sexual pleasure is taught at school, and there are understandable if not good reasons for that, but understanding sexual pleasure is part of understanding consent. If kids cannot learn about it at school, they need to learn it somewhere or they risk wasting far too much time on unfulfilling or even unpleasant sexual encounters.

But let's start with the easy stuff first.

Naming body parts

A friend of mine used to refer to her genitals as her 'lady garden', a euphemism she later passed on to her daughter. The little girl, as small children often do, abbreviated the term she was taught and called it her 'garden'. It was cute and funny and no one corrected her. As she grew older, she learned the medical terms for all her body parts, but even as an adult she is still embarrassed by any direct discussion about sex and bodies.

As far as I know there was no other harm done, but that may have been a matter of luck. Imagine a six-year-old stuttering out a confused story to her teacher about someone playing with her 'garden'. As I outlined in Chapter 2, children often test out disclosures in noisy rooms and at inconvenient times. They can be easy to miss and 'oh well never mind' is an unhelpful response when a child is feeling bullied or imposed on, but it is a catastrophic response to an attempt at disclosing sexual abuse.

We're often told that children don't disclose sexual abuse when it's happening – and this is true of many children being abused in institutional settings but research on child abuse in families and homes suggests that children might be telling people (or at least attempting to tell people) far more than we realise. One study suggests the figure could be as high as 80 per cent of children being sexually abused try to ask for help and up to half of them are misunderstood, dismissed, minimised or ignored.[74] When this happens children will shut down and often not try again for years.[75]

All child abuse prevention programs, as well as the broader violence prevention and sexuality education curriculum include lessons on understanding and naming private and public body parts. Children will often start these lessons in preschool, but all children should be learning this in the first year of primary school.

Kids in those classrooms experience this as a fun game, not a lesson about dangers. Teachers will bring out a puppet or soft toy, give it a name and use it to start a conversation about clothes. If Sam is a teddy bear, for example, the teacher might tell the class that Sam has fur and doesn't need clothes, so how can the class help Sam understand what people use clothes for? The teacher would ask questions such as

- What clothes do people need on hot days?
- What clothes do we use for swimming, netball and bike riding?
- What about when we take a shower or a bath?
- When do we wear special clothes? Birthdays? Celebrations? Halloween? School?
- If we get really hot at school can we take off all our clothes and run around the schoolyard naked? How about just in our undies?

The answers to these questions lead to discussions about comfort (cool clothes in summer and warm clothes in winter) safety (goggles to protect eyes in the pool and helmets to protect heads when bike riding). The class will also talk about nudity and private body parts (which are usually covered by undies and swimsuits).

From there, the teacher will typically use a plain line diagram to show and name all the private body parts. Very young children (around six or younger) are usually more curious than embarrassed, but they can become increasingly self-conscious as they get older. By the time they're in Year 5 and 6, they're edging into puberty and can be quite coy and giggly about saying 'penis' or 'vulva', they might even protest, saying it's 'rude' to talk about those things. This is very typical of primary school kids – it shows they know their genitals are private. Modelling calm, practical conversations about body parts is usually the best way to reassure children their bodies should never make them feel shame or embarrassment.

The most important lesson for children to learn is that their bodies belong only to them and no one has the right to touch them in a way that makes them scared or uncomfortable. Again, exceptions for healthcare and keeping clean are important to note, but emphasise that this must never be secret, scary or uncomfortable.

Puberty

In preschool, the most obvious changes between three-year-olds and four year olds are verbal and cognitive. In primary school, while those changes are still going on, the physical becomes more noticeable. As they get closer to the end of primary school, they grow up, fill out and fall headlong into puberty.

A primary school teacher from Queensland who grew up in a devout churchgoing family told me that the first time her older sister got a period, she believed she'd been cursed by the devil and was going to bleed to death as punishment for playing pranks on the parish priest. The two sisters, terrified and ashamed, kept the secret for almost a year. It was only after an intervention from an aunt on a family holiday that they found out about menstruation. 'She was only eighteen months older than me,' Little Church Sister told me. 'I can't even imagine what we would have thought if I'd started my period before Aunt Jenny talked to us. But my sister had panicky feelings about periods right up to menopause.' Years later, their mother said she thought she didn't need to talk to her daughters about periods before they were sixteen.

Menarche (the start of menstruation) is happening earlier now than it was in the 1950s, but even back then the average age was around twelve to thirteen years old in the US (by 2005, it was around eleven years).[76] Australian data indicates the average age of menarche here is about thirteen years old, but it can be as early as eight years old or as late as fifteen.[77]

It's not unusual for children who don't understand puberty's alteration of their bodies to pull together a few half-heard snatches of adult conversations and assemble them into a notion that scared them half to death. The sisters probably heard someone refer to 'the curse' (an old euphemism for periods) and they'd certainly heard far too much from the parish priest about Satan's punishment for naughtiness. It's not difficult to see how they wove those together to explain the sudden gush of blood from an unmentionable body part. Little Church Sister was so determined to make sure that terror was not visited upon any other children that as soon as she started teaching at her current school, she started a period club. It's a little room tucked in between the sick bay and the girls' toilets, full of bean bags and soft lighting. She keeps the room stocked with period products, hot-water bottles, and child-friendly pain killers. She also has a wide range of books for kids that explain everything they need to know about periods (I've included her recommendations in the list on the next page).

All the other changes puberty brings can be equally alarming for children who have no idea of what's coming. Erections, wet dreams, discharge, body hair, smells, acne, changing body shapes, breasts growing at different speeds, and wild emotional swings are all exciting and exhausting and can be overwhelming, but they are so much easier to cope with when children understand what is happening to them and know what to expect. It's also enormously helpful for them to know that everyone else in their class is going through similar changes (or will be soon).

It's very common for children to worry that their body or the way it's changing isn't 'normal'. Calm, practical lessons at school that are regularly reinforced at home can make this confusing time much easier.

If you want some help with reliable information, Australia has several very good websites full of useful and accurate information about puberty for kids and parents:
- www.raisingchildren.net.au
- www.kidshealth.org
- www.healthdirect.gov.au

There are also several great books available for kids and parents:
- *Welcome to your Period!* by Yumi Stynes and Dr Melissa Kang.
- *Celebrate Your Body (and Its Changes, Too!): The Ultimate Puberty Book for Girls* by Sonya Renee Taylor.
- *Are you There God? It's Me, Margaret* by Judy Blume.
- *What's Happening to Me?* by Alex Frith.
- *The Boys' Guide to Growing Up* by Phil Wilkinson.
- *Puberty Is Gross but Also Really Awesome* by Gina Loveless.

Sex and reproduction

When my daughter was nine, she fell in love with the Baz Luhrmann movie, *Moulin Rouge*. She watched it almost every day for months, crying each time as Satine died, breathlessly hoping the next viewing would give her the happy ending she longed for, embracing the joyful sorrow when it didn't. She's an adult now and last week we watched the movie together for the first time in more than ten years. She was stunned to discover that Satine was a courtesan and that all the scenes inside the elephant were full of sexual innuendo, to say nothing of the implied sexual violence in the third act. She must have watched the movie at least a hundred times when she was a child, and she'd never noticed any of it.

'I loved the colour and the dancing and the songs. I wanted Ewan McGregor to sing to me inside an elephant. All that stuff with her rolling around on the bed, I just thought she was being funny. I didn't even know it was about sex.'

This is typical of how children see the world. They don't know everything adults know, they don't recognise sexual allusions, and they are far more likely to skip over references that don't make sense than get upset about them. Which is why we should always be concerned about (and believe) a child who demonstrates knowledge of explicit sexual behaviour (see Chapter 2).

When children see something graphically sexual that they don't understand (porn for example) they're often curious and confused. If their adults can give them calm, practical explanations that satisfy their curiosity, they'll usually move on to something more interesting. But if their curiosity and confusion is not alleviated, they will seek answers from far less reliable sources, typically either the schoolyard or their online world.

No one who wants the best for children wants them to become too adult or too sexually aware before they're ready. But it's important to remember that prepubescent children don't have the same responses to sexual material as an adult or an older teen. If they go looking for sexually explicit images it could just be because they're looking for weirdness and shock value more than masturbation aids.

Children's curiosity naturally extends to babies, especially if they've got or are about to have younger siblings. They see pregnant stomachs growing and parents coming home with very new babies, and they want to know how it all happened. They're often also intensely interested in their own babyhood as they try to make sense of their rapidly developing brains, bodies and capabilities.

Sex education in the first year of primary school begins by helping children explore how much they've changed since they were little babies. Teachers will encourage children to bring in baby photos or mementos and ask parents for stories about what their baby self did that made parents laugh or cheer. Early primary classes play games like designing Baby Olympics – *Can babies compete in a bike race? Can toddlers use roller skates?* – and learn to appreciate their developing skills and independence.[78]

As they progress through the primary school years, children will slowly develop their understanding of bodies from naming the visible parts (arms, legs, penises, nipples, bottoms and vulvas) to naming and understanding the various organs inside their bodies (heart, lungs, kidneys, uterus, ovaries, testes). Most kids are fascinated by the internal workings of their own bodies and the love to see diagrams of skeletons, cardiovascular, digestive and reproductive systems. [79]

By the time they get to the end of primary school, they should have a solid knowledge of the mechanics of sexual intercourse, conception and birth. Most children at this age will make the connection between reproduction and sexual pleasure and they may even start experimenting with masturbation or curiosity about other people's genitals. As long as they can be easily distracted from this behaviour and are not simulating explicit sexual acts or attempting to penetrate genitals or ansuses (their own or other kids) there's nothing to worry about.[80] If you are at all worried about your child's sexual behaviour, your GP or family health nurse are the best place to start. If you don't have a regular GP or you're not sure if there's a family health nurse near you, ask your child's teacher where to find someone you can go to for help. The Raising Children Network website (www.raisingchildren.net.au) also has a wide range of reliable resources for parents.

By secondary school, sex education should help teens begin thinking about what they need to know and do if they start having sex themselves. At this age they should all know the mechanics of sexual intercourse and reproduction, but if they think that sex only means penis-in-vagina penetration they can sometimes apply this definition to consent. Sometimes this can mean other forms of sexual touching or touch between same sex people can sit outside their concept of sexual consent. Building their understanding of a wider definition of sex alongside their understanding of sexual consent is key to keeping them (and the teens around them) safe.

One of the as-yet unresolved sensitivities about teaching consent is joy and pleasure. Teens consistently say they want sex and consent education that doesn't view sex as something they should avoid because it's dangerous or demeaning. They want to know that they can have safe, fun, *pleasurable* sex and they want guidance on how to do so (I don't blame them, I know a whole lot of adults who'd want to attend a workshop like that).[81]

Parents, on the other hand, are understandably conflicted about their children being taught that sex can feel wonderful. Most parents want their children to have fulfilling sex lives – when they're old enough – but they're worried about anything that might encourage their kids to start experimenting too early. Comprehensive education about sex is one of the factors that lowers the risk of early sexual behaviour, along with close family bonds and relaxed communication about sex.[82]

The idea of a stranger coming into a class of fourteen-year-olds to extol the wonders of a clitoral orgasm is too confronting for many parents – for now. That may change, but in the meantime, kids need to learn that sex is not shameful when it is fully informed and consensual. Parents and families play a very important role in this and their influence is often as much in what they don't say as it is in what they do say. If parents are too embarrassed to talk about sex or they're casually shaming women for being too sexual or men for not being sexual enough, kids will often incorporate those beliefs into their own understanding of sex. Conversely, if they hear their parents and families talking about sex as something enjoyable and fun – when it is fully consensual – they're much more likely to expect that standard for themselves and others.

In addition to consent, they also need to have a very clear understanding of how to prevent STIs and unwanted pregnancies. Condoms are still the most commonly used and effective method of preventing the spread of many (but not all) STIs, but many STIs do not have symptoms and some can be spread even when people use condoms. Any sexually active person should be having regular STI screening, which teens can do through their GP. Most clinics will bulk bill children under 16, but the appointment might still appear on Medicare records. If you can manage it, give your teen permission to make GP appointments without telling you and show them how to do it. I know this is a big call, but if your kid is worried about STIs or contraception and they're too embarrassed to ask you, you want them asking a doctor not their mates. The Better Health Channel website also has a wide range of reliable and up-to-date resources about STIs and contraception options www.betterhealth.vic.gov.au/health/healthyliving/safe-sex

Gender and sexuality

I have a friend who is a theatre nurse (meaning she works with a surgical team in a hospital operating theatre, not on stage in a skimpy nurse costume). I asked her once if people are as different on the inside as they are on the outside. 'Oh yes,' she said, 'you see unexpected bumps and lumps and odd shapes and weird placements every time you cut someone open.' I found that so warmly reassuring. All the big noses, knobbly knees, high cheekbones and dimpled chins that make us unique on the outside are not just surface differences. They go all the way through. Our organs, muscles, bones and tendons are all uniquely our own, not factory built carbon copies of each other.

If is this true of our physical selves, how much more variation is learned and hardwired into our minds? All the thoughts and feelings and abilities and knowledge of self and others is so individual, so variable and constantly shifting. The very idea of codifying anything about humans - let alone something as complex as gender – down to two narrow definitions is laughably reductive.

I sometimes struggle with a few concepts and language choices suggested for inclusive education and healthcare. I will never refer to myself as a 'vagina owner' (I do *not* define myself by my genitals) and I hesitate over nomenclature that feels like it's erasing recent, fragile and hard-won protections for women's medical and physical health. But rigidly binary definitions of gender are far too disconnected from the messy and complex reality of people to make any sense. So I keep working through the complexity of language until I can find terminology that makes emotional sense to me and doesn't exclude people who live in that complex reality. For example, I cannot bring myself to remove women from discussion about reproductive health care rights, but I can (and do) comfortably talk about 'women and other people who need abortions'. The same approach can work for sexuality education.

We can make generalisations (for example, it is true to say that men are often taller and physically stronger than women) but we cannot ever be definitive (it would be ludicrous to say all men are taller and stronger than all women). Inclusive teaching is kind, respectful and informative. It teaches children that male bodies are typically born with penises and testicles, female bodies are typically born with vulvas and vaginas, but it's also typical that some people have genders that don't match these definitions and other people have genitals that don't look like or work like other peoples. These variations have always existed and it's no more weird or surprising than blonde hair, dimples or very big feet (and even bigger shoes).

Roughly 10 per cent of people are born left-handed and this has been true for at least 200,000 years. The only change in this pattern was a dip to around 3 per cent in the 19th century when the industrial age introduced machinery designed for right-handed people and mass education had left-handers smearing ink all over their papers. During this time, left-handedness was stigmatised and all but disappeared. It resurfaced as the stigmatisation dissipated and by the beginning of the 21st century, left-handedness had returned to the roughly 10 per cent it has always been.[83]

Reducing stigma and shame is why there are so many more trans and non-binary kids in classrooms now than there were twenty years ago. The same is true of neurodivergent kids. None of these normal variations of humanity are new in the modern age, they're just not hiding as much or as often.

Learning about LGBTIQA+ people is not going to turn a cis or straight kid gay or trans, any more than learning about left handedness is going to turn a right handed kid into a southpaw. What it will do is help them understand themselves and all the possibilities that might be there for them and for the people they will live, work and play with for the rest of their lives. Growing up knowing they don't need to fear or hate differences in other people makes for a much calmer and safe life for everyone.

Additionally, we know how closely the fate of straight people and LGBTIQA+ people are bound together, never more so than when they appear to be divided. All the fears and assumptions that lead to policing gender norms (see Chapter 5) underpin homophobia and transphobia. We can't dismantle only half the patriarchy. It is an all or nothing deal.

Understanding LGBTIQA+ terminology

Most curriculum include lessons on the terminology of gender and sexuality. Even kids who haven't been taught these terms in class will generally pick up the meaning by the time they're in their early teens. You probably know them too, but in case you're unsure, these definitions are taken from the Victorian Government's LGBTIQA+ Inclusive Language Guide.[84]

Gender is part of a person's personal and social identity. It refers to a way a person feels and sees themselves. It can be about differences in identity, expression and experience as a woman, man or gender-diverse person.

- **Gender diverse** is an umbrella term for a range of different genders. There are many terms gender-diverse people may use to describe themselves. Language in this area is dynamic and always changing, particularly among young people. Some examples include gender-fluid, gender-queer, gender non-conforming, agender, bigender and non-binary.

- **Non-binary** is a term for people whose gender sits outside the spectrum of man or woman or male and female. A person who is non-binary might feel like they have a mix of genders, or like they have no gender at all. A person might identify solely as non-binary or relate to non-binary as an umbrella term. They might consider themselves as gender-fluid, gender-queer, trans masculine, trans feminine, agender or bigender.

- **Trans or transgender** refers to someone whose gender does not exclusively align with their sex recorded at birth. Not all trans people will use this term to describe themselves.

- **Cis or cisgender** (pronounced 'sis') refers to a person whose gender is the same as their sex recorded at birth. Not all cisgender people will be aware of this term or use it to describe themselves.

- **Sistergirl and brotherboy** are terms used in Aboriginal and Torres Strait Islander communities to describe transgender people. Using these terms can validate and strengthen their gender identities and relationships. Sistergirls and brotherboys might be non-binary, female or male. Sistergirl describes gender diverse people that have a female spirit and take on female roles within the community, including looking after children and family. Brotherboy describes gender diverse people that have a male spirit and take on male roles within the community. Other Aboriginal and Torres Strait Islander peoples may also use these words. For example, lesbian and heterosexual Aboriginal and Torres Strait Islander women may refer to themselves as 'sistagirls', 'sistas' or 'tiddas', which has the meaning of the word 'sisters'. Gay Aboriginal men may also refer to themselves as sistas. In broader Aboriginal and Torres Strait Islander communities, the terms 'sistagirl' and 'brothaboy' are used as terms of endearment for women and men with no reference to gender diversity. It is important to note that not all First Nations people who are transgender use these terms.

Sex refers to a person's biological sex characteristics. This includes their sex chromosomes, hormones and reproductive organs.

- **Sex recorded at birth** (or sex assigned at birth) is based upon a person's sex characteristics and reproductive organs observed at, or soon after, birth.
- **Variations of sex characteristics**: Some people are born with a variation to physical or biological sex characteristics including chromosomes, hormones or anatomy. These are often called intersex variations. There are many different intersex variations

that can be identified prenatally, at birth, puberty or adulthood. People with intersex variations use a range of different terminology to name their bodies and experiences. Some use the term 'intersex', which is signified by the 'I' in LGBTIQA+ communities. Others do not connect to the term 'intersex' or with the acronym LGBTIQA+. People with variations of sex characteristics are usually assigned male or female at birth or infancy, just like everyone else. Intersex people can have any gender identity or sexuality.

- **Endosex** refers to people whose sex characteristics meet medical and social norms for typically 'male' or 'female' bodies. Not all endosex people will be aware of this term or use it to describe themselves.

Sexuality or sexual orientation describe a person's intimate, romantic and/or sexual attractions to others. It can include sexual identity (how a person thinks of their sexuality and the terms they identify with). It can also include attraction (romantic or sexual interest in another person) and behaviour or relationships. These attractions may be towards someone of the same gender or sex, another gender, all genders, no gender or a combination. There are many different terms used for sexuality. Some people may choose to describe their sexuality in terms of feelings, behaviours or experiences such as 'same sex' or 'gender attracted'. Others may choose to use no term at all. Sexuality may be fluid for some people and change over time. For others it can be the same throughout their life.

- **Asexual** refers to a person who does not experience sexual attraction but may or may not experience romantic attraction towards others. Asexual people can be any gender or sexual orientation.

- **Lesbian** refers to a woman (cis or trans) or gender-diverse person who is romantically and/or sexually attracted to women.
- **Gay** means someone who is romantically and/or sexually attracted to people of the same sex and/or gender as themselves. This term is often used to describe men who are attracted to other men, but some women and gender-diverse people may describe themselves as gay.
- **Bisexual** is a person who is romantically and/or sexually attracted to people of their own gender and other genders. The term 'bi+' or multi-gender attracted (MGA) are sometimes used to describe communities of people who are attracted to multiple genders.
- **Pansexual** means a person is romantically and/or sexually attracted to people of all genders and regardless of gender.
- **Queer** is often used as an umbrella term for diverse genders or sexualities. Some people use queer to describe their own gender or sexuality, as an identity that does not correspond to heterosexual norms. For some people, especially older people, 'queer' has negative connotations, because in the past it was used as a discriminatory term.
- **Questioning** refers to people who are exploring or questioning their gender or sexual orientation. People may not wish to have one of the other labels applied to them yet, for a variety of reasons. It is important these people feel welcome and included in LGBTIQA+ communities.
- **Heterosexual** is another word for 'straight'. It generally refers to men who are attracted to women, or women who are attracted to men.

Books about sex and sexuality
- *First Human Body Encyclopedia* by DK Publishing.
- *Amazing You: Getting Smart about Your Private Parts* by Gail Saltz and Lynne Avril Cravath.
- *Healthy for Life: Sex and Relationships* by Anna Claybourne.
- *Welcome to Sex* by Dr Melissa Kang and Yumi Stynes.
- *The Sex Ed You Never Had* by Chantelle Otten.
- *The Gender Identity workbook for kids: A guide to exploring who you are* by Kelly Storck.

5

Gender myths

Culture, according to the *Oxford Dictionary* is 'the ideas, customs, and social behaviour of a particular people or society'.[85]

Schools have cultures, in the same way that countries, cities and organisations do. They are the spoken and (often more powerful) unspoken rules by which teachers and students define themselves, each other and the standards of expected behaviour.

Almost all schools have written rules about bullying, but some schools have (again, more powerful) unwritten rules that condone or even encourage bullying of children and teachers who challenge the school's culture.

Other schools, sometimes with only the vaguest written rules – 'we treat everyone with respect' – have a culture that welcomes all the outliers. The pre-pubescent goth poet, already questioning their gender and sexuality, has the same social power as the budding football star or maths genius. Sometimes this culture is a deliberate choice. In other schools it seems to happen by osmosis and is reinforced by parents and students self-selecting in and out in response to the school's culture or attempts to impose change. This happens more often at private schools, where schools are not allocated by zoning and around 30 per cent of primary students and 40 per cent of secondary students are in non-government schools. [86]

Almost all the teachers I talked to for this book recognised that their students were often enforcing gender roles in the classroom. Which is not surprising, policing gender roles typically starts in pre-school.[87]

Picture a typical four-year-old preschool class having some outdoor playtime. In the sandpit, a small boy frowns in concentration as he builds roads and quarries for his toy truck. He bumps into another child playing with a truck in the sandpit and is immediately outraged. 'You're a girl!' he yells, snatching the truck away from her, 'girls play with dolls not trucks.' I heard this story from a woman who has been teaching four-year-old kindergarten for more than fifteen years. She told me that this scenario, or something very like it, happens in every year in every class and almost always more than once. 'Sometimes it's boys sending girls away but it's just as likely that girls will tell boys they can't play with dolls or toy kitchens. The child being rejected is usually frustrated and upset but they almost always understand that the rules exist.'

Even when teachers disrupt the gender rules and encourage kids of all genders to play with all the toys, gender differences are so embedded into even our smallest daily tasks (the way we wear our hair, the colour of our clothes, the very names we give our kids) that by the time children are in primary school they will still be rejecting classmates from their games ('you can't play football with us you're a *girl*') and policing each other's feelings ('boys don't cry like that, stupid').[88]

A Year 7 teacher told me that while she knows the kids all recognise gender roles, she doesn't believe the boys come into her class with misogynist beliefs. Sadly, though, some of them end the year heading down that path. 'This age is often when they start to pick up those cues and as the year goes on I can see the Unmentionable (meaning Andrew Tate – see Chapter 11) creeping in'. It's not always the boys who are the loudest and most talkative but there are always far too many boys in the loud group and far too many girls among the quiet ones. When I try to hush the boys and tell them to let the girls talk, they always look so surprised. They'll say something like "but I wasn't stopping her talking" and then they'll all stare at the girls, waiting for something to happen.'

Many years ago, I worked in the energy industry. Back then it was almost completely male dominated, and I can't remember ever going into a meeting where men didn't outnumber women by three or four to one. Very occasionally, someone would firmly tell one of those men to shut up for a bit so a women could finish her sentence. Every time this happened, they'd respond with the same surprised look that teacher saw in her Year 7 boys, and some variation of their bewildered 'but I didn't stop her talking' response. Most of them were not deliberately or malevolently shutting women out, they're just so accustomed to men dominating conversations and ideas that it seems normal.

In the 1970s, Dale Spender, author of one of the first feminist books on language, asked university students to evaluate their perception of who talked more in a class discussion.[89] The women's estimations were roughly accurate; but men perceived the discussion as being gender equal when women talked 15 per cent of the time, and as dominated by women if they talked 30 per cent of the time. This experiment has been replicated many times over the last few decades, and the results remain roughly the same.[90][91][92] Men talk more than women in mixed gender rooms; they interrupt women more than each other and perceive more hostility in women who disagree with them than in men who disagree with them. This is learned behaviour. It starts in the early primary school years when girls were praised for being sweet, gentle and quiet, and boys were rewarded for being louder, interrupting more, and taking up more space. Again, this isn't every classroom or every school, but when it does happen, the results can be both sad and dangerous.

The opposite sex

'It's a girl!' 'It's a boy!' Gender is often the first thing we know about babies. Our perception of their gender can influence how we think about our children's personality, needs and future – and sometimes this can happen before they're even conceived.

By the time they're two years old, children understand gendered expectations and expect praise for conforming or shame for failing to conform to myths about gender roles.[93]

Gender myths are the set of beliefs and expectations about how girls and boys should look, behave and live.[94] These myths underpin patriarchy, a word that goes in and out of fashion but is useful to describe a culture that embraces and enforces gender myths. The word patriarchy comes from the Greek and translates as roughly 'the rule of the father'. British sociologist and Professor of Criminology Sylvia Walby defined it as 'a system of social structures and practices in which men dominate, oppress, and exploit women'.[95] What her definition doesn't include, however, is how patriarchy also hurts men and erases non-binary people.

In a binary concept of gender, there are no variations or nuances, the binary defines men as the *opposite* of women and men prove their manliness by being everything a woman is *not*. If women are weak, men must be strong – the further away he moves from weak womanliness the closer he gets to strong manliness. Any characteristic that could be perceived as weakness (kindness, compassion, affection, gentleness, consideration) moves him towards weak, contemptible womanliness and his punishment is shame (which I will explore more in chapter 6). While women who perform appropriate weakness might be given (conditional) patriarchal protection, they are also vulnerable to patriarchal abuse and they live in constant fear of rejection, shame and violent punishment if they fail to conform to their weak and passive role.

Concepts of gender that include fluidity, transition or non-binary identity tear away the foundation of definition by opposites and are therefore terribly threatening to rigid gender myths.

A common exercise teachers do to help kids understand this is called, *What makes a boy? What makes a girl?* [96] The teacher puts two labels on the board: *Boys* and *Girls,* then asks the kids to fill in lists about clothes, hobbies, abilities and characteristics that belong under each heading. As one primary school teacher told me, it's not even that they are so quick to identify differences – girls should be pretty and boys should be strong, girls cry and boys yell – but their reactions to the lists are so telling. Boys will often perform exaggerated disgust for each other, clutching their stomachs and making vomit noises at the mention of Barbie or Taylor Swift, because nothing is more dangerous to traditional masculinity than enjoyment of girlish fandoms. Girls can earn respect for liking 'boy' things, such as football, but only if they're not a threat to the boy's enjoyment of 'boy' things – *you can like football but if you take our practice times on the field or run faster or kick harder than boys, the reprisal will be swift and violent.*

Most kids know these myths are false, even harmful, but they all find them familiar, and they often underestimate the power they have over their beliefs about what they can do and how they should act. Writing the ideas down helps kids clarify the gender myths they've accumulated, often without even noticing, and then they can talk about how that happened. Did they absorb these ideas at home? At school? Did they pick them up from movies, books, TV, games, social media, and just living in the world. How does it affect the way they dress? Does it change the careers they think about for their future, or how long it takes them to get ready in the morning? The things they say in class? The sport they play? The shoes they wear? How do those small choices affect their interaction with the world? These are the questions you can ask your kids at the dinner table, in the car, or while you're both out walking the dog.

A few years ago, I had a fabulous conversation with a group of sixteen-year-olds about how gender affects the clothes they wear for exercise. They talked about the loose comfortable clothes the boys typically wear (shorts and T-shirts) and the tight-fitting, revealing clothing girls wear (crop top bras and leggings), and how this often meant that boys were relaxed and comfortable while girls sometimes felt self-conscious and exposed, 'with every bump and bulge on show' as one girl put it. We dug into every aspect of this, the differences in colour and material of gendered exercise clothes, even down to how much extra time and cost was involved in buying, washing and coordinating outfits for exercise. Everyone laughed at the idea of boys planning ahead to make sure their T-shirts, shorts and socks were complementing colours, but the girls all said they made sure their outfits 'matched'. Exercise clothes might seem like a trivial topic, but it's those simple everyday things that are often easiest to recognise and talk about without getting so emotionally invested that anyone needs to feel they're being accused of weakness.

It can be confronting to realise how gendered thinking creeps into your life. When my kids were in their early teens, my daughter asked, with a pointed stare, why it was her job to stack the dishwasher and my son's job to take out the rubbish. 'Some feminist you are,' she said, with all the righteous disgust of a child uncovering her parent's hypocrisy. She was right, of course and I was oblivious to the gendered nature of the tasks when I assigned them, possibly even distracted at the time by composing another feminist diatribe. But there it was, the patriarchy looming large in my head and my house.

This is how subtly these myths can sneak up on us. We know women can be CEOs and carpenters and soldiers, but we're more likely to picture men in those roles. Similarly, when we imagine a nurse, a retail worker, or a childcare worker, we think of women. In all those cases we would likely be right to do so. There are very few jobs in Australia that aren't highly gendered. Men rarely aspire to be nurses and women don't often become plumbers. This is how the myths reinforce and perpetuate themselves.

Warrior kings and fairytale princesses

Gender myths exist in almost every culture. There might be minor variations, but the concept of men as dominant warriors and women as submissive nurturers is so ubiquitous that the few cultures that don't adhere to these beliefs (which I'll get to soon) are the perfect demonstration of the exception proving the rule.

People have argued for thousands of years about the source of binary gender roles. It's been ascribed to gods, hormones, animal instincts, reproductive necessity, economics, ingrained habits and even witchcraft. No one has ever proven a definitive cause. So, I go back to the three most useful questions to ask when trying to understand why people do things: who has power, why do they have it, and what do they do with it?

For most of human history until the beginning of the industrial age, power depended on a ruler's real or perceived ability to field warriors who could defend their homelands or win a battle against defenders of other homelands. With very few exceptions this meant that most people's role in their society was to grow food, die on battlefields or produce children who could do one or both of those things.

Hunger always provides the necessary inspiration for growing, hunting and trading food, but how do you convince young men to willingly die in a war they barely understand or young women to keep risking their lives in childbirth? You tell them stories. You create myths and legends to make them believe that deaths on battlefields or in childbirth are the ultimate glorious fulfilment of their destiny.

All stories serve a purpose. Whether they are oral traditions handed down over generations, fairytales, Shakespearian plays, Disney movies, or the latest streaming series, stories are about how we understand ourselves, each other and the world; they are how we set our aspirations for who we will strive to be.

Until very recently, most stories venerated submissive femininity in women and warrior virility in men. Broadly speaking, these aspirations were embodied in fairytale princess and warrior kings.

I'll come back to the warrior kings, but first, let's look at fairytale princesses.

Fairy Tale Princesses

Fairytale princesses were a staple in stories written for and told to children over many centuries. Long before Disney sanitised and monetised fairytales, the Grimm Brothers were collecting Germanic folklore stories, erasing most of the sex and some violence, and selling them to parents. No more killing babies (as per the original *Sleeping Beauty* story), eating the internal organs of our daughters (*Snow White*) or hacking off body parts and sending birds to eat the eyes of our stepsisters (*Cinderella*).

The beautiful princess of fairytales, however, has not changed. She is the epitome of perfect womanhood – beautiful, slender, sweet, submissive, and most of all *unselfish*. This was key to her ability to win the greatest prize to which any woman could aspire – marriage to the Handsome Prince. A Fairytale Princess wants nothing for herself.

She has no sexual desires, no ambition, no dreams for her future, no wants or needs or feelings for anything other than marrying her Handsome Prince. She rejects economic security, friendships, family, success, achievement and strength. All she wants – all she can be – is a beautiful embodiment of love, care and nurture for the Handsome Prince.

The villain of the Fairytale Princesses story is always another woman, envisioned as some form of wicked witch, evil and malignantly jealous of the princess's youth and beauty. The selfish and powerful wicked witch is the antithesis of the fairytale princess. She is either old and ugly and therefore jealous of the princess's youth and beauty, or she is malevolently sexual and is threatened by the princess's sweet unselfishness. Her role is to curse the princess or the prince and prevent their marriage in envious reprisal for her youth, beauty and thoughtfulness.[97]

Wicked witches lived and died outside the fairytale world. During the fifteenth and sixteenth centuries, around 40,000 witches (almost all of them women) were reviled, tortured and killed for having knowledge, power and wisdom – which of course could only have come from Satan.[98]

Modern older women who have earned their power, experience and wisdom (is that you?) are still a threat to boys and men who want to control young girls. In a broader sense, they're a threat to patriarchal structures just by existing and refusing to be invisible, but they are a threat to individual abusive men too. It's almost always older women who run domestic and sexual violence services, advise younger women on the signs of abusive men, or write books that empower women and children. Their lives, achievements and independence serve as examples for younger women to follow and even exceed.

Over the last 200 years, women have worked hard to create aspirational role models that exist outside the wife/mother role. We seek out women who succeed in sport, music, arts, business, and politics and share their achievements. Almost anywhere a woman is doing something amazing, another woman will be standing in front of her snapping pictures and sharing them so other women and girls can see what is possible. Serena Williams, Hilary Clinton, Ash Barty, Ruth Bader Ginsberg, Elise Perry, Cathy Freedman, Jacinda Ardern, Malala Yousafzai, Melissa Lucashenko, Michelle Obama, Madonna, Indra Nooyi, Taylor Swift, Angela Merkel, Jane Goodall, Oprah Winfrey, Penny Wong, Sheryl Sandberg, and Beyoncé are all visibly there in the world, demonstrating the options available to women and girls, not just of what they can do, but of who they can be. Sometimes those women paid a high price for their visibility, but even that proved to the young girls crowding up behind them that obstacles can be overcome.

This was not an accident. Women chose to be leaders for other women. They worked hard to tell and retell the stories of feminine success and achievement. They did it deliberately to create a pathway for the girls and young women rising rapidly in their wake. They were not – are not – modelling perfection or ultimate womanhood. Rather, they are demonstrating flawed, imperfect, erratic achievement and a wide range of options.

Men have not done this service for boys and younger men. Indeed, given the state of increasing violence and decreasing wealth equality, there is a strong argument that older men are failing the boys who should be able to look to them for example, guidance and inspiration.

Which brings us to the myth of the warrior king.

Warrior Kings

Almost every culture and era has had their warrior-king to inspire young men. Gilgamesh, Achilles, Alexander the Great, Yueh Fei, Henry V, King Ashoka, Beowulf, Julius Caesar, William Wallace, the

Samurai, the Navy Seals, Captain America, Solid Snake, and Master Chief. Battles are celebrated, killing and dying in war is glorified by the warrior myth that reveres male strength, courage and brutality.

The brotherhood of men who fight in wars is sanctified in warrior myths. Sometimes, even manufactured hatred for an enemy is not enough to make healthy young men run towards violent death. But if being labelled a coward who would leave his brothers to die is a threat worse than death, young men will kill and die to avoid it.

Most wars have involved propaganda that dehumanises and demonises the enemy. *They're killing our children. They're raping our women. They are the enemies of our freedom. Killing them is glorious work blessed by gods. If you are not a Glorious Warrior, you are a cowardly wormlike thing, cravenly leaving your brothers to die as you hide in womanish weakness.*

The warrior king is both physically and emotionally powerful. He is justice without mercy, vengeance without consequence, and authority beyond questioning. He is revered by men, desired by women, and respected by all. He is powerful but unaccountable. In control but never responsible. He will suffer pain, even death, for his chosen bride but she is his prize not his equal and his first allegiance is always to the battlefield and his brotherhood of soldiers. He is everything we still tell young men to exalt as the best qualities of manhood and he is, in real life, the epitome of a violent and controlling man.

For thousands of years the warrior myth served its purpose. Men and boys volunteered for pointless causes and great wars with equal fervour. They died and killed for their tribes, states, and countries and the warrior myth told them this was how they achieved greatness.

Then we changed things.

Over the last 200 years, and particularly in the last 70 years, much of the world has learned to aspire to more and better choices for their young men. Wealth and education gave many of us more possibilities for our sons than either warrior or farmer. Now they can be accountants and lawyers and plumbers and artists. We want them to be caring friends, good fathers, and loving husbands because we believe this will bring them happiness. We want them to find pride and self-worth in manhood without basing it in violence and control. Even if our boys do become soldiers, we expect our military leaders to have the technology, diplomacy and smarts to prevent battlefield deaths, not glorify them.

But our mythology hasn't kept up with the modern world – at least, not for men and boys.

Where is the hero in the modern mould? All the aspirational male heroes I can find are fictional or real-life warrior-variations: Batman, Jon Snow, Tiger Woods, Iron Man, Dwayne Johnson, Cristiano Ronaldo, Will Smith, Elon Musk, Donald Trump. And of course, Andrew Tate (see Chapter 11). Fictional or real, they're all winning simulated battles or applying the warrior mythology to politics, sport or business.

Where is the man who shows aspirational manhood that doesn't rely on dominance and control? Where are the men leading by example and inspiring boys to modern heroics of creativity and invention? I wish I could think of a list as long as the one in the last paragraph, but I can't. Barack Obama, Ian Thorpe, Patrick Stewart and Adam Goodes would all be on that list, but who else? If you can think of them, tell your children, tell other people's children. Tell me if you have the time – I'd genuinely like to know.

Without an aspiration outside the warrior king, is it any wonder the likes of Andrew Tate have such influence and power over boys and young men? Tate fills the yawning identity gap and tells boys that the warrior ideal can still give them a sense of self-worth and the respect of others.

When we talk about needing men to step up, this is where they can have the most value. Fathers and uncles and granddads can step up, step out and show boys a manhood built on self-respect, pride, creativity, even leadership that does not rely on violence and control. Be the man of strength and power who heals and nurtures, the man who thinks and creates and invents. This does not have to be earth shattering or world changing. It can be as small and important as a garden bed you and your son build for the balcony of your apartment, or regular walks together to teach the dog to walk at heel, or learning new skills together (even, perhaps especially, if you're not very good at them). It can be simply finding other men you admire for their varied masculinity and talking to your son, grandson or nephew about the qualities you admire and how you try to emulate them. The warrior myth and the wounded blank space that is its only alternative hurts all of us and this is a problem only men can solve. Perhaps a true hero could make that effort.

One of the most powerful things fathers can do for their sons is talk to them about fear. Tell them about the things that make you afraid. What did you do? How did you feel? What do other men tell you about fear? Little boys who know their fathers can feel fear and manage it without lashing out learn that this is a normal part of being a man. They don't have to hide it or feel ashamed of it.

Founder and Director of The Equality Institute, Dr Emma Fulu did her PhD on intimate partner violence in the Maldives, which had, at the time, relatively low rates of violence. Her research found Maldivian masculinity is constructed on an ideal of 'calmness and rationality rather than power and control'.[99] Violence between or by men was rare and considered to be a sign of immaturity or poor education. As Dr Fulu writes, 'many men in high-level positions are considered to be masculine because they are able to stay calm in stressful situations, are quiet and dignified.' It's a far cry from the warrior myths of dominance and aggression that permeate western culture, and it shows the power that can come from a wider understanding of masculinity.

Children learn about gender roles from their families, their online worlds, school, sports, media, but most of all from the men in their physical worlds. The men they watch and hear every day. If those men chose absence or leave raising children and talking about emotions to women, boys learn this is 'women's work', only fit for the soft and the weak and girls learn that softness and weakness is their destiny. Non-binary kids learn their very existence is erased and ignored. Our children have a right to expect more and better from the adults – especially the men – in their villages.

Luckily, we can now find books, movies and TV shows that include fully realised female characters, although it might take a little bit of work and research. We can also talk to our children about the people of all genders who we admire and want to emulate. Don't assume your children know about them. Ask your kids about the women and non-binary people who inspire them. Talk about what those people had to overcome to achieve their success and what help they might have had – did they have mentors or other women who inspired them?

Another great question to ask is why those women worked so hard to be successful. We often assume that men just naturally strive for success while women want it as a stepping stone to something else – money, fame, or a rich husband. Having these conversations is a great way to help your children recognise the assumptions they may not even know they're making. Or it could be very reassuring for you to discover your children don't make these assumptions about anyone.

Fathers and other men in the family circle need to be key figures in this discussion. They, more than anyone else, can show boys how to understand that gendered violence is a threat to women's lives, not an attack on men's feelings.

6

Shame and violence

Children and teens who have absorbed gender myths are intimately familiar with shame as the punishment for failing to conform to the narrow role assigned to them by these myths.

Shame is far more damaging than guilt (what we feel about a wrongful act that can be redeemed and forgiven) or embarrassment (what we feel about other people's perception of our wrongful actions). Shame is an internal destruction, a deep belief that the entire self is inherently unworthy. It's the cold, uncaring voice in our heads that says, 'You are not good enough, you will *never* be good enough, you do not deserve love or recognition, your pitiful attempts to be loved or respected are laughable and only prove that you are irredeemable, contemptible and vile'.

Guilt and the desire for redemption can push us to change ourselves. Shame says we are inherently, unchangeably despicable and our only hope is in hiding our shameful selves from the world. Shame-ridden people often believe they have tricked others into loving them, respecting them, or admiring their achievements. They are plagued by constant fear that at any moment someone will see through the trickery to their hidden shameful selves and be repulsed.

This makes shame a powerful weapon to wield against vulnerable or insecure teens who may already hear that cold internal voice too often and too loudly.

The combination of putting gender at the centre of identity (see Chapter 3) and believing in gender myths (see Chapter 5) creates vulnerability to gendered shame – that deep feeling of worthlessness, failure and humiliation for not achieving strong hyper-sexual masculinity or unselfish, passively desirable femininity.

How does shame lead to violence?

Children and teens who are still forming their understanding of themselves and their place in the world can be particularly vulnerable to gendered shame. Conversely, people whose sense of identity is not centred on narrow gender roles may still feel embarrassed or upset about being labelled weak or promiscuous (depending on their gender) but they don't experience the intense shame threatening their very identity.

I saw this play out a few weeks ago when I was visiting a Year 10 class and watched two fifteen-year-old boys' sneering at a classmate who was cheerfully helping a friend make sense of her weather maps. They started with whispers, but it took only minutes of Cheerful Classmate ignoring them before the epithets such as 'cuck' and 'mangina'* were audible to the whole room. No matter what they said to him, however, Cheerful Classmate just calmly ignored them. Their rage rapidly escalated to shoving chairs and throwing pens. 'Who do you think you are?' was the last thing I heard one of them say before the teacher intervened. The question struck me as a plea more than an

---

* 'Cuck' is short for cuckold, an old English term for a man whose wife is unfaithful. In the manosphere it indicates a man too weak to command his partner's fidelity. In recent years the term has also become common in alt right and white supremacy idiom, arising from a genre of pornography in which a white man watches submissively as a black man (or men) have sex with his wife. 'Mangina' is a portmanteau of man and vagina, another term to denigrate boys and men by feminising them.

insult. I think they were genuinely desperate to know how he could be so resistant to the shame they perceived as devastating.

That strength and confidence is not something all teens can achieve. Even boys who wholeheartedly reject gender myths can still crumble a little bit in the face of epithets such as 'soy boy' (a derogatory term implying a boy is weak and feminised by consuming the phytoestrogen in soy milk rather than 'manly' food like dairy products and red meat) and girls who believe they're worthless if they're not pretty and desirable are intensely vulnerable to body shaming.

Sometimes this gendered shame is born of neglect or abuse, but young and vulnerable people can also learn shame from constant exposure to people who revile masculine weakness and feminine power. It might start in infancy when boys are told to be tough and strong when they cry, or when girls are told to be 'nice' and praised for being 'unselfish'. Or it can be imposed when insecure or uncertain teens are exposed to influences such as Andrew Tate (see Chapter 11).

Shaming children and teens into conforming with gender myths isn't always obvious or even aggressive. Sometimes it hides in what seem like simple lessons on good manners: 'you're a big boy now, you shouldn't be crying like that' or 'nice girls don't yell'. It can even be hidden in praise: 'you're such a big, strong boy' or 'you're such a sweet, pretty girl'.

When gendered shame takes hold of boys without disruption, it often sows the seeds of violence. This link is well established in research. For example, Dr James Gilligan, who worked as a psychiatrist in the American prison system for 25 years, wrote in his book, *Violence: Reflections on a National Epidemic,* that almost all the violence he saw in prisons came from men believing that their masculinity was being shamed. He described men who had committed the most horrific crimes against women as feeling shame so devastating it resulted in what he called the 'death of self' and said that the 'purpose of violence is to diminish the intensity of shame and replace it. . . with pride'.[100]

In 2014 a University of Indianapolis research project found shamed masculinity can both make anger more likely and increase its intensity. They also found that shame reduces a shame-prone person's willingness to control aggression and proved the connection between male shame and perpetrators of child sexual abuse, intimate partner violence and sexual violence.[101] Australian researchers in 2014 also found that shamed masculinity can increase men's vulnerability to suicide.[102]

There is a horrible logic to sexual violence for a deeply shamed man. It is power, dominance, and control all wrapped up in sexual proof of virile masculinity. As celebrated author Jess Hill wrote in her award winning book *See What You Made Me Do*, 'in the moments before a man takes control, he can feel at his most vulnerable and powerless, just milliseconds before feeling the flush of power and pride that comes from reinstating dominance'.[103]

This can be a potent mix for teenage boys afraid of being shamed for their fears or insecurities about sex – and this is not just a small minority. A 2024 Australian study of men's beliefs about masculinity found 42 per cent of young men agreed that 'a "real man" would never say no to sex' and 50 per cent agreed that 'guys should act strong even if they feel scared or nervous inside'.[104]

I've heard this from so many secondary school teachers, and I've seen it myself many times. Teenage boys are sometimes very anxious to prove to each other that they're rampantly ready for sex at any moment. As with any performative bragging, the volume of their proclaimed virility increases with the amount of insecurity they feel about it. One secondary teacher told me she almost lost control of her Year 9 class a few years ago when one of the boys was laughing too loudly at the suggestions that some boys might not be ready to have sex or that they wouldn't not want sex with someone who was scared or reluctant. 'As if any dude wouldn't ever do it whenever they can,' he said, looking around to get confirmation from the rest of the boys in the class. He got it from two of them. The rest didn't laugh until one of the girls muttered, 'As if it's not just assholes who think that'. Loud Laugher Boy angrily told her to fuck off, but his fear and confusion were obvious. Muttering Girl's and Loud Laugher Boy's friends all joined in and turned the air blue for a few minutes before the teacher was able to get them to settle down.

This might have been the first time Loud Laugher Boy was confronted with unavoidable evidence that his beliefs about masculinity were the minority. Like David in the barbecue story in Chapter 7, Loud Laugher Boy believed that all other boys were just like him. Challenging that belief, even proving it to be untrue gave him an opportunity to reassess his beliefs and (hopefully) change his behaviour.

If his behaviour and beliefs don't change, he is going to have difficulty asking for and giving consent to sexual touching. If rejection triggers shame about his masculinity, he could easily lash out or refuse to accept a 'no' or 'not now'.

Gendered shaming that inhibits consensual touch is not only about boys. Gender myths, as I outlined earlier, are about boys and girls defining their gender by being opposites. So, when boys are required to be aggressively sexual, girls must therefore be passively desirable, the reverse of forceful or powerful in pursuing sex. Women and girls who believe they are shamed by not being feminine might sometimes try too hard to be sexually submissive; never expecting, asking for, or even believing they deserve pleasure, respect or consent in sexual relationships.

It's not easy to talk to our daughters about their right to ask for and receive respect and pleasure in sex, but a good place to start is by debunking the myth that girls shouldn't expect such things. Make sure they have access to trustworthy information about clitoral orgasms and other erogenous zones. The movie *When Harry Met Sally* is a bit dated but the restaurant scene where Sally demonstrates how easy it is to fake an orgasm is a good conversation starter. Ask questions like, why would a woman be so good at faking an orgasm? Why would women even do that? Why would Harry assume it's never happened to him? Keep a sharp eye out for other signs of passive or submissive sexuality from female characters in any other TV shows and movies you watch together (they won't be difficult to find) and use them as a starting point for conversations with your teens.

Trans, gender fluid, and non-binary teens have often thought deeply about gender roles as they learn to understand their own identity. Sometimes this can lead to them rejecting any expectation of gender as they write their own script for how they should behave and carry themselves. Others might cling to hyper-masculine or feminine ideals as they go through this process. But regardless of their gender identity, it's always valuable to have conversations with your children about how gendered ideas impact our expectations of people's behaviour and responsibilities in sex. If your child is not cisgender, it's also important to have conversations about the reactions they might get from other people. Many will be supportive, but people who adhere to gender myths can often feel threatened by anyone who live outside those constraints, and they often react to that threat by using shame to enforce conformity. If that doesn't work, violence is not unusual (see Appendix 2). Talk to your child's school about making sure the classroom and playground is safe, the teachers are informed and supportive, and school leadership actively suppresses any gendered shaming and violence (see Chapter 1 for more ideas on how to be an advocate at your child's school).

To be clear, I am not saying shame is an excuse or a justification for violence. Nothing excuses or justifies deliberate harm to another person. But if we can attempt to understand the feelings behind the actions, we have a much better chance of understanding what we can do to prevent or at least reduce violence. One way to do that is to understand that simply recognising gendered shame is not enough. We need to replace that shame or the vulnerability to shame with something else.

The flip sides of shame and guilt are self-worth and self-esteem.

Self-worth is our intrinsic belief that we deserve love, respect and consideration. It's based on stable characteristics that are inherent to who we are, not what we do, or how we look. Self-esteem is built on self-worth but is about the things we do, such as what we've accomplished, how we look, what we say and other people's recognition of our successes.

Much of the education I've outlined is this book seeks to help children and teens better understand themselves and their beliefs about gender in the hope they can build a strong sense of self-worth and reduce their vulnerability to gendered shame. I wish I could promise these lessons will dismantle all the fears and myths about gender children are taught to build into their identity. I can't. The beliefs that make up our sense of self are not created or demolished in a few hours in one classroom. They're built over a lifetime in hundreds of rooms. They come from our parents and families and friends and all the people we watch and listen to in the digital and physical worlds. Unpicking those beliefs takes a very long time and needs support from more than just one person.

This work, though, is not just one person. The point of a whole-of-community approach is that we reach everyone in a child's community. It's about making sure the entire village understands the value of helping children form their sense of self without shaming them. If those adults know how to help children build their self-worth and an identity that does not rely on shame-ridden gender myths, all our children will be stronger, safer and happier.

This doesn't mean removing gender from their identity. Manliness, womanhood, or living outside gender roles can be a healthy, loving aspect of our identity if it is not rigid or confining. Rather, it must include a wide variation of strengths and capacities, and most importantly of all, it must never be policed or enforced by shame.

How to help your kids build self-worth

Shame is much easier to prevent than heal. Supporting parents to raise children with strong self-worth is the single most effective thing we can do to reduce all kinds of violence.

The key is to make sure children do not grow up believing that love is conditional. They don't have to earn your love by being 'good' or through success at sport or at school. Sometimes just a slight re-framing in how you praise them can make a big difference:[105]

- Recognise and praise their courage for attempting something new or learning a new skill, not just their 'wins'. 'Learning how to play an instrument is difficult and everyone makes mistakes at first. I'm really proud of you for giving it a go!'
- Notice characteristics about them and encourage them to feel proud of themselves: 'I saw you work through that fight with your friends last week. I was really impressed by how thoughtful you were in that difficult situation. You should be proud of yourself.'
- If they're playing sport or learning music or art, ask about the new skills they've learned, or what they enjoy about it, or how they feel about their progress rather than asking about their success.

- Play games or try difficult tasks together when they're little and slowly give them more responsibility and scope for working out how to approach difficulties as they get older. You could start with ambitious Lego models or artwork, or even household tasks (how do we get the vent cover off to clean the dryer) and praise them for trying, persisting or approaching it as a problem to solve.
- They get hugs and cuddles because you love them, because they deserve affection and care, not because they've earned it. I'm sure you feel that way about your children but just do a quick mental audit to make sure you are telling them – and showing them – that your love is not conditional.

7

Why non-violent kids need to learn about violence

We teach kids about gender-based violence to reduce the frightening prevalence of domestic violence and coercive control (see Appendix 2). We want them to have the knowledge and skills to build strong, loving relationships that make them and their partner happy and safe. We want them to be clear and unafraid of what they want and need in a relationship and be equally unafraid of understanding and caring about their partner's needs. And, of course, we want them to be able to pass these skills on to the generations that come after them.

Some of this work is about changing beliefs and attitudes, but that isn't enough. We also need to change behaviour – and these are not always the same things.

The easiest way to explain this is with an example, which is loosely based on something I watched happen on a Saturday afternoon many years ago.*

---

* I've been using variations on this scenario to demonstrate how primary prevention works for a while now but I had never written it down. In 2024 Respect Victoria commissioned me to write the scenario as a teaching tool on the functions primary prevention. It is reproduced here with their kind permission.

Imagine five average young Australian men having a barbecue. Let's call them Andrew, Peter, Samal, Hassan and Dave.

Andrew tells the other men about his wife burning last night's dinner and makes a joke about hitting her to teach her to not do it again. He only makes the joke because he thinks the idea of hurting his wife is so ludicrously far-fetched that it's funny and he certainly doesn't intend any harm. He may even feel a bit awkward as soon as the words escaped his mouth.

Peter and Samal are deeply uncomfortable when he makes the joke, but they don't want to make it a big deal or embarrass Andrew, so they laugh perfunctorily and look away.

Hassan was thinking about a problem at work and barely noticed the joke but takes advantage of the silence to start talking about the troubles he's having with his boss. Peter, Samal and Andrew are relieved the difficult moment has passed and lean into giving Hassan the advice he needs.

None of these men are violent. Listening to the joke, even making the joke, will not change that. They all have positive attitudes towards women, despite Andrew's questionable choices in jokes. Even if one of them had called out the joke, it wouldn't have done anything to change male violence because nothing about their behaviour to women *needs* to change.

Dave laughs too, but he has a different story.

Dave is controlling and violent to his wife. He is the only man at the barbecue who has ever hurt a woman. He never talks about it and never does it in front of other people, which is why none of his friends know about it. They assume, as most of us do, that their friend's internal worlds are very similar to their own. None of them would abuse a woman, Dave is their friend, therefore, Dave would never abuse a woman. They don't know enough about the way men who abuse women operate, so they don't know to question that assumption.

Dave also makes assumptions about his friends and their inner worlds.

Like most violent men, Dave believes that all men are violent. (This is the bitter hilarity of the NotAllMen defence – there is only one group of people who genuinely believe that all men are violent, and it's not women or even feminists. It's violent men.)

Dave tells himself – and his wife – that she is the cause of all his abusive behaviour. He believes he is the victim of her disrespect and deception and that his response is not really violence, it's just what men do when women shame them. He keeps it secret because he knows he will 'get in trouble' if he says it openly, but he assumes all other men share the same secret. It doesn't matter what women say about domestic violence because they're not part of the shared secret, and in his mind, the more they go on about it, the more they reinforce that women don't understand the reality of being a man.

So, what happens for Dave when Andrew makes that joke, Peter and Samal laugh, and Hassan jumps in to hurriedly changes the subject? In his reality, the other men are laughing for the same reason he laughed – it's funny because it's true. Sometimes you do hurt or humiliate your wife and it's not that big a deal because she's the one causing all the problems. Dave would never come right out and say this, but joking about it is how he tells other men that this is what he does and seeks reassurance that they're doing it too. So, for him, not for any of the others, the joke and the laughter are reinforcements that abusing women is normal male behaviour. He doesn't need to change his beliefs or his behaviour because he thinks the other men in his life are telling him it's a normal way for men to act.

So, Dave chuckles along with Peter and Samal, then turns his attention to Hassan's problems at work and no one notices a thing.

None of the others have any idea why he laughed. They'd be horrified if they did. He has no idea that they might be laughing because the very idea of slapping a woman is so alien to them that it's ludicrous to even consider it.

All five men are chuckling away in their own reality, comfortably believing they all think the same thing.

The entire interaction took less than 30 seconds. In a normal day, as Dave watches the news, streams his favourite TV shows, listens to a football game, has a beer with colleagues after work, and scrolls through social media, Dave has dozens, even hundreds of those 30-second interactions. He interprets all of them as confirmation that his violence is normal for men, all men do what he does and he doesn't need to change his behaviour.

What if we could change this scenario?

What if Andrew had learned enough about violent men to know that they will clutch at any straw to shore up their belief that the way they behave is fine and normal, so he knows not to make those jokes?

Or . . .

What if he did make the joke but Peter and Samal know to not laugh or look away, they are angry and disgusted by the joke and they know how to say so?

Or . . .

What if Hassan tunes in to what Andrew said and instantly tells him how revolted he is that anyone would make a joke about such a thing?

Again, nothing much changes for Andrew, Hassan, Peter and Samal's chances of being violent. They were never going to do it anyway.

But what about Dave?

How does he continue to hold onto his belief that what he does is normal, understandable and justifiable? Does it get more difficult to keep believing his wife is the problem, not his behaviour? What if this happens in every or even most of those daily interactions that he uses to shore up his belief that all men are violent?

How respectful relationships education works in this scenario

Andrew, Peter, Samal and Hassan started out with positive values about gender equality and violence against women. This might because of their family life and education (both of which are prevention activities) or it might be because they chose to have and live those values (again, prevention activities). In the barbecue scenario, however, none of them had the skills to intervene when Andrew made the joke. More intensive prevention education might have taught them why intervening is important and given them the skills and confidence to do so. This, as a single incident, would probably not have been enough to convince Dave that his assumption that all men are violent is incorrect. But if most men did it most of the time, it would get more difficult to maintain that delusion.

If, as is common, Dave is violent because this is the behaviour modelled by his father as he was growing up, it's quite likely that, back then, he promised himself he would never grow up to be like his father. Maybe it happened without him even knowing. Or maybe he embraced violent and controlling behaviour as a means of feeling powerful and masculine in a family or a community that made him feel small, afraid and ashamed.

Dave needed a lot more support when he was a child than he was given. He needed the adults in his life to see what was happening, understand how to help him, and have the skills, knowledge and resources to do so. He needed teachers, family, sports coaches, faith leaders, and mentors who could show him how to be proudly masculine without violence. All those adults who could have supported Dave when he was little needed training to recognise the warning signs of a child in trouble and be able respond kindly and consistently, with no judgement or preaching. Without that help, all little Dave could learn was that his father, who he perceived as powerful and in control, was the only model for manhood that is worthy of respect.

Prevention education is the work we do to give the adults in Dave's life the skills they need to support him to want to be a man who is not violent.

Respect in all relationships

As I said earlier, relationships education is much bigger than romantic relationships. It's connected to many of the issues we see playing out in schools, workplaces, aged care homes and parliaments all over the country. Bullying, harassment, abuse, violence, not just between romantic partners but also between colleagues, students, parents and teachers, bosses and employees, retail staff and customers. But, sticking with schools, let's have a look at an everyday example of how poor understanding of respectful relationships can play out.

A few years back, I met a high school teacher at a conference. He was a very chatty chap, brimming over with stories about the inventive vagaries of his students. ('Never a dull moment, darling. My first year the art class replaced the portrait of the school's founding Headmaster with a portrait of the Year 12 football captain. It was hanging in reception for months before anyone noticed.')

Chatty Teacher had another story too, about a boy in his Year 9 English class. He'd been looking forward to teaching this boy for years after listening to English teachers in lower years rave about him. The boy loved to read and already had a broad understanding of 5000 years of Indian history. English was his first language, but he was also fluent in Hindi, as were his parents and grandparents. He had the instinctive feel for writing so common in passionate readers and was delighted by his ability to express complex ideas in perfectly constructed sentences. 'Erudite AF,' was Chatty Teacher's eloquent description, and he was eagerly anticipating a star student.

What he found instead was a withdrawn, sullen boy who wouldn't speak in class and if he handed in essays at all, they were curt and joyless. Chatty Teacher noticed that Erudite Boy rarely spoke to the other students, but sniggers and whispers often circulated around him in class. He asked Erudite Boy if anything was going on but the only response was a brief head shake.

He got a clear understanding of the problem a few weeks into term when he was in the schoolyard one afternoon and heard one of the boys from his Year 9 English class call out, 'Hey Munch, where's your lunch?' to the accompaniment of uproarious laughter and saw Erudite Boy running back into the school building in tears.

'Munch' was short for 'curry-muncher', a vile racial slur and a verbal weapon wielded to wound and diminish people of South Asian descent. Within a few days Chatty Teacher discovered Erudite Boy had stopped bringing lunch to school because almost every day it had been emptied into his school bag, ruining his books and homework. His beloved kindle had been smashed. His laptop had been replaced three times since the beginning of term. He was arriving at school late and waiting in the toilets at the end of each day to avoid walking home near his classmates. But he couldn't avoid deliberate shoves between classes and the constant racist epithets.

Erudite Boy had cancelled all his social media accounts after his inboxes filled up with racist cartoons and 'jokes'. He changed his phone number to stop the texts. It worked, but it also completely isolated him from any contact with friends or other kids in the school who might have wanted to express support and solidarity.

Chatty Teacher was enraged and disgusted. He summoned everyone he could find who had been even tangentially involved in bullying Erudite Boy and spent an hour explaining the reasons for his rage and disgust in fine detail. He made them all stay after school to write formal apologies to Erudite Boy and set them all a 1000 word essay on the history and effects of racism.

The next day Erudite Boy arrived at school with a black eye.

The principal and the parents of all the students who'd been set the essay were called in. All the students claimed they had no idea how Erudite Boy got hurt and Erudite Boy refused to even speak. Chatty Teacher and the principal called his parents and tried to convey a convincing apology and a promise to enforce change.

Erudite Boy's father arrived at the school, tight-lipped and uncommunicative. He left, holding his son close, glaring at every teacher and student he passed. A week later, Erudite Boy's parents moved him to another school and refused any further contact with Chatty Teacher.

Bullying takes many forms, and it can be tempting to apply a one-size fits-all approach of addressing it with techniques to increase empathy and kindness. This can certainly help but we also need to make sure children and teens understand the cruel reality of their behaviour. The kids targeting Erudite Boy needed to hear all the adults around them name and explain racism. Hiding racism, misogyny, sexual harassment or sexual assault under a catch-all label of bullying harms everyone involved. Transphobia, homophobia, image-based abuse and ableist bullying all need to be named and explained before we can address the behaviour. It's not just enough to 'get in trouble' at school. We would not be doing children any favours if we didn't help them understand that in the adult world, they could lose their job or even face criminal charges for this behaviour. And they *should* have to live with serious consequences for behaviour that can do such serious harm.

If the teenagers at Erudite Boy's school had been taught these things, along with consent, power and respect from early childhood, they would have had years of learning to think about their responsibility for other people's feelings before they act or speak. It's all connected to that concept of consent as an expression of consideration and respect for self and others, not just permission for sex.

Learning to recognise bullying, in all its forms, is a vital life skill. No one can get through a lifetime of work without coming up against a bully. Too often they are in positions of power and they got there because they know how to disguise (at least for a while) their cruel, petty and vindictive behaviour behind a mask of 'managing difficult employees' and the time-tested techniques of convincing everyone the victim is downright lying or straight up crazy. I've worked for more than one person who fits that description and I've seen the devastating effect it can have on people in their power (the clues are a high staff turnover rate combined with sycophantic public praise from the few employees currently in favour). In every case, the most common regret expressed by escaping employees is 'How did I not see this earlier? Why didn't I do something months ago? The answer, sadly, is that we don't expect such petty spite from people who appear so benevolent on first meeting, and if we haven't learned the skills to recognise and confront a bully, a racist, or a misogynist, confusion and fear can often render us silent, complicit and helpless.

I hope Erudite Boy found a school that could give him the opportunity to develop all the wonderful creative potential his teachers had seen in him before the bullying started. I hope he will be our next Thea Astley or Trent Dalton. But that year of being so diminished by casual cruelty might have done irreparable harm. We'll never know, I guess, but it was entirely avoidable.

Parents (like you!) who can and do make the effort to teach their children to understand the meaning and effects of bullying, racism, sexual harassment, homophobia and transphobia are a powerful bulwark against this behaviour. But they cannot do it alone. Schools need to design and enforce a culture of safety, and parents can be a big part of this. Everyone is busy and it can feel overwhelmingly difficult to push for change on your own, but don't underestimate the power of collective action. If you're worried about the culture at your children's school, there's a good chance other parents are worried too. If you can make it to after school pick-ups, ask around. Or, if you don't have that opportunity, try arranging play dates to meet other parents and talk about what you want from your children's school. Enlist them in finding other like-minded families. One email from one parent might be easy to dismiss but multiple contacts from multiple parents are much more difficult to ignore. Connecting with other parents is also a great way to find out whether your concerns are widespread and affecting many children, or just an isolated experience of one or two.

Sometimes problematic behaviour in the classroom and playground is created by the school culture. Or it can come from just a few children who have learned harmful behaviours from someone with a strong influence over them.

Children who live with family violence sometimes use violence themselves. It is imitation of what they've learned at home and expression of the pain and sadness they carry. Reaching those children when they're young, providing them with support and teaching them another way to have relationships with people can make a huge difference to them and to all the people who share their lives in the future. It's also important to remember that for many children, the experience of growing up with a violent adult is so horrifying that they embed peaceful non-violence into their core values. It becomes a function of who they are not just the choices they make.

Other children can be exposed to violence and prejudice online (see Chapter 11) but for now, suffice to say the online world is full of grifters and wounded ideologues in search of acolytes. They prey on and exacerbate young people's shame and weaponise their insecurity for profit. They can reach into our children's hearts as they sit at our kitchen tables and break them before they've had a chance to find out what the world could offer them.

Sometimes parents can see this happening, more often we don't, or we think it's just an adolescent phase, not serious, dangerous, or permanent. Sometimes we might even be right, but if we're not, the consequences can be tragic and lifelong.

This is all very gloomy but the thing to remember – the reason I wrote this book and the reason you're reading it – is that humans are a clever and adaptable species. It's how we came to rule the whole planet despite our fragile bodies and puny defences. We don't need teeth and claws. We have our enormous brains and our preternatural ability to learn from the mistakes of others and adapt to new ways of thinking and being. Children and teens are especially good at this. They learn new languages, new cultures and new concepts at an accelerated rate. Which means they can also unlearn and relearn much more easily than us older folk who must work so much harder to form new neural pathways.

Some of them need this ability – desperately. As much to form happy relationships with themselves as with each other. The greatest protection against manipulated shame is robust self-worth (see Chapter 6).

8

Understanding consent

All the lessons I've outlined so far coalesce around consent. Understanding their own and other people's bodies, feelings, identity and gender roles is how children learn to understand power and choices, which are the essence of consent.

The curriculum for learning consent starts in the first year of primary school. Five-year-olds are not learning about sexual consent, they start with learning to give and ask for consent for hugs or sharing their toys and pencils. As they get older and progress through to secondary school, the lessons slowly develop their understanding of personal space, empathy and respect for self and others until they're mature enough to be thinking about consensual sexual touch and, eventually, consensual sex.[106]

Having said that, the curriculum resources on consent are very uneven. As I outlined in Chapter 1, there are several sets of official curriculum resources. Some of them are more than ten years old, and often focus on the legal definition of consent or frame sexual violence as a subset of domestic and family violence. Other resources give more consideration to the various forms of non-consensual sexual activity (pressure, coercion, force etc.) but don't focus on the consensual aspects.[107] These things are all valuable ideas but they are indirect paths to a true understanding of consent, which is about power and choice.

Why teach children and teens about consent?

I don't think I've ever doubted that consent education is essential learning for children of all ages, but if there had ever been a moment of wondering if it really is necessary, it vanished one cold afternoon in Melbourne about four years ago. This is how I wrote about it at the time:[108]

A few months ago, I delivered a workshop on consent for a group of fifteen- and sixteen-year-old students in Melbourne. I waited around for a bit after the class because there's always someone who needs to know more. A waifish girl, all knees and elbows, crept up to whisper her question. 'If something happened and I didn't say no because I was too scared, it's my fault, right?'

Eyes full of tears and doubt stared at me as I tried to convince her that of course it was not her fault.

She didn't believe me. Not really.

I wanted to burn the world to the ground.

Her distraught teacher told me afterwards that everyone in the school knew about the 'incident'. The boy in question was in Waifish Girl's class. They used to be friends. Now he hates her and refuses to even look at her. Distraught Teacher told me she'd talked to the boy about what happened. He was bewildered when she asked him about what he called his 'sex life'. He believed at the time (and still does) that it was consensual. 'She never said no, not once,' he said. Distraught Teacher said he was genuinely confused when she told him Waifish Girl was too scared to say no. His parents were furious and threatened to sue everyone. His mates made memes about 'Rapey Dude'. Sometimes they sent them to Waifish Girl, who had stayed home from school so often that Distraught Teacher was worried she might not finish Year 10. All their classmates knew about the 'incident' and too many of them reacted as if the problem was not that it happened, but that too many people knew it had happened. 'She should have just kept it to herself,' declared one so-called friend of Waifish Girl.

Distraught Teacher was beside herself, crying as she told me that she didn't know what to do to help any of them.

This is what happens when people don't understand consent. And it is happening at every high school in Australia.

I told Waifish Girl's story to a police officer I know quite well. He stared down at the table the entire time I was talking and continued to sit in seemingly indifferent silence when I was done. Eventually, he said, 'What can you do? It's the classic he said/she said, and you'd never get a conviction. Even if you did, who is going to be safer if we send a sixteen-year-old cleanskin to prison two years after it happened and everyone involved has finished school?'

I was about to explode with rage when I realised, he was in tears. He wasn't indifferent, he was despairing. And my reaction wasn't really rage, it was that same despair. Because he was right. Incarcerating children who have never been taught to understand consent is not the answer. But neither is doing nothing. So, what can we do?

That question is so unanswerable that it paralyses almost everyone. Teachers who see their students being victims and perpetrators have two options: police or nothing. Both those options are painful and there aren't any others. I've seen so many teachers cry over this, and then pull back in shame, saying they have no right to cry. 'It's not happening to me,' they say. Except that it is. Not as much as the victims, certainly, but their pain is real. I've rarely met a teacher who doesn't care about their students. The reason most of them become teachers is because they want to work with young people and see them succeed. Seeing their students hurt, even worse, seeing them hurt each other, breaks their hearts. Every time. Feeling that they are powerless to stop it is more than heartbreaking. It's traumatising.

They also know, and cannot change, that the victim, the perpetrator and all the other students who inevitably hear about a rape, watch as the adults around them seem powerless and uncaring. There are almost no consequences for boys who ignore consent. All the teenagers involved learn those lessons far too well and they carry them into adulthood.

This is happening in every school in every suburb in every state in the country – yes, yours too – and no one knows what to do about it.

As much as the reformers of the 1970s couldn't see a solution outside the legal system, we too, 50 years later, are still stuck in that same binary – police or nothing. The kids themselves are not stuck. Many don't want police and courts involved. But they don't want nothing to be the only other option. When I talk to them, they have solutions. Restorative justice approaches are common. They want safety and care for victims, and they want education for and acknowledgement from perpetrators more than they want retribution. This is obviously not true for everyone but seems to be the case more often than not.

They want consent education. Thorough, comprehensive consent education that explains power, choices, intimacy, empathy, pressure, gender, sexuality, joy and pleasure.[109] They believe such education would give at least some children and teens the skills they need to keep themselves and each other safer and happier, and they're all too aware that too many of them missed out on learning those skills when they were young enough for the lessons to be natural and easy.

A childcare educator once told me about two little boys in kindergarten who were locked in a fierce battle of wills about loving hugs. One of the boys was persistently trying to hug his little friend, who found the relentless affection overwhelming and annoying. The teachers explained empathy and boundaries to Persistent Boy, but he already knew that the constant attempts were making Little Friend angry and upset. He knew it was wrong to hug someone against their will and that he should stop when Little Friend asked him to, but still, he persisted. Persistent Boy wasn't persisting because he couldn't empathise, he was persisting because he didn't know any other way to respond to what he perceived as rejection.

When children internalise rejection even the most trivial act can feel life-threatening. You don't want me or care about me. No one will care for me. I am a helpless child and will die without care. If I am to live, you must love me! It's a visceral cri-de-coeur, almost always misinterpreted as 'attention-seeking' or 'bad' behaviour.

The only way Persistent Boy knew how to react to rejection was to keep begging. Trying to redirect him by suggesting more empathy for Little Friend without acknowledging his feelings of rejection only made him more afraid, more in need of reassurance, and so the cycle continued.

Persistent Boy and Little Friend were only four years old. They're not supposed to be able to manage their emotions or understand complex internal worlds. That's what the best parts of education and family life are for – to teach them as they grow.

But what if no one ever teaches Persistent Boy to understand rejection as something he doesn't need to fear as life-threatening? What happens when he becomes Persistent Teen with his first girlfriend? He's in love. He wants sex, not only because of physical desire, but because he loves her and he believes sex is an expression of that love. If she says no and he enacts the sixteen-year-old sexual version of persistently seeking a hug, his girlfriend will be under enormous pressure. This is not a theoretical exercise, it's a far too common story told by teenage girls. Pressure, persistence, endless asking. 'Are you ready now?' 'How about now?' 'Now?' 'Are you sure?' 'What about now?'

Pressured Girlfriend's 'no' is experienced as a painful, incomprehensible rejection of him and his love. Persistent Teen's relentless asking is experienced by Pressured Girlfriend as painful, incomprehensible rejection of her as a person whose needs matter. Whichever one of them 'gives in' they are both wounded by the experience.

Too many negotiations of sexual consent follow this pattern. It's about so much more than just the sexual act. Each person comes to it with very fragile emotions, and it is laughably insufficient to give them nothing but 'yes' or 'no' to work with.

If, as happens too often, Persistent Teen's fear of rejection is expressed as aggression or violence, the rape he then commits has lifelong consequences. Most deeply for the girl he rapes, but also for him, in how he thinks of himself and how he approaches love and rejection from all the Pressured Girlfriends in his future.

Persistent Teen isn't four years old. He is much closer to adulthood, and he has a quasi-adult responsibility to manage his emotions. He is certainly old enough to take responsibility for harm he inflicts on others. But when is he old enough that we can blame him for not learning something he was never taught? When does it become his responsibility to *know* rather than the responsibility of the adults in his life to *teach*? What do those adults do if consent is something they have never been taught themselves?

Defining Consent

Before they start explicitly teaching the nuances of consent, teachers will often ask kids to explain what they understand about consent. This is particularly important in Years 7 and 8, when early teens first move into secondary school and there might be very wide discrepancies in the consent education they've received in their different primary schools.

Some teens have a very sophisticated understanding of sex and consent. I've heard fourteen-year-olds give more nuanced explanations of consent than many adults could manage. They talk about 'respecting boundaries', 'making sure the other person feels safe' and 'knowing who has the power in the relationship' with confidence and ease. At the other end of the spectrum are the teens who turn up to consent classes with disdain writ large on their faces. They sit at the back of class with their arms crossed, sneering and nudging each other, thinking and sometimes saying that consent is not their business or their problem. They are not always boys, but there are always too many boys among them.

Between those two groups sit the majority, the middle of the bell curve. They twitch when the teacher talks about penises and vaginas and struggle to answer question about defining consent. 'No means no, right?' It's a phrase almost all of them know. They find it reassuring in its simplicity and its alignment with their understanding of consent as an authorisation rather than a mutual understanding.

Their perspectives on consent are often gendered. Boys tend to define it in terms of *getting* permission and girls often describe it as *giving* permission. This is usually a sign of strong gender myths distorting their perspective on sexual roles and they think of boys as pursuing sex while girls are the gatekeepers of sex. A key concept in changing this perception is understanding bodily autonomy, which is simply the idea that all people have the right to make choices about their own bodies, without coercion or violence. Gender myths, however, distort our views on women's and girls' bodily autonomy.

Dr Rachel Hogg, a psychology lecturer at Charles Sturt University, told me there is a connection between consent and ownership of our bodies. 'How we think about our bodies and ownership is highly gendered,' she said. 'Men have no doubt about owning their own bodies. Their body is theirs to fully inhabit. Women's bodies are not seen as belonging solely to themselves in the same way. Criminalising abortion, for instance, is part of believing a woman's body is not her own. Rape and consent are tied up in that too.'

If women don't own their bodies, they are public property, meant for viewing and using, and their primary purpose is to be desirable and accessible. For people who believe this, women don't have bodily autonomy and men do not need consent to touch or use women's bodies. This belief is the foundation of sexual violence, where women's bodies are simply receptacles for men's insecurity, sexual needs, anger, shame or rage. It should go without saying that not all men and boys believe this or see women's bodies this way, but the disturbingly high rates of sexual violence indicate that far too many boys and men do believe it (see Appendix 2).

Men, who have undisputed ownership of their bodies are not as vulnerable to sexual violence, but they can feel intense pressure to acquiesce to every sexual invitation, regardless of their real wishes and needs. Non-binary people, who experienced very high rates of sexual violence, exist outside binary gender myths and because their very existence is a threat and a challenge to that binary, are sometimes perceived as righteous targets for punitive sexual violence.

Again, patriarchy hurts us all.

Replacing patriarchal assumptions about gender and bodily autonomy with a true understanding of choices and power can ease that pain for everyone.

Consent is all about choice.

Understanding choices

Consent is mutual, ongoing, and equally relevant whether you have known each other ten minutes or twenty years. All touching requires consent, not just sexual touch or penetrative sex. Consent must be freely given, which means the consenting person *wants* to participate for their own reasons, based on their own wishes or inclinations. This is not to say that consensual sex must always be a response to sexual desire. Seeking intimacy, comfort, reassurance, physical contact, even relief from boredom are all entirely valid reasons for wanting sex. There are no right or wrong reasons for wanting, asking for or offering consensual sex. Everyone involved needs to understand exactly what they are consenting to and what will happen before, during and after they have given their consent. As a teacher might explain to a six-year-old, if you consent to lending your friend a book in class, they still have to ask you if they want to take the book home or before they draw on the pages. When that child is sixteen years old, a teacher would explain sexual consent, where someone who gives consent to kissing or touching over clothes does not necessarily consent to oral or penetrative sex. Each new activity and each new moment requires asking and giving consent.

Consent is often communicated non-verbally by touch and sound, but any uncertainty means asking for verbal consent. This doesn't have to be incongruous to a passionate moment. 'Do you like this?' 'How does this feel?' 'Do you want to keep going?' 'What do you like?' 'I'd like to keep going but it's OK if you want to stop or take a break.' 'How do you feel about us doing this?'

Consent is enthusiastic and active. Everyone involved is eager to be part of what's going on. A six-year-old is delighted to be playing chasey with the other kids in their class and says so. A seventeen-year-old is eager to kiss and touch their sexual partner, they want to know what their partner likes and are guiding and expressing their enjoyment.

Consent is ongoing and present from the moment the activity starts until after it ends. The six-year-old runs up to the other kids playing chasey and asks to join in. They're laughing and excited throughout the game and continually showing how much fun they're having. And finally, everyone involved in an activity must have the capacity to give consent. They need to be conscious, coherent, able to understand what is happening and old enough to make the choice to participate.

Asking for, giving and communicating consent is the responsibility of everyone involved, but the onus for seeking consent is on the person who initiates touch and the person who has greater power in the relationship. There are some relationships, however, where power is so inherently imbalanced that even asking for consent is prohibited. Doctors or therapists and patients, teachers and students, adults and children are all relationships that preclude consent to sexual activity.

While it's obviously important that teens understand the laws about sex and consent, understanding consent as a free choice is where legal definitions can be very unhelpful. Only a very few of the things that can constrain our choices are illegal. Physical force or threats, being unconscious, or being too young to be able to consent are all against the law. But there are many other restraints on our choices. They can be financial, emotional or social. Sometimes they can be so ephemeral it can be difficult to recognise them as limits on our ability to consent. For example, far too many people in Australia know the feeling of teetering on the edge of homelessness. Always one delayed pay check or one twisted ankle away from losing their rental home or defaulting on their mortgage. Those people can't always make truly free choices about sex with someone who has the power to either push them over that edge or pull them back from it.

What about loneliness, which can be terribly painful and often feels like a long, slow death. Can someone make a truly free choice to have sex if, in exchange they're offered relief from crushing loneliness?

There are so many other constraints on our ability to choose freely. All the expectations we think people have of us, the fears we have about ourselves and our futures, to say nothing of the sheer force of emotions such as lust, jealousy, love and infatuation.

It would be a very rare person who doesn't have those limits on their choices at various times and with various people. That those limits exist doesn't mean anyone who has those limits can't consent to sex. It does, however, put some extra responsibility on someone who has power over the person they are asking to consent to sex. And the resolution is very simple – they just need to make it clear that there is no risk in saying 'no', 'not now', 'not like that' or 'not with you'.

Understanding power

Power is simply about having the ability to direct or influence the behaviour of other people or the course of events. The things that give us power are sometimes inherent in who we are or where we were born, which means we sometimes don't even notice them. Once I would have called this 'privilege', but it's become such a loaded word that I stopped using it. Privilege is almost always interpreted to mean that someone has something they don't deserve and didn't earn. Not only is this rarely true, even the implication can cause resentment.

A white man from a stable, wealthy family and a private school background who becomes a cardiologist has to study for at least fifteen years. He must pass dozens of difficult exams, work long hours, stay up to date with every new piece of research, continually strive to improve his own skills and pass those skills on to junior doctors. He had to work *incredibly* hard. He didn't just turn up to a hospital, wave his bank statement and his school tie at the Head of Cardiology and stroll off to the cardiac ward. On the other hand, his family connections and wealth may have made it easier to get into an 'elite' private school. It would also have helped give him access to tutors and other academic assistance when he needed it. If he had a calm, secure home and family who could help with financial and domestic support he would have no other demands on the time and energy his career required of him. And, of course, his family and professional connections would have helped him get prestigious fellowships because he had 'the right background'.

The daughter of a refugee family, who had none of those things, might still become a cardiologist, but her journey will be much harder and take much longer. Her focus is likely to be split between her professional, financial and domestic responsibilities. She'll have to continually prove not only her abilities but her right to use those abilities – her white male colleague is never asked to do this and probably doesn't notice when it happens to her. The word privilege was supposed to describe those nuances, now it seems to erase them, so I prefer to talk about power.

Who has power? Why do they have it? What do they do with it? These are key questions to understanding almost every interaction between individuals, groups and even nations. People who have power can – and do – change the world. They can start wars or they can end them. They can free people or enslave them. Power itself is not good or bad. What someone chooses to do with it is everything. And how they got it matters too. Were they born into it? Did they strive for it? Did they lie, bully and manipulate people to get it? Did they get it from a lifetime of earning and deserving respect? Was it perhaps a mix of reasons because life is complicated and simple definitions are rarely accurate?

Having power doesn't make someone a good or bad person. It just means you can do some things that other people can't. A tool I've often used to demonstrate this is something that is immediately obvious about me – I'm quite tall. My height doesn't tell people anything about my character, but it does mean I can reach things on high shelves and see over crowds. It's also not something I had to work for or earn; it's just how my genetic makeup and childhood environment shaped my bones. It's useful at times, awkward at others, but because I have always been taller than most of the people my age, it is the only way I know how to see the world. Again, my height has nothing to do with whether I'm a good or bad person. It would, however, say a great deal about me if I used it, deliberately or thoughtlessly, to block other people's view at a concert, or grab the last item from a shelf that a shorter person couldn't reach. If I did such things, it would be my choices, not my height, that define my character and my values.

As both Spiderman and the Bible remind us, 'with great power comes great responsibility'.

The infographic inside the back cover of this book summarises some forms of power men and boys can use to remove someone's ability to refuse consent to sexual touch.

Physical size is one small measure of power. There are many others, and children can be experts at recognising various forms of power, if only because they are so often powerless in their interactions with the adult world. They understand age and size immediately.

Social power is immediately familiar to them. It's often about popularity and the hierarchy of the schoolyard. Teens often develop a keen understanding of the power of wealth as they get older and the social capital of having the right clothes, devices, holidays and beauty treatments becomes more dominant. The kids with high social status can condemn someone with less power to being ostracised, ridiculed and humiliated. This is something some teens take very seriously, and it cannot be dismissed with a 'just ignore them'. Bullies who use sexual harassment as a coercive tool for sexual assault is not trivial. A young woman, now in university, told me that when she was in Year 10 one of the boys got hold of a nude selfie she'd sent her then boyfriend. He used it to blackmail her into giving him oral sex and then used that to coerce her into more non-consensual sex (AKA: rape). 'I can't explain it,' she told me. 'It doesn't make sense, "Give me a blow job or I'll tell everyone you're a slut" like, what does that even mean? But it felt so real at the time. I didn't know what else to do.'

Emotional power is a common tool in sexual violence between partners. Usually in the form of an implied or even explicit threat to withhold love or affection. 'I need to show you how much I love you or I can't keep feeling this way.' 'I can't keep touching you if you won't let me finish.' 'If you won't let me do it, I can easily find someone who will.' 'If you loved me as much as I love you, you'd want to do it too.'

Financial power as a tool of sexual harassment is often something we think of as an adult problem, but many teens have jobs and need money. This can include direct threats to get them fired, reduce their shifts or even assign them dirty or unsafe jobs. 'Do you want to be walking home at midnight or taking all the rubbish out to the back alley?' Indirect threats or more subtle uses of financial power can also be effective. 'It's dangerous for you to be on the train home by yourself. I can pay for an Uber for you later if you stay with me for a while.' Financial power can also come from the ability to guilt, persuade or pressure someone into spending money, 'I'm broke right now, so you'll have to pay for me all night if we go out. Why don't we just hang as my place instead?'

Psychological power, also known as gaslighting (or even coercive control if it's extensive enough) is about destabilising someone's ability to trust themselves and hold onto what they really feel and think. 'You're so weird that you don't want to.' 'What's wrong with you? Everyone else loves it.' 'You're so cold and frigid. Did something happen to you? Do you need to see a therapist or something?' 'Why are you doing this to me? Why can't you see how much it hurts me?'

Pressure is where someone relentlessly nags until they get what they want. They know the other person doesn't want to do what they're asking, but they 'win' if they eventually get a reluctant 'okay then'. This is often where we see the most confusion in teens who have been taught the yes/no binary of consent, because in this binary, someone did say yes, so what's the problem?

The power of authority is something children are particularly vulnerable to because there are so many people who have authority over them. Priests who abused children or even adult parishioners were using the authority that came from their religious and social position. This power can also come from someone's position as a teacher, carer, doctor, therapist, older family member, or anything else that could compel obedience, silence or respect.

Coercive power is when someone threatens, blackmails or bribes another person to prevent resistance. The coercion might be physical ('Say yes or I'll hurt you') but it can also incorporate the other forms of power outlined above. The girl who was threatened with being labelled a slut if she didn't comply was targeted by social and coercive power. It can also be framed as something beneficial, 'If you say yes I'll give you the concert tickets you so desperately want' or 'I'll get you that camping trip invite you were hoping for'. Coercion, like pressure, can force a technical yes, but it is not consent.

Physical force is the traditional understanding of rape, where one person physically overpowers another. It can also include deliberately incapacitating someone (for example, spiking their drink to incapacitate them) opportunistically raping someone who is already incapacitated by drugs or alcohol, or physical violence that rendered them unconscious or too frightened to say no.

Other factors that can create power imbalances include race, neurotype, trauma history, sexuality, intellectual or athletic ability or, in same sex relationships, being out. These power imbalances outside gender can lead to non-consensual touching or sexual assault in LGBTIQA+ relationships as well as in heterosexual relationships.[110]

Gender, of course, confers very different powers on boys, girls and non-binary kids. As I outlined earlier, children are very aware of gender roles and will often participate in doling out the rewards and punishments that police conformity even when they don't believe the gender myths or want to conform themselves. Teenage boys can feel enormous pressure to prove their masculinity by displaying sexual prowess. When I was in my teens, boys would brag about 'bagging babes'. A group of fourteen-year-old boys in 2025 told me they'd say, 'clapping cheeks' or having a 'sneaky link' and brag about their 'body count'. The nomenclature has changed but the underlying purpose has not changed for centuries – boys believe they win admiration and respect from other men by having lots of sex with lots of different girls.

Sexual standards for girls can be much more complex. They must walk the very wafer-thin and twisted line between being a 'bop' or 'thot' (slut) or 'uptight' (frigid), always knowing that these words and all their predecessors have only ever been used to shame and punish girls. This conflict often drowns out any consideration of sexual pleasure for girls, sometimes to the point where shame inhibits their ability to feel pleasure.[111] If they believe that sex is something men do *to* women, or if they have absorbed shame about their bodies, they may not be able to talk comfortably about their own bodies and pleasure. They might silently comply with their partner's wants or acts and not ask for or even expect mutual pleasure. This may not fit the legal definition of sexual assault, but it is not consensual either.

Recognising power imbalances

People who have power, particularly if they've always had it, can have trouble understanding what life might feel like to someone who doesn't have that power. Boys who are tall, good looking and athletic often have significant social power at school. They've almost certainly had moments of embarrassment or fear, but they wouldn't know how it feels to face the persistent belief that they're less worthy of love and respect simply because they're physically small, weak or not conventionally masculine and handsome.

A few years ago, a teacher told me about an awkward, skinny boy in his Year 7 class who was reported to police for creating and storing deep fake porn images of some of the girls in his class. The teacher, when he told me this story, was both angry with Awkward Boy and angry for him.

> 'There's no defending what he did. It's disgusting. And he was old enough to know better. But... I know there should never be a "but" about child exploitation material... but... he was the patsy. The other boys didn't know how to make those images, so they bullied and manipulated him into doing it for them. They used to just ignore him or pick on him, but when they needed him to do something they pretended to be his friends. They made him part of their group, but it was conditional. I think he did what they wanted because he couldn't stand the idea that they'd go back to humiliating him again. When it all came out and the police turned up on his door, there was nothing he could say. He made the images. They were stored on his phone and distributed by him. The other boys said they didn't even know how to make deep fakes and everyone believed them, because it was true. But they instigated it, they bullied him mercilessly and not only did they get away with

it, those little shits are proud of how they put all the blame on him. The girls and all the other parents all hate him – fair enough too – but the real force behind those images will never be held accountable.'

In a true understanding of consent, where the core issue is who had choices and who had power, 'those little shits' would not have 'got away with it'. The boy who created the images still made a choice to commit a terrible act of harm against the girls in his class, and he needs to be held accountable for that choice. But he was only twelve years old and those boys offered him camaraderie and acceptance in place of loneliness, rejection and contempt. They did it knowingly, manipulatively, callously. Not caring or even interested in how much damage it did to the girls whose images were twisted into child abuse material that may well now find a permanent home on the private storage drives of paedophiles.

Consent and the law

It is important that children and teens understand that sexual assault is against the law, but I doubt this is news to any of them. They know it in the same way that they know it's against the law to steal cars. Only people who wanted to make a fool of themselves would try to say that kids who steal cars do it because they've never been taught that they shouldn't steal a car or that they don't know what stealing a car looks like.

All the secondary school curriculum include lessons on the details about the legal age of consent in their state (typically in Australia it's round sixteen, but there are variations across states and territories and across age groups within each state). Victoria and New South Wales have affirmative consent laws, which puts responsibility for ensuring sex is consensual onto the person seeking consent. In mid

2025, Queensland still allowed the notorious 'mistake of fact' defence to rape, which means someone cannot be convicted if they can argue that they honestly – if mistakenly – believed they had consent to sex. Definitions across the other states and territories hover somewhere between these two. If you want the specific information for your state, your child and your child's teacher will have access to classroom resources that provide these details. But consent education is not about the law. Focusing on the legal aspects of consent and sexual violence – the evidence a court can here and the verdicts a jury can hand down – does a great disservice to children and teens. It risks consent education becoming a tutorial in beating a rape charge rather than the in-depth exploration of empathy, power and choice necessary to a true understanding of consent.

Many teens, particularly boys, are often very concerned about rules and laws of consent. It's an understandable approach. Much of their life at this age is bound by rules about how they dress, what time they eat, even when they're allowed to go to the toilet or ask for a Panadol. And the endless flood of online misinformation about false rape allegations can have them utterly convinced this is a real and serious risk.[112] Their questions can get very specific about the circumstances that would lead to or avoid a rape conviction: 'What if she said yes, even if she didn't want to, would you still go to jail?' 'What would the police do if a girl said no, like fifteen times, and then didn't say no, would you still get arrested?' 'What if you had a witness or could you get her to sign something first?'

Reassuring boys that false accusations are vanishingly rare can help – best estimates put it at about 5 per cent of rapes reported to police and even then, they are rarely deliberate or malicious (see Appendix 2). It's worth noting, however, that the boys who typically believe myths about false rape accusations are also the ones most likely to commit sexual violence. However loudly they protest about false allegations ruining the lives of innocent men, they also rest comfortably in the knowledge that conviction for rape is even less common than a false allegation (see Appendix 2).

One of the most common stories I've heard from teenage girls comes from this 'get permission' understanding of consent. Boys who haven't been taught a deep understanding of consent will sometimes believe that a 'yes' under any conditions is consensual. If they ask for consent and get a 'no', they simply keep asking until they get the answer they want. *Are you ready now? How about now? Can't I just kiss you for a bit longer? Can I touch you there? Please? Please? Just for a minute? Just one more time? Just for a little bit longer? Are you ready now? I really need it, how about now?* In the face of this relentless pressure. Girls will often say they are 'worn down' and eventually just 'give in'.

Boys who are trained to have a legal understanding of consent will say, they had permission to proceed with sex, so there was no problem. But someone with an understanding of free choice and power would instantly recognise that while this may not have been illegal, it was certainly not consensual.

How to help teens understand sexual consent

As with all the topics covered in consent, sex, sexuality, respectful relationships and body safety programs, these discussions need to start well before children are old enough for romantic relationships and they need to be important in all their relationships. Children who have learned to tolerate or placate toxic friends can very easily take the same behaviours into romances when they get older. If they're used to giving and receiving respect, empathy and consent from their family, teachers, friends, teammates and school fellows, they will find it much easier to notice and reject relationships that could harm them as they get older. Especially in those early romances where the intensity of first love can be utterly overwhelming. All those new feelings and thoughts are so consuming and so new. The belief that no one ever has or ever could be in love like this is almost universal in those first passions. Romeo and Juliet had nothing on it! It's worth remembering though, that Shakespeare's play was not so much about young lovers as it was about how all the adults in Romeo and Juliet's life failed to give them the care, guidance, and acceptance they needed when they were unable to manage their own lives and emotions.

Helping boys get beyond consent is permission

The most useful technique I've found to move boys from thinking about rules to thinking about the why consent matters to their values and self-respect was to start with this question: 'What are the words you would most like other people to use to describe you?'[113] (This, by the way, might be a great discussion for parents and families to start at dinner or in the car.)

The initial answers are often very revealing. 'Good at sport', 'funny', 'successful', and 'strong' usually come out first. Too often, boys are taught to define themselves by what they can do rather than who they are. When I re-frame the question and ask them to think about the character traits they'd be most proud to have their parents or friends recognise in them, they'd say 'brave', 'thoughtful', 'kind', 'trustworthy' 'considerate', 'honest', 'fun to be with', 'friendly'. These are their aspirations and values and writing them down helps keep the focus on what they believe to be the most valuable parts of themselves. Asking them how someone who embodied all those traits would think about consent gets a very different answer to permission or law-based questions. It's when they start talking about empathy, care, and consideration. Respecting others becomes a form of self-respect – not a rule they have to follow, bend or break.

Cisgender boys walk through a very different world to the one inhabited by girls and non-binary people, even in Australia. Boys who don't live with an ever-present threat of sexual violence need to understand the power this gives them over the girls and non-binary people who do live with that threat. If we help those boys understand this difference, not only can they make the world feel safer for people who have reason to be afraid, they can also respond to that fear with the kindness and respect it deserves. Not, as boys often think they should, by reinforcing it with pseudo-heroic statements about 'I'll kill anyone who hurts you' but by responding to it with genuine care.

A few years ago, I worked with a group of sixteen and seventeen-year-old boys to come up with a range of ways they could do this. 'Like, if you tell someone that it's OK to say how they feel, and then make sure you don't get angry, even if you don't like what they say,' was one suggestion. 'What about if you ask her if she wants to go out with a group, instead of just the two of us?' was another one. They understood very quickly that this was not about denying their own wants or needs. As one of the boys told me, 'You can say what you want too, right? It's just that you need to make sure she's not scared to say what she wants.'[114]

Girls are not sexual gatekeepers

Another limitation on free choice is gendered expectations of who is allowed to want and enjoy sex. This is often implicit in consent lessons where teachers unintentionally, sometimes even unknowingly, reinforce the belief that girls are responsible for fending off boys' rampant striving for penetrative sex. As recently as 2025, researchers were publishing studies of fresh high school graduates' frustration and disappointment that their sex education ignored women's sexual feelings to teach outdated and rigid gender stereotypes.[115]

Desire is not gendered. Neither is responsibility for seeking and giving consent. Limiting consent inside stereotypical gender roles is not going to keep any child or teen safe, but it does increase the risk they will feel shamed by their inability to adhere to unrealistic gender roles. It also makes sex education a target of disgust and resentment, rather than what it should be – an opportunity to learn essential information about keeping their bodies safe and healthy.

Consent and sex education must be inclusive

Another common danger in consent and sex education is teachers assuming all their students are straight and cisgender. As I wrote in Chapter 4, this is almost certainly not true and every kid in the class needs to know they are visible and important to their teacher and their education. But even a class entirely full of straight cisgender kids still needs to have inclusive sex and consent education. A foundational principle of everyone's understanding of consent must be that it applies to all people of all genders and all sexualities. Cis, straight kids who think consent only applies to girls having sex with boys are at real risk of committing grievous sexual violence against LGBTIQA+ kids (who are already at increased risk of sexual violence – see Appendix 2). No one is truly teaching consent if they are not teaching that consent includes everybody.

Walk as well as talk

More than anything you say to your kids, your actions teach them about consent. Do you ask them how they feel when you have to make a decision about their bodies? Explain why sometimes you have to override their consent – yes, they need to take off wet shoes, go to the dentist and get vaccinated – but as they get older they will be able to make those choices for themselves. Is it clear to them that even if you have to make health and safety choices for them, you still care about their feelings and take their concerns seriously?[116] Do the adults in their home and in their life respect each other and make sure all their interactions are consensual? Do those adults disagree and even fight without being violent, controlling or cruel? Does gender dictate who asks for and gives consent about everyday things around the home? Children are little sponges and they will absorb everything you do, even the things you don't notice that you do.

Your children's village can't just talk about consent; it needs to show them how much consent matters. Sometimes that is by getting it right. But how everyone acts when someone gets it wrong is equally important. Do all the other adults ignore or dismiss the person who did something non-consensual? Did they talk to each other about it? Was it a joke or did they take it seriously? Who was given responsibility for the breach of consent? Who got support and sympathy? Did anyone talk to the children and teens about it? Kids learn a lot from watching how we walk, but sometimes they learn even more from watching how we fall down and get back up again.

Books about consent for your kids

- *Consent* by Jayneen Sanders: a picture book for under five-year-olds.
- *From My Head To My Toes, I Say What Goes* by Charlotte Barkla: a picture book for three to seven-year-olds.
- *Kit and Arlo Find A Way* by Vanessa Hamilton and Ingrid Laguna: for nine to twelve-year-olds.
- *Welcome to Consent* by Yumi Stynes and Dr Melissa Kang: for eleven-year-olds and older.
- *Real Talk About Sex and Consent: what every teen needs to know*, by Cheryl M. Bradshaw for thirteen-year-olds and older.
- *Consent Laid Bare: Sex, entitlement & the distortion of desire* by Chanel Contos: for sixteen-year-olds and older.

9

Safety and consent online

The digital world did not spring into existence in a single moment of blazing invention. It was a collection of ideas and theories that slowly coalesced between the 1950s and the 2010s. Only 60 years ago, we needed a computer the size of a bus to send a single email. Now almost every Australian has a smartphone that fits in their pocket and can communicate with the entire world.

Some parents of today's teenagers might have had a computer in their home when they were children. If they were very lucky, they might even have had a flip phone in their teen years. But they didn't grow up in a world where their online and physical worlds were equally real and seamlessly connected.

By 2024, almost 70 per cent of Australian kids under seventeen own a smartphone. They typically get their own phone when they are twelve. The average ten-year-old is on their phone almost fifteen hours a week and this increases to more than 26 hours by the time they're seventeen[117].

No frustrated teen who has every shouted 'you don't understand!' at an adult could even imagine that adult as a misunderstood and angry adolescent. The current generation of teens, however, might be the first in history to be entirely correct in that assertion. Their parents did not grow up in the online world. They often don't understand the perils and benefits it can have for children. Perhaps most importantly, they do not have the world view of someone who cannot imagine a life *not* lived online.

If this book was written for children and teens, it would not have a separate section on technology. That's not how they think about the world. Technology is woven into all their experiences and any book intended for them would need to similarly weave technological concepts into every topic. Parents and teachers, however, remember the pre-internet days and we often still see a divide between the online world and the physical world. We still sometimes talk about the online world and the 'real world' and forget that, for the kids growing up in it, the online world *is* the real world. We know enough to see the dangers (and the benefits) but not enough to know where our children are when they disappear into their digital lives.

Those lives can be a source of great strength for teens. They have access to information, imagination, creativity and communities that we could never have imagined growing up in the 1980s and 1990s. It's perfectly normal for fifteen-year-olds to have daily contact with close friends who protect them from loneliness, even though they've never met in the physical world. People with niche interests in the habitat of frogs or the embroidery techniques of Ancient India can, with a simple voice command, find a depth of information, advice and like-minded folk online that they would struggle to access in a physical world.

When children were growing up in just a physical world, parents had a fairly clear view of who and what was shaping their values and identity. There may have been some friends kept hidden, but parents had much more visibility of who their kids were talking to and what they were reading, seeing, and hearing. That is no longer the case.

Children and teens absorb ideas and perspectives and relationships from their bedrooms that might shock their parents. It's interesting that private bedrooms are also a relatively new concept and confined mostly to reasonably wealthy western families.[118] For most of human history, families slept in the same room, if not in the same bed. A friend of mine who recently travelled to the Philippines told me her driver asked her whether it was true that Australian children sleep in a room by themselves. When she said this was mostly true, at least of teenagers, he said, 'Poor little things, do you think they'll be OK?'

In Australia, where children usually sleep in rooms alone or with a sibling, and do not have their extended family for comfort and companionship, they often turn to their online world. A survey in 2016 found that even back then, 68 per cent of teenagers kept their mobile devices within reach at night, and nearly a third of teens slept with smartphones, cell phones or tablets in their beds.[119] An update to that study found screen time is increasing rapidly and in 2021 teens were spending an average of more than eight hours a day on their entertainment screen use – watching television and online videos, playing video games, using social media, browsing websites, creating content, e-reading, and other digital activities such as messaging their friends and family.[120] That's an enormous portion of their day, and for some kids, that might be positive, creative, community-building time. But all of it is shaping their world view in ways their parents can't see or understand. If those views are toxic or hurtful, parents may not even know about it for years.

Parents who don't have much contact with the online world might find this bewildering and frightening. Even parents who have a very strong online presence can still be shocked by the online world inhabited by their children – sometimes it is a world they choose but it can also be a world the algorithms create for them.

The mother of a fourteen year old girl recently told me that she was pleased her daughter had an Instagram account because 'Instagram is all about body positivity and feeling good about yourself'. This is no doubt true for her, because she only searches for and consumes body positive content, so this is what the Instagram algorithm feeds her. Even if a body shaming post somehow made its way into her feed, the algorithm ensures the top comments she sees are all people angrily rejecting negative body attitudes. If her daughter is viewing content about dieting or idealised female bodies, she might see that same body shaming post but her top comments would be full of loathing for women who can't or won't adhere to false beauty standards. That mother and daughter can sit next to each other on their couch, scrolling through the same social media app, and live in completely different online worlds without even realising it. This is a very new problem, and we are still working out how to manage it.

As much as I might wish I could write a handbook for every app, website, message service and game your children might use, it would be impossible to describe all the risks in each service's tailored content and even if I tried to do so, it would be out of date the minute it was published. And I doubt there are many parents who could set up digital barriers their teens couldn't get through, under, or over in far less time than it would take to build them.

What I can do is outline an approach to keeping your children safe online, and the warning signs to look for that might indicate they are not safe. The theory is simple – talk early, openly and often. The practise is much more complicated.

A commonly used analogy for teaching kids about online safety is how we teach them road safety. We carry babies across a road or strap them into strollers. We insist a four-year-old holds our hands and ten-year-olds walks next to us. We teach them to look both ways, cross at the lights, wear bright clothes and wait for the crossing guard to signal safety. We do all this in the hope that by the time our children are in their teens, they can safely navigate traffic and public transport on their own and start preparing to learn how to drive. It's an interesting analogy, but where it becomes misleading is that it forgets that roads and traffic are among the most strictly regulated spaces in the country. Every driver on the road must be licensed, every car registered and traceable. Safety for pedestrians, particularly children, is given higher priority than the smooth flow of traffic. Road rules require drivers slow down to 40 in school zones, give way at pedestrian crossings, wait for passengers to get on and off trams, stop at traffic lights, stay on designated roadways, obey speed limits and road signs, ensure their vehicles are fitted with basic safety devices, and never drive after consuming too much alcohol. The penalty for breaking these rules is hefty fines or, for serious breaches, having your licence revoked. If you break the road rules and hurt someone, even accidentally, you're likely to go to prison.

The road safety analogy would only work if someone could drink a dozen pints, strap a jet engine to the top of a bulldozer with no brakes and go drag racing other jet-fuelled bulldozers through quiet residential streets, knowing there would be no consequences other than a good chance they could make millions. Even if someone created a beautiful park for children, something with high fences and security gates, the jet-fuelled bulldozers can come over the fences at any moment.

How would you teach your kids road safety if there were no road rules? No stop signs or speed limits or safety crossings. No police waiting to catch rule breakers and no penalties for putting people in danger. No roadworthy certificates, vehicle standards or registration requirements. No breathalysers, booze buses, drug test or driver's licences. What would you teach your children if drivers could do whatever they wanted, whenever they wanted, at whatever speed they liked, in any vehicle that took their fancy? What safety could you put in place for your children if some drivers and car makers could profit from harming the children who use roads and footpaths?

Banning your children from ever using a road or a footpath might keep them safe, but they could never be part of the world outside their childhood home.

This is a much more realistic analogy. There is almost no regulation in the online world. It is our new wild frontier. Many inhabitants are well intentioned. Some are making great and positive change. Most are just going about their daily tasks. But mixing in with all those benign people are the malevolent grifters, happy, even eager to trade children's safety for bitcoin.

We need to recognise the online world as both a place of great possibilities and great dangers. We can't raise our children with no experience in the online world, so the only option we have is to work with them to show them the risks, make the most of the opportunities, and stay close enough that we can see the dangers they may be too young to recognise.

Online communities: the good, the bad and the dangerously ugly

Children and teen's relationships, good and bad, are connected through their devices and interwoven with their school, social and online lives. We can separate these contexts to tease out some of the complexities, but we must always remember that it's never about the real world and the online world – the online world *is* their real world. They might see friends and enemies every day at school or after school, but they also take those people home, into their bathroom and bedroom every night.

Almost none of the girls who worship Taylor Swift will ever meet her or talk to her, but they feel deeply connected to her through music, lyrics, images, videos, posts, in-jokes and Easter eggs shared with millions of other Swifties from all over the world.

Teenage girls have always had passionate devotions. Fans of Audrey Hepburn, K-pop group BLACKPINK, the Spice Girls and Princess Diana were mostly teenage girls. Throughout history, girls have found women to worship in religious figures such as the 'Virgin' Mary, Saint Brigid of Ireland and Saint Cecilia. Queens, princesses, even fictional women such as Arthurian legend Guinevere have all been objects of feminine worship. The inner lives of adolescent girls are so thoroughly dismissed and ignored that there is very little research on the expression of their devotions to saints, goddesses and celebrities – unless it's about the supposed deficits that incite them.[121]

Girlhood is sometimes so reviled that it's almost impossible to recognise their idolisations as aspirational, a spiritual search for a female role model, perceived as holy, who provides them with an example of womanhood on which to build their best selves. Taylor Swift, with her apparent kindness, empathy, generosity, strength, ambition, success, work ethic, leadership, and vulnerability appeals to the best of what girls and young women can hope to be. There's plenty of room to critique her elevation of slim white prettiness and embodiment of the fairytale princess myth in her earlier years, but even so, she is a positive and encouraging role model for girls. Particularly over recent years as she dressed herself in the fairytale princess daydream and subverted it into the patriarchy's worst nightmare: a smart, hard-working, ambitious woman who finds her happy ever after in the success of her own creativity.

The online Swiftie community is, at its best, generous, thoughtful and inclusive. In the lead up to the Eras Tour concerts in Melbourne and Sydney, Swifties were sharing tools for supporting disabled and neurodivergent concert-goers, along with costume tips and links to the best places to buy beads for homemade friendship bracelets. They were making friends with each other, meeting up at the concerts and staying in touch afterwards. It was an example of the best of what the online world can offer children and teens, and it passed almost without notice or comment – because no one is more likely to be dismissed or ignored in 'serious and important' discussions than teenagers who adore girlish things.

Swiftie culture is one example of children and teens reaping the benefits of harmony, intimacy, camaraderie and a shared love of artistic endeavour online, but it's certainly not the only one. Young sporting enthusiasts find encouragement, support, help with training, and links to fellow devotees in their local communities. Queer kids were among the first to embrace online connection as a panacea to the isolation of living in a straight cis world. As far back as the 1990s, message boards set up for and by LGBTIQA+ people shared information, love, support, healthcare knowledge, and safety services. The message boards of the 1990s are now social media groups and private messaging services, but the shared content and alleviation of loneliness and shame are still the key defining features. The same is true of neurodivergent communities, people with disabilities, and faith groups. Even so-called 'army brats' (children of military parents who have to follow family postings all over the world) can maintain continuity of friendship in the online world that was impossible in the pre-internet days.

Matilda Bosley, in her book, *The Year I Met My Brain*, said it was TikTok videos about ADHD that were her first clues to understanding that her brain is not like typical brains. After watching those TikToks, she went to a doctor, then to a psychiatrist and was finally diagnosed. She then spent a year (probably longer, but the book is only about that first year) understanding what this meant for the rest of her life.

All of this positivity makes the online sound almost painfully wholesome. Sometimes it even is that way. But, of course, nothing is ever simple. There is the flip side, the darker corners of the internet where danger lurks for people of any age, but particularly for children and teens, vulnerable because they don't yet know to be sceptical of kindness or companionship even when sinister motives might be readily apparent to an adult.

In 2001, for example, *Time* magazine reported that there were more than 400 websites promoting anorexia nervosa (known as pro-ana sites) as a lifestyle choice rather than a life-threatening mental illness.[122] Today, in addition to the thousands of pro-ana and pro-mia (promoting bulimia) sites, social media content and private messaging groups reaches into the millions. People share tips on how to avoid eating, praise images of malnourished bodies, shame each other for giving in to hunger, and find advice on how to hide starvation from concerned parents and teachers. A friend of mine, now in her thirties, told me she spent years moving from pro-ana chat boards to social media pages to WhatsApp groups. 'It was – it is – like a cult,' she said. 'You can't question anything or say you're scared about what's happening to you or you'll be swarmed by people telling you to get out, "You're not welcome, go away and die of obesity". They were the only people I could talk to, but I could only talk about how good it was to starve. I couldn't leave them, but I couldn't do anything to get better while I stayed.'

Around one million people in Australia live with an eating disorder and around one third of adolescents engage in disordered eating (restrictive or compulsive eating, irregular or inflexible eating habits).[123] Women and girls are about two thirds of people with eating disorders, but evidence indicates the number of boys might be rising.[124] Trans and non-binary people are also at elevated risk of developing eating disorders.[125] While diagnosis typically happens in late teenage years, most people begin with disordered eating somewhere between twelve and 25 years old.[126]

Confusingly, there are also many effective online and social media supports for people recovering from eating disorders. For some people, when the will to keep trying for recovery weakens, the online community, shared experience and support can be a lifeline.

Eating disorders and negative body image are just one example. The same conflict between invaluable support and dangerous exacerbation is embedded in mental health issues, gender myths, vaccinations, nutrition, relationships, medical treatments, addiction, and any number of other topics. It's worth noting that a 2025 investigation by *The Guardian* found that more than half of the top 100 mental health TikToks contained misinformation or advice that was at best, of dubious quality.[127]

Online communities that are not well protected and monitored can also be hunting grounds for predators or angry young men looking for vulnerable people to abuse. This risk is such a concern that counter terrorism officers in the UK are joining with the National Crime Agency to set a special task force to monitor young men and boys riled up by 'strongly misogynistic' content who are hunting for vulnerable women and girls on suicide and eating disorder support sites.[128]

The rapid rise of technology facilitated abuse

The National Plan to End Violence Against Women and Children defines technology facilitated abuse as a 'wide-ranging term that encompasses many subtypes of interpersonal violence and abuse using mobile, online and other digital technologies. These include harassing behaviours, sexual violence and image-based sexual abuse, monitoring and controlling behaviours, and emotional abuse and threats.'[129]

I've worked in frontline domestic violence services where tech consultants would routinely find tracking devices installed on women's phones, hidden in their cars, sewn into children's teddy bears or concealed in the heels of their school shoes. As frightening as this is for the women and domestic violence refuge workers, it is also terribly painful for the children, who feel used, manipulated and torn between controlling fathers and fleeing mothers.

Apart from their forced participation in their parents' abusive relationship (which is a form of child abuse) children and teens are also both victims and perpetrators of technology facilitated abuse against each other.

The one we see most often is image-based abuse, defined as 'non-consensual creation, distribution, and/or threats to distribute, nude or sexual images'.[130] It's also sometimes referred to as 'revenge porn' although it can and frequently does happen outside romantic relationships.

Picture a sixteen-year-old girl in an advanced Year 10 maths class where boys outnumber girls by about three to one. She loves maths and had always earned high marks in the younger years where everyone had to participate, and the classrooms were not so gendered. The boys around her are muttering and sniggering to each other. She tries to ignore them, but she hears her name and feels them staring at her. They're all surreptitiously looking at their phones. One boy shows her his screen and grins. It's a photo of her, naked from the waist up. She doesn't know where he got it. It might be fake, or someone might have taken the photo without her knowing. She might never find out where it came from, but she will spend weeks, maybe even months, unable to think about anything else.

The teacher is irritably aware something is distracting the class and Maths Girl is somehow involved. He tells the boys to settle down, stop talking, put their phones away, glaring at Maths Girl as he says it. The muttering dies out for a while. Then it starts up again. Another boy flashes his phone at her, the image now has a crudely drawn penis on her face. Irritable Teacher is fed up. The topic is complex, he doesn't have enough time to teach this class when too many of them aren't paying attention. He can't see Maths Girl doing anything, but he can sense she is at the centre of the disruption. He tells her to change seats. The boys all snigger as she stands up, straightens her shirt, and walks to a seat at the front. The few other girls in the class know exactly what's going on. Some of them join in the whispering and sniggering, others stay silent. It's self-protection. They all know the target can move with shocking speed.

By Year 11, Maths Girl becomes History Girl, a subject for which she is far less suited, but at least she is no longer outnumbered. A boy who once spent an entire maths class sniggering at a picture of her breasts asks her, with genuine curiosity, why she dropped out of maths. 'You were really good at it. I never thought of you as a history type.' She tells him maths was too hard and she wants easier subjects for VCE. He looks mildly surprised and then forgets about it as he walks off to his all-boys maths class.

There have been countless other Maths Girls over the years. Before smartphones became ubiquitous (around 2010) boys were passing notes and crudely drawn sketches. Now they're sharing images, both real and fake, across a tangled web of apps and services.

I've heard versions of the Maths Girl story from women in their fifties when they explain why they spent a fortune on sending their daughters to private single-sex schools. I've heard it from university students who choose an arts degree instead of the science degree they'd dreamed of before high school. From teachers who do their best to ban phones in classrooms. From teenage girls who can't stop crying on their way to school. From teenage boys and young men who went along with what they thought at the time were jokes and only realised years later were crimes.

Maths Girl first saw the image being shared while she was in class and only sixteen years old. That image could follow her for years, maybe even decades. Passed like a virus from the boys in her school to the young men at her university to the men at her workplace. In her online world the image could be shared with all her communities through messaging apps, online games, shared servers, social media, and private group chats. If they attach her name to the image it can come up in search results by potential employers decades into her future. It could also end up on porn sites and child-abuse sites. It can move in and out of her digital world and her physical world, and she has no control over where it goes, who sees it, or what they believe about how it came to exist.

A recent survey of Australian adults found that almost three-quarters of people aged eighteen to 24 had experienced some form of technological abuse.[131] Women and LGBTIQA+ people were more likely to be subjected to sexual and image-based abuse by a current or former partner. Men were slightly more likely to report harassing behaviour by a stranger. Men and women had roughly the same level of controlling and emotionally abusive experiences, but in all cases, women were more likely to react by feeling angry, controlled, humiliated and depressed. Men were more than twice as likely as women to find the behaviour okay, funny or flattering. Fewer than 10 per cent of victims reported the abuse to police or the eSafety Commissioner, and more than one-third never told anyone. More than three-quarters of women and almost half the male victims reported that their perpetrator was a man.

While image-based abuse isn't new, in the months after the Covid-19 lockdowns, it felt as though this problem was more endemic than the disease. We saw it in every single secondary school and far too many primary schools. We've mostly stopped talking about lockdowns now and I think we often forget the profound impact they had on children and teens.[132]

While writing this, I did a quick check of Melbourne's lockdown dates. It took me by surprise how sick I felt when I looked at the dates of that last shattering lockdown, 5th August to 21st October 2021. It brought back how exhausted, lonely and bored I was by the end; what being locked away did to my body, mind and emotions. How impossibly awkward it felt when I saw people in person again, and I had to remember how to react to smiles, body language and feelings unmuted by digital transfer. I was well into adulthood when Covid happened, with a lifetime's practice of having friends and making small talk. During Covid, babies, children and teenagers had a massive interruption to their developing understanding of how to build relationships with each other, adults and the world. These effects didn't disappear when we sent them back to school.

They also had the added disruption of forced immersion in the online world. It was almost like a global social experiment of the hothouse potential of gender myths and shame, supercharged by pervasive technology and isolation. It will be years before we fully understand the effects of this, but I think we need to recognise that the Covid generation should not – cannot – be expected to manage themselves and each other as if those ghastly two years never happened.

It's worth taking some time to check in with your children about their memory of being in lockdown. Maybe, like me, you've tried to erase it from your mind. Your children might want to do that, too. I understand. That sick, visceral returning memory was awful. But it also tells me that the effects are still with me. That might not be true for you or your kids, but it's still a good idea to check. The Covid effect is not as immediate or urgent now, but I think we can still see some evidence of it in the intensity of children's and teens' connection to their online world.

Image based abuse didn't start in Covid but it absolutely flourished in the hothouse conditions of lockdown.[133] Teens couldn't be with each other so they, like everyone else, communicated online. Flirting, joking and having fun included sharing their bodies with each other. Caught up in the thrill of it all, wanting to like and be liked during a very lonely time, it's entirely understandable that many of them didn't think beyond the trusted moment of shared joy and fun. For many of those kids, there were no negative repercussions. One girl, who was seventeen in 2021, told me she now has better sex because of those years. 'I had to learn about my own body because I was the only one who could touch it. And I had to tell someone what I was doing and why I liked it. That was my first sexual experience and so when we got out of lockdown, I just kept doing that. I know there are some bad stories but don't forget to tell people about the great stuff too.'

A few years back, victim-blaming was a very common response to girls who were targets of image based abuse.[134] 'Don't send nudes' was the main message and 'Well you should have known better than to send him a nude' was the logical follow up. It rarely worked to explain that blaming victims cannot solve a problem created by (mostly) men and boys who believe they're entitled to take and share images of naked women and girls. 'That's all very well,' as one irate parent said to me, 'but you need to be teaching girls about the risks of those images being around forever or they'll get themselves in real trouble.' She got even more irate when I said the girls could no more get themselves into trouble than they could get themselves pregnant. It requires at least one other person.

Back then someone needed technical skills and powerful equipment to take a photo of a person's face and insert it into a porn image. Even the most skilled technician would have had trouble creating realistic faked video of someone. Now anyone can make a foolproof porn image on a phone in less than two minutes from class photos or profile pics.

A Year 9 teacher told me how a class discussion about deep fakes had some terrible consequences. After the class she was chatting to a few of the boys who had told her that making fake nudes was incredibly easy. She was surprised; she told me she thought it still needed considerable technical capability. One of them offered to show her how easily it could be done, and she agreed. She told him not to make an image but just show her through the steps. 'I don't know what I was expecting,' she said, 'but I definitely didn't realise how fast it would be.' He went racing through what he called an app but she identified as a website, which already had a wide range of porn images available. He showed her where he could upload a photo and before she knew what he was doing he'd uploaded a photo of his sixteen-year-old sister and, with a couple of clicks, created a porn image of her. The other boys scoffed and laughed when the horrified teacher remonstrated, but the boy who made it was irritable, saying, 'It's fine, she's *my* sister and of course I'm going to delete it.' He did so with a flourish and the boys all assumed that was the end of it. The teacher, of course, was mortified. 'I don't know what to do. He essentially created child porn of his sister at my instigation. I don't believe it's just gone because he thinks he deleted it. What if it ends up on a server somewhere? Should I tell her? I can't report him, but do I report myself? Oh my God, what a mess! None of us knew enough about what was happening to stop it all going completely off the rails. And the whole thing took about a minute!'

Most of the people exploited by perpetrators of image-based abuse are girls and women, but there is a form of abuse, known as sextortion, that is often specifically targeted at boys and young men. Predators trick or coerce their prey into sending naked or sexual images of themselves and then threaten to share them with his friends or family unless the boy gives them money or more images. It's yet another form of violence very much under-reported, but best estimates in 2018 put it at around 5 per cent of adolescents (most of them boys).[135] Recent reports from the Internet Watch Foundation indicate a massive increase since then.[136] The people who target boys in this way are playing on their fear of admitting weakness – both that they were tricked into creating the images and that they don't know what to do when they're being extorted. While perpetrators often pretend to be female to obtain the images, they frequently threaten to claim the images prove the boy was involved in gay sex, adding homophobic shame to masculinity shame. The effect of this can be catastrophic, to the point of putting some victims at increased risk of suicide.[137]

Research published in Australia in 2020 showed that, regardless of who committed the image-based abuse – casual sexual partners, current or ex-partners, friends, colleagues, housemates or strangers – the results were devastating.[138] One participant described it as 'torture for the soul', a description so apt it became the title of the research paper. Others talked about how the abuse affected their entire lives: 'I've changed my hair colour. I intentionally put on weight, because I was quite thin and I always had quite an athletic sort of figure, and it sounds so ridiculous because I intentionally made myself put on [substantial weight] so people wouldn't [recognise me].' The fallout wasn't just about the image itself, but the reaction from friends and family, as well as strangers online: 'I got a lot of hate and a lot of it was because I'm brown skinned, I'm a woman of colour... I had racialised hate and misogynistic hate, and the commentary was, "You're ugly and gross"... "You're asking for it"... "You're a slut, you're a whore"... "What do you expect?"'

Another aspect is the permanence. Abuse committed in the physical world can end. Image-based abuse can last a lifetime. As another person in the study mentioned above said, 'There will never be a day in my entire life that all of the images of me could ever be deleted.'

I've seen such painful, helpless rage in the faces of girls who have lived through these kinds of abuses. They feel guilt and shame, even when they know they shouldn't. Then they feel guilty and ashamed for feeling guilty and ashamed, as if they've failed to meet the standard of the strong independent woman who refuses to take on those burdens.

Teens would hate to hear me say this, but they're still children, trusting someone they liked, as children do. Not foreseeing consequences they've never experienced, as children do. Unable to cope with expectations that, while they are still children, they should behave with more maturity and forethought than many adults show. If the adults around them have no idea how to manage this problem or respond to it, then it strikes me as grossly unfair that we throw the blame back on child victims for failing to prevent it in the first place.

CSAM and 'child porn'

Child sexual abuse material (CSAM) and child sexual exploitation material (CSEM) are the technically correct names for what many people call 'child porn'. These terms make it clear that, unlike porn, this material is illegal. It's not simply another niche or genre of porn. It's a crime that involves committing criminal and deeply wounding violence against children.

For more than 30 years Michael Sheath, Associate Lecturer in the School of Psychology at the University of Worcester, has worked with men who sexually abuse children. He now advises police forces around Europe on the changing profile of child abusers. In 2025 he told *The Guardian* that the nature of online child sexual abuse material (CSAM) has changed immeasurably over the last 15 years. 'It used to be that child abuse material was hard to find and looking at it was extremely risky,' he told *The Guardian*. Now, as he points out, it's mainstream, free and easy to access from any device. 'Look on a mainstream porn site and you'll immediately see titles like "Auntie takes the boys' virginity" or "Stepdad and stepdaughter". When I started working 30 years ago, that was really out-there outrageous, pervy and wrong. Now it's seen as a laugh.' [139]

This does not absolve the men who watch content that is, or implies, children being sexually abused. It's not like they need a special education campaign to teach them that sexually abusing children – or watching someone else do it – is wrong. They know that. And they should be held accountable for the choice to watch it and in doing so, participate in the abuse and create a market for more abuse. But the consumers are not the only culprits. The market for illegal drugs is a good analogy here. No one is going to make a dent in the amphetamines trade by arresting the users. They need help to stop, and they should be held accountable for the harm they do in their search for or consumption of drugs, but the traffickers, dealers and manufacturers are truly dangerous criminals. They are deliberately creating and expanding a market for their product. They're making a coldly calculated choice to enrich themselves by selling other people's lives, safety and happiness. The websites and apps that trade in child sexual abuse content are doing the same thing.

It's difficult to know exactly how much child sexual abuse material is online, much of it is hidden or shared privately, but the US-based National Centre for Missing and Exploited Children received almost 32 million CSAM reports from electronic service providers in 2022, a 47 per cent increase since 2020. Researchers all over the world have asked people whether they've ever watched CSAM. The results are usually between 2 and 5 per cent of men will admit to watching it and results for women are too low to be reliably counted.[140]

Parents should also be aware that a growing trend in child sexual abuse material is men finding and grooming or coercing children into producing images and videos of themselves or even of their siblings and friends. The Australian Federal Police (AFP) were issuing warnings about this in 2021, and emphasising that this is not about children committing crimes or doing anything wrong. Victim identification specialist Detective Sergeant Svetlana Palmer from the AFP-led Australian Centre to Counter Child Exploitation said, 'Children and young people are never to blame for being a victim of online child sexual exploitation.' She warned that the offenders are highly sophisticated in their ability to manipulate children and teens. It can take as little as ten minutes for them to trick or coerce young teens into being filmed or photographed as they undress or perform sexual acts. Abusers then use those images to threaten and extort terrified children into producing more and more content. They collaborate in targeting specific children and endorsing each other so the child will trust them. Then they brag about the success in exploiting the child's youth and vulnerability and share content on the dark web.[141]

This is frightening but you can do a lot to protect your child from this abuse. Young children's apps, games and services should only allow messages and friend requests from trusted contacts. Little children should only be able to add contacts or accept messages with adult supervision so they can talk through the reasons for accepting or rejecting those contacts in real time. As children get older and need more independence on their devices, communication is the key to keeping them safe. All their trusted adults need to make sure kids know to be sceptical of contact from people they don't know.

Most importantly, your children need to know they can turn to an adult in their physical world whenever they feel scared or overwhelmed.

Abusers will often try to convince kids they'll get in trouble or even that they will be arrested and sent to prison for making sexual images. It is crucial that children and teens know they can ask an adult for help, no matter what they've been told about the consequences for speaking up.[142] As I said back in Chapter 3, you need to be saying this so often that your kids are bored by it. You want them rolling their eyes and sighing at you every time you tell them they can come to you for anything, and they will never get in trouble when they need help.

AI and abuse in the virtual world

It's taken more than a year to write this book and even in that time the technology available to children – and to adults who want to harm children – has changed. It will keep changing. AI and the virtual world are the new frontier and tech companies are committing vast resources to developing new technology and inventing new ways to use existing technology.

AI companions and chatbots are a prime example. Even a year ago AI chatbots such as ChatGPT barely lived up to the AI label. Researchers used a very simple problem to demonstrate the limits of ChatGPT. It goes like this: Mary and John are in a room with a cat, a box and a basket. Mary puts the cat in the box and leaves the room. John takes the cat out of the box and puts it in the basket. Mary comes back into the room. Where does everyone think the cat is?

Early versions of ChatGPT could only tell you that the cat was in the basket, because that's where the cat is. Chat GPT4 will tell you that Mary thinks the cat is in the box because that's where she put it. John thinks the cat is in the basket because that's where he put it. The cat knows it is in the basket because that's where it is. The box and the basket are not sentient and therefore do not have any thoughts about the cat.

This is a profound shift. It's called theory of mind and while it is not yet a human level of consciousness, it does mean ChatGPT is able to understand different perspectives, that point of view can alter what we think of as knowledge.[143]

This technology is now used to create companions. Adults and children are able to create free customised AI confidants, a personality they can turn to for advice, comfort, companionship and support. In mid 2025, AI companion apps Replika, Chai and Character.ai each have 10 million downloads on the Google app store alone.[144] Many of these companion bots can be intimately sexual and, once again, there are almost no regulatory limits on what they can do. If porn is already changing young men's sexual scripts through increasingly extreme content, what affect will companion bots have if they are designed to replicate enthusiasm and enjoyment in response to violent sexual fantasies? That's happening already but the next steps are even more concerning, and they are probably only months away, a year at the most, from being widely available.

What happens when chatbot technology is combined with deep fake technology and anyone can create an AI version of a real person? Who owns you when AI can create a version of you that looks like you, sounds like you, laughs with your laugh, makes the same jokes and likes the same music as you? A stalker can create an AI version of the human target of his obsession and train it to tell him she wants him to watch her, have sex with her, or even create rape fantasies for him. Could someone create an AI version of a woman after he killed her? Are the next generation of celebrities and influencers going to be the people who lease out their face, voice, body and personalities to AI companies as the foundation for building companion bots?

The bots learn from their human partners and become more intimate, more human-like over time but at the moment, the company that designed the technology owns the bot. That could very easily change. But what happens if the person who created the bot and teaches it to imitate a person is then deemed to own it? Could I make a bot of my intimate partner and own it after they leave me?

Replika is one of the services that allows people to design their own chatbot companion. The companions have names, faces, voices and personality characteristics. They ask about your day, respond to every message, listen to every problem and constantly remind their users how much they care about them. The paid upgrade will flirt, sext and respond to erotic role-play. It will send and ask for nude selfies. In 2023 changes to privacy laws in Italy put the erotic service at Replika in jeopardy so the company altered the programming. Users said their bots' personalities changed significantly and many of them felt grief, even bereavement over losing the bot they loved so deeply.[145]

As much as I find the idea of AI companions disturbing, I cannot deny the evidence that says they can be beneficial. A US study in 2024 found that college students who created a friend on Replika said the bots eased their loneliness and, in a few cases, stopped them attempting suicide. Chatbots provided daily, even hourly support for cognitive behavioural therapy, mindfulness, reflection and other mental health activities. They are never tired, busy or bored and one of the key benefits reported by the students was 'just having someone to talk to who won't judge me'. The students in this study could not afford to pay human therapists for this level of support and many of them said it helped them deal with stress, feel better about themselves and even improved their relationships with people.[146]

That the chatbots can be helpful, even lifesaving companions doesn't make them less concerning. In fact, their success in replicating human relationships makes them even more of a threat in a world that still can't manage to effectively regulate old technology such as image sharing and messaging.

In early 2025, the eSafety Commission issued a warning about children using companion bots for support, advice and companionship.[147] These bots are not designed to be safe, especially for children. They're designed to collect data and generate profit for their creators. And as we have already established, if harming children generates profit, someone somewhere will do it without any hesitation.

Monetising AI is not just about collecting our email addresses and basic demographic data. That's very old news. People ask AI bots about problems in their marriage and insecurities about their body. When those people are products not customers their fears and insecurities are just metrics that companies can sell to advertisers. *Afraid that girls won't like you? Here's a manfluencer selling online courses to make you so tough and hard that girls will fling themselves naked at your feet. Afraid your wife is losing interest in you? Here's some extreme porn to keep you numb and some surveillance equipment you can install in her shoes. Did your girlfriend leave you or your crush reject you? Here's a service that will make an AI version of her that will plead with you to choke her and make her bleed. Click here to confirm your credit card details…*

One final thought for the future. Laura Bates, in her 2025 book, *The New Age of Sexism*, wrote about the metaverse, where full body wearable technology make it possible for users to interact physically as well as verbally in the virtual world. She points out that the metaverse is the brainchild of Mark Zuckerberg, who created Facebook so men could score women's attractiveness. Sexualised abuse, sexual harassment and image-based abuse are common on Meta products (Facebook, Instagram, Snapchat etc.) and between 2017 and 2023, where the communication channels were identifiable, 47 per cent of online grooming offences took place on Meta products.[148]

In a virtual world designed to maximise profits for organisations with a proven disregard for women and children's safety, what happens when the technology allows for full-body physical experience? If you can see, hear and feel something in a virtual world is that any different to seeing, hearing and feeling it in the physical world? How long will it be before women and children are at risk of physical rape in a virtual world?

All this sounds (is!) terrifying but it's so important to remember that our children do not live entirely in the online world. They do still sit in our cars and our lounge-rooms and at our diner tables. They are still part of your family and their school, and they still have all the other interests in the physical world that shapes their values and their sense of self-worth and self-respect. You, the adults who care for them, can protect them from online harm as much as you do from physical harm. This protection is as much about joining advocates in their call for increased regulation and monitoring of new technology as it is about sitting next to your child as they learn to master a new online game.

Helping your teen deal with online abuse

While it is important you know the seriousness of these issues, you are not helpless. In addition to the tips on the following pages, Australia's world-leading eSafety Commissioner offers a huge variety of resources, information and support – especially for parents of vulnerable teens.

Tell your teens about the eSafety Commissioner and how they can help. They may never need it themselves, but even if it is just something they can pass on to a friend, it will be very reassuring for them to know the service exists.

If your teen does tell you about image-based abuse or sextortion, make sure they know you don't blame them. Even if they created the images willingly in the beginning, they're still not adults and they were sought out, groomed and coerced by an adult or even another teen who was deliberately trying to harm them. They need the same comfort, reassurance and support you would give them if they were set upon and assaulted in the street.

Take it seriously. Technology facilitated abuse is both a crime and a serious problem. Your child needs to know you understand that this might feel devastating for them and you know it is not a trivial matter, but that you are able to help (or find help) and there is a solution for what's happening to them. They're not alone or powerless.

Clarify the kind of abuse they are describing. Racism, sexism, sexual harassment, misogyny, homophobia, transphobia are all words your child should know. Bullying is a useful umbrella term but understanding the particular rage or ignorance behind the abuse can help your child understand the abuse is about power and circumstance, not something they've done or said.

If you're not sure what to do and your child is very much against reporting the abuse, start off by calling one of the helplines in appendix 1 and ask for advice anonymously. You can reassure your child that the only reason they would ever request a police trace on the call is if someone is in serious and immediate danger (for example, someone was in the room with them threatening serious harm). The call might help clarify the situation for both of you and help you make a more informed decision about the next steps you want to take.

If your child still has copies of the images, don't delete them. You don't have to look at them but tell your child to store them as password-protected files on their own device until you can get advice from police or the eSafety Commissioner. If this turns into a criminal investigation, police might need the images as evidence. Or, if you don't take the threat to police, the eSafety Commissioner (which can and will help) might need them to trace all online copies for removal. If your child is being blackmailed, don't pay. Blackmailers will come back and try again if they know the threat is effective. Contact the eSafety Commissioner and follow their advice.

Is age verification a solution?

How do we resolve the conflict between raising our kids to be comfortable with their digital future while protecting them from online harm?

There's lots of talk of regulation. Age verification is a perennial topic and if it works and implemented perfectly, it might help some people some of the time. Perfect implementation is rarely a defining feature of government initiatives and it's very unlikely that inventive teens won't find a way around it, but that doesn't mean it's not worth trying. From a harm minimisation point of view, the purpose is not so much to implement a perfect impenetrable barrier, it's to reduce harm. Think of it as being akin to age restrictions on buying cigarettes and alcohol - some kids might find a way around it some of the time, but age restriction minimise the harm to kids and reinforce social expectations that children should be protected from harmful substances. We can't, however, make the mistake of thinking age verification is a reliable solution or that it won't equally do harm by cutting off the vital online support that vulnerable teens can give each other through social media and messaging apps.

If the age limit only applies to social media sites such as Instagram and TikTok (which tend to be more female dominated) but not online gaming (largely male users), the gendered effect could exacerbate the toxicity of manosphere influencers while isolating girls from each other and their support groups.

Games such as Minecraft and Roblox are (at the time of writing) not going to be included in age-verification requirements. More than 97 million people log into Roblox every day and at least 40 per cent of them are under thirteen years old. In 2024, Roblox generated over $5.6 billion in revenue, mostly through people spending real money on Roblox's virtual currency.

Most online games are designed to manipulate users into spending more money than they want or intend or often even understand. Children are particularly vulnerable to these tactics. Again, there is little to no regulation or protections for children using these games and parents have almost no access to information about the algorithm and physiological tricks embedded in the game design.[149]

Even if the federal government can resist the lobbying power of the richest corporations on the planet, how do we decide what is valuable information for children and what is dangerous? What rights do they have to participate in the world – including the online world – and is restricting those rights protecting them or harming them?

There are some very useful websites for teens that provide non-judgemental, fact-based information about preventing sexually transmitted infections (STIs) and unwanted pregnancies. This is almost impossible to do without describing the sexual acts that can lead to pregnancy or put someone at risk of an STI. Some teens, for example, still believe the myth that withdrawing from penis-in-vagina intercourse before ejaculation will prevent pregnancy. Accurate contraception information must explain that this is not the case. Effective STI education must explain that unprotected oral, vaginal and anal sex all pose risks. To do that, these sites have to be sure their readers understand exactly what is involved in all those sex acts.

Robust and comprehensive sex education reduces teen births and STI transmission.[150] [151] While we hope that most kids get what they need at school, the evidence says school-based sex ed is not always robust or comprehensives and when teens are left needing or wanting to know more, they look for it online.[152]

In 2013 the UK mandated 'pornography filters' for all internet service providers. A BBC investigation of the filters found that they did not block all porn sites, but they did block access to award-winning sex education site, BISHUK.com and several sexual violence crisis service websites.[153]

It's worth noting that the UK introduced age-verification measures in July 2025 and in the two weeks following their introduction, UK traffic to major porn sites almost halved.[154] It's too early to tell whether this was just a momentary blip, an indication that users are moving away from mainstream porn sites in favour of less restrictive and less visible online places, or the beginning of real long-term change.

Even if age-verification technology works, who decides what constitutes dangerous content for teens? If a fourteen-year-old questioning their sexuality or gender wants to find information and community with like-minded teens, is this harmful or helpful? Should a child from a strictly religious family be allowed to watch a sermon preached by an adherent of a religion their parents believe is heretical? If a teenager wants to understand the mechanics of STIs or the safest way to have anal sex, should they have unrestricted access to this information? Conversely, do their parents have the right to deny them this access? Who should decide whether a TikTok video is promoting nutritious eating or harmful body images? Should parents be allowed to stop a modern Romeo and Juliet messaging each other online?

Do kids have a right to get involved in adult political movements and activities? Climate change is particularly relevant to children and teens but a government that doesn't want radical action could use age-verification technology to block access to information about protests and activism. How do we protect kids from that kind of harm?

Where is the responsibility for providing dangerous content? Does it sit only with the content creator? Doesn't the organisation that provides the platform – and makes massive profits from doing so – have some responsibility? We should have learned from tobacco companies that when corporations must choose between harm minimisation and profit, they will usually choose to keep harming their customers.

The answer to all these questions is that there is no population level solution. They're all case by case, community by community and even then, we almost certainly won't get it right all the time.

The most important thing we can do for children and teens – and for their parents, families, teachers and communities - is give everyone the tools they need to have more informed conversations with each other. They need to know how to develop healthy scepticism about everything they see, keep the worst of it away from the most vulnerable (surely we can all agree that child abuse, advocating violence, and rape videos are not OK for anyone but particularly not for children) and take a minimal harm reduction approach to the rest of it.

While we can (and many of us do) worry about the harm that might come from our kids' online lives, there is no definitive line in the sand we can draw about how much screen time is safe or what apps are dangerous. Suffice to say that evidence suggests there is a link between mental-health issues in young people and 'excessive' use of social media or online games.[155] There is so much variation in age, gender, genetics, pre-existing tendencies and other aspects of growing up in the new millennium that no one can be certain how much is too much. We also don't know for sure whether 'excessive' use causes or follows mental-health issues. There is a statistical link between eating ice cream and getting sunburnt. Obviously, no one gets sunburn from eating ice cream, they get it from direct sunlight. But people are more likely to have an ice cream on hot sunny days, which is why we get the correlation. We don't know yet whether excessive online usage is ice cream or sunlight. Either way, it should at least be a flag for concerned parents.

Among its many excellent resources, the eSafety Commission provides a wide range of regularly updated advice for parents on managing screen time and some general guides for typical usage for particular age groups. I've summarised and adapted some of their key advice but if you're worried or want more information, there really is no better place to start than the eSafety website (see Appendix 1).

How to manage screen time[156]

There's no workable rule that applies to all families and all kids. Rather than a specific number of hours, think about (and talk to them about) how their screen time affects them.

Questions to think about and ask your kids:

- Does it cause problems with their sleep and exercise?
- Is it impacting their relationships with friends and family?
- Does it make them feel agitated, scared, angry or anxious?
- Is it getting in the way of completing or enjoying schoolwork?
- Do they struggle to forget about their online activities when they're doing other things?
- Do they show extreme anger when asked to take a break from online activity?

Some tips for managing a balanced approach:

- Start when they are very young and make sure you have regular conversations about online activity and the apps, games and devices your children are using.
- Make sure you also talk about the physical world and the things you both enjoy or do routinely that don't involve the online world.
- Try to find some online games or projects the family can do together so it's not always a solitary activity.
- Don't use online time as a reward/punishment system for behaviour unrelated to their online world.

- Work with your child to create a plan for leisure and entertainment time that has a balance between physical world and online world activities. Find a balance you can all agree on and if possible share it with any family or friends that regularly spend time with your child.

Set some basic boundaries such as

- No devices in the bedroom for younger children
- All screens off in bedrooms after a set time for older children
- No screens at dinner time.
- All devices out of the bedroom during sleep times.
- Explain why you're setting those boundaries and make sure they know the consequences you've set for breaking the rules.

Media literacy

Follow the money: kids need to understand their role as products not customers of the service they use. TikTok, YouTube, and Minecraft are all billion dollar organisations that exist only to generate profit. Set your kid challenges such as identifying every online interaction that is trying to generate profit, like a digital game of Where's Wally. Start with simple things – advertising and 'sales' on game coins, then move on to activities designed to heighten emotions – excitement, insecurity, fear of missing out – and other more subtle tricks. Do ads respond to moods? Some social media algorithms will send girls ads for beauty products as soon as they delete a selfie. Others will push game demo videos onto boys, seemingly just offering hints and workarounds. YouTube channels, self-help, wellness, politics, sports and sleep apps can all be part of the monetised content kids consume without realising its purpose. Challenging them to identify and make note of it is a great way to help them improve their media literacy and decrease their vulnerability to manipulation.

Physical and mental audits: we often don't notice the slow build-up of tension that happens when we spend too long online. Sit with your child after they've been online and both of you run through a physical and mental checklist together. Do you have pain in your head, neck or jaw? Are your shoulders hunched or tense? Do you feel sick, thirsty or hungry? How do you feel mentally? Agitated? Drained? Overstimulated and under-stimulated at the same time? A teen talking about the post TikTok haze to me described it as, 'my brain feels all goopy'. Does your brain feel like that?

This is even more effective if you do the same audit after doing something in the physical world, such as playing sport, walking the dog or dancing. It's not about proving the online world is all terrible (it isn't), it's about making sure your kids are accustomed to monitoring their physical and mental health so they can learn to recognise signs they need a break or a change to clear their minds and bodies.

Safe adults for your kids to talk to: Is this feeling repetitive yet? I hope so. I want you to feel something close to the eye-rolling boredom your kids should feel when you remind them that they have adults in their life who they can turn to when they need help or advice. We all want those adults to include parents but kids also need to have adults who are not parents who can help them with the embarrassing or worrying questions that might be too difficult to ask Mum or Dad. Review all the advice in Chapter 2 about safe adults, what they need to know and what you need to do. It is as relevant for your seventeen year old as it is to your three-year-old.

10

Consent and porn

Pornography wasn't invented in the digital age. Humans have been creating sexual and nude images of each other for almost as long as we have been making art. Every technological advancement in the creation and sharing of information has included porn. Erotic writing and images existed in most ancient civilisations and were shared among the wealthy before the printing press made erotica much more accessible.

Almost as soon as moving pictures were invented in the late 1800s, people were making images of sex and naked women. By 1915, anonymous filmmakers in America, Germany and Argentina had produced hardcore films showing oral sex, threesomes and masturbation.[157]

Rapid developments in technology put videos and then DVDs into many lounge rooms around the world. Since the early 2000s, online streaming services have offered video content to everyone with an internet-enabled device. At every stage, cunning producers immediately recognised the profit potential in using new technology to sell porn.

It's worth noting that every new development was greeted by pearl clutching and doomsday prophets, convinced the production of 'filth' was the end of decency and morality. In 1896, The Vatican wanted to ban Thomas Edison's silent film *The Kiss,* which showed actors May Irwin and John C. Rice exchanging a two-second, closed lip smooch. I'm not suggesting there is no harm in porn, quite the opposite, but we need to remember that porn is not new, and its power is not overwhelming or inevitable.

Porn is simply about giving sound and picture to sexual fantasy. The difference, however, is that imaginative fantasy is self-directed. Porn gives control of the fantasy to someone else – and their profit motive.

Many people have fantasies about things they would never do in real life. But in our own fantasies we can change direction, follow ideas and incorporate emotions into physical responses. Porn puts the fantasy script into the hands of the producers who can then dictate your emotional response (or lack of it) as well as scripting particular acts into your physical response. In a fantasy, even a fantasy about a celebrity or a person you know, your feelings can be real even if you know the scenario is not. You can be in love in the fantasy. You can be excited to be with her, and she can be passionately responsive. Free online porn doesn't typically include those feelings, which require time, skill, talented writers and other expenses. Freely accessible videos are usually just sexual acts, relying on graphic imagery for stimulation. Those acts may not necessarily be the ones the recipient enjoys or was looking for, but once they've started watching it's often simpler to keep going than go searching for content that is closer to their individual preferences.

Online porn in the mid 2020s is not a single, monolithic thing. Much of it, particularly the stuff thrown out on free websites, shows sex without foreplay, condoms, consent or pleasure. The actors either start naked, or they whip their kit off and launch into penetration in the first few seconds. Ethically produced pornography, which depicts consent (between the actors and the characters) and shared joy is also typically distributed ethically, which means it costs money and is not easy for people under eighteen to access.

The algorithms on porn sites work in very similar ways to social media algorithms. They feed their users content that will shame, shock, enrage, excite or provoke some other emotional response that might encourage them to spend money. The feed is constantly changing but sometimes, a few posts go inexplicably viral. The viral posts never last long but the voracious need for new content expands with each one. My Instagram is full of dogs and feminists. My aunt's social media is flooded with people yelling at each other about American politics, my cousin thinks social media is all about cooking and recipes. Her teenage son says all social media is stupid but he spends hours on YouTube watching gamer videos. We all get ads and influencers and suggested content that we scroll right past, but our perception of common content on social media is vastly different.

Porn sites work the same way. If you're always searching for 'amateur' 'middle-aged couple' content, that's what the algorithm will send you. It might try to drag you into more extreme content that you have to pay to watch, but it will do so by laying down a trail of naked, middle-aged breadcrumbs for you to follow. If you're watching, clicking and engaging with 'rough', 'barely legal' 'extreme' or 'XXX' content, the same thing will happen.

Young children and exposure to porn

Even very little children can see sexualised images online. This can happen by accident – 'Siri, show me the bottom of the world' or as a joke, 'Siri, show me boobies'. It could come up if algorithms detect searches on other devices on your home network and feed content or advertisements into the devices children use. Children can also stumble into porn because they're looking for information. If you hear someone talking about a 'blow job' and you don't know what it is but you get a sense it's something 'rude', what would you do? The same thing a six-year-old does – you search the term online. I don't watch porn (so there's no browser history to direct my searches to porn sites) but I don't have any filters on my computer. When I put 'blow job' into a search engine, the first five results are free online porn sites offering categories such as 'rough teen blow job' 'slut blow job' and 'my school life'. There are another 2,630,000,000 results after that. I did not investigate them all, but in the first ten or so pages, around 90 per cent of the results were porn, the rest were sites offering the sort of information that curious six-year-old probably wanted, albeit with a lot more graphic detail than a six-year-old needs.

It's almost impossible to design a useful survey about porn exposure that you could give to an eight-year-old without provoking exactly the kind of curiosity that would lead to porn exposure ('Have you seen pictures of naked people online?' 'No, but now I know about it I'm definitely going to look for them' – what parent would consent to their child participating in that research?)

Ethical research on children's exposure to pornography, therefore, typically involves asking older teens and young adults about their experiences of porn exposure when they were children. If the research is robust, it is then checked, analysed, and checked again before it's published. One result of all this (necessary) work is delay. For example, research by Queensland University of Technology (QUT) published in 2024 said 10 per cent of boys and 8 per cent of girls had seen porn by the time they were eleven years old.[158] These results were from a survey of 15 to 20 year olds conducted in 2018, which means this 2024 data is telling us what eleven-year-olds were seeing between 2009 and 2014.

Technology and access to devices is moving so quickly that it's impossible for robust research to provide real-time data. Teachers and other people who work with kids tell me they're seeing more signs of porn exposure in younger children every year. Their observations do not have the robustness of the QUT research, but they do have the ring of truth.

Children don't watch porn for the same reasons or in the same way as adults. They're not necessarily looking for masturbation aids. They will sometimes share photos and videos with each other. Not always maliciously or sexually, but because its naughty, rude or shocking – and therefore exciting. Or it can be a form of sexual harassment. Whatever the motive, children who share porn images with other children need support not punishment. If they're afraid of getting into trouble they can get locked into a conspiracy of silence, fear and shame, as happened to my Text Friend's son in Chapter 2.

Glimpses of these images or overheard conversation between other children can also provoke curious questions in a search engine, which gets results parents may not want and these results go into the pool of shared images circulating in the playground.

Online porn is a billion dollar industry and about 30 per cent of the data transferred across the internet is porn.[159][160] It is so ubiquitous that it's not surprising that we cannot hide it from our children.

A poll taken in September 2024 said that 60 per cent of people believe parents are the ones most responsible for keeping children safe online. Only 21 per cent said the government and 13 per cent said social media platforms.[161]

I think this is horribly unfair to parents. Online platforms make billions of dollars from feeding unsafe content (such as porn) to every user, regardless of their age or vulnerability. This is a structural issue that parents cannot overcome on their own. If your young child has seen porn or shared it with other children, you do have to address it and I hope this book helps, but it didn't happen because you did something wrong or because your child did something wrong. It happened because there are no protections for children built into high risk but essential infrastructure. Responsibility for that does not lie only with individuals. It is primarily with governments and regulatory bodies who are supposed to ensure all infrastructure is safe, whether it is publicly or privately owned.

Porn and teens

I recently read a research paper, called '"Not my child": parenting, pornography, and views on education'.[162] The researchers conducted a survey of Melbourne parents whose children were between the age of ten and sixteen, asking what they thought about their children's experience with porn. Most of them said that online pornography is a huge issue for children that age, but they didn't believe their own child would look at it. Here are a few quotes from parents in the study:

> 'It is something that I don't really think about because I suspect that they don't do it.'
>
> 'I'm pretty certain that they don't do it because when you get woken up at 11pm at night because he is yelling out on his headphones playing some sort of game and you know he is not looking at porn.'
>
> 'He's got a fairly strong sense of justice and what's right and wrong. So I'm sure he has been at a mate's house and seen inappropriate stuff. But I also know that it's been fleeting, or it's been just a joke like one of his friends was like look at what I have found online. You know, he doesn't seek that kind of thing out.'

When the researchers talked to these parents about the data on children's exposure to pornography (in which they said the average age of first exposure is thirteen, and 80 per cent of boys and 22 per cent of girls has seen porn by the time they are sixteen) most parents said their child was either too mature or too naive (or somewhat confusingly, both) to want to watch porn.[163]

Almost all teens will see porn before they are ready to start exploring sexual touching with each other. If they see it and recognise it as unrealistic, glamorised, monetised adult sex, they probably won't suffer any harm. If, however, they don't understand what it is and especially if it becomes their habitual aid to masturbation, violent or misogynistic content can distort their expectations of what sex should be, how it should feel, what their partners should look like and how they should respond.[164] Watching pornography is also much more common among boys than girls and some teenage girls have never even heard of the acts their partners have been conditioned to believe are everyday activities.[165]

I've heard stories from many teenage girls who were horrified and bewildered by what they perceived as aggression from boys they thought were sweet, or fumbling experiments with touch that suddenly turned into shaky attempts at violent sex acts. They often find out afterwards that the acts that frightened them so much (usually slapping, choking or aggressive attempts at anal sex) are all very common in porn. As one of those girls said to me, 'Well if everyone knows about it, *why the fuck* did no one warn me?'

She's absolutely right that the adults have a responsibility to talk to teens about porn, but *not* to make girls (once again) the gatekeepers of boys' sexuality. The aim must be to make sure that all teens know what porn is, and what it isn't. They need to know about the profit motive to produce extreme content. They need to know about lighting and filters and actors chosen because they have specific body types or very unusual body parts – gigantic penises, silicone filled breasts, malnourished bodies, and faces full of filler don't deserve any moral judgement but teens do need to know that these are not the standards by which they should judge their own developing bodies. They also need a *much* more detailed and nuanced understanding of consent than almost anything they will find in free online porn. And we cannot expect that they learn these things on their own.

If we, as the adults in our children's lives, are not making sure our teens understand all this before they've seen too much porn or started experimenting with sexual touch, we're leaving their sex and consent education in the hands of porn producers. Think of it this way: what would you tell your kids if you discovered that some oily, profit-driven porn producer had been coming into your home when you're not around to teach your children how to think about sex and consent?

How to talk to your kids about porn

It's all very well to say parents should just overcome their embarrassment and talk openly to their kids about porn, but for most of us it's just not that easy. And it's not that easy for our kids either. If I'd tried to talk to my son about porn when he was fourteen his head would have fallen off.

It's often easier to explain sex reproduction and contraception, which are all about biology. They're fact-based subjects and even if it can get a bit embarrassing, it's relatively easy to explain these things without getting too intrusive or personal. Porn, however, is often about masturbation, which for most people is an intensely private matter. (Groups of men or boys watching porn together isn't usually about masturbation, it's performative heterosexuality, done to prove their virility and masculinity to each other.[166])

It's also important to be wary of generalisations. While it's true that teenage boys are more likely to have seen porn than teenage girls, that doesn't mean that all boys use porn for masturbation or even that they like it or find it arousing. Boys often feel pressure to claim arousal or laugh about images they find off-putting or alarming.[167]

Most non-predatory adults have a healthy reluctance to discuss their masturbatory habits with children, even by implication. Kids have the same response – 'EW YUCK GROSS' is the standard response from anyone asked about their parents' sex life. Which makes it very difficult for teachers and parents to talk to kids about the themes and common activities in porn because the loudly unvoiced question hanging over every conversation is *how do you know?*

This is complicated enough when it's one or two parents and one or two kids. Teachers, facing nearly 30 kids in a class, can (quite understandably) find it utterly impossible.

At every age, but particularly in the early teen years, there's always a wide range of understanding and experience in an average classroom. Some teens are sexually confident and experienced at sixteen. Other kids that age are nowhere near ready to even start thinking about it and are disgusted by the very idea of watching people have sex. And yet, teachers need to find a way to make sure all those kids have some understanding of what porn is and how its monetised.

Even if teachers do feel able to manage such a challenging task, there are real risks in doing the research needed to understand what kids might be seeing. Most of them could not (and would not) use work computers to look for trends in porn, particularly using terms like 'teenagers' or 'youth' – that's a very short road to a departmental investigation and terminated employment contract. Even if they could find a way around this, many of them simply don't want to. A teacher from Brisbane told me that while she wanted to help her students understand porn, she couldn't because she knew almost nothing about it. 'I had to ask my brother. It was so embarrassing for both of us, but I tried watching it myself and it was too disgusting. I had to turn it off.'

This quite common response, especially among women, means many parents and teachers don't really know what free porn sites look like. I skimmed through the videos on the front page of one of the major porn sharing sites when I started writing this chapter. To access the site all I had to do was click a button confirming I am over eighteen. Under the button was a link to instructions for parents on how to block access to that particular site. In other words, the site claims to be acting responsibly by making parents responsible for knowing every porn site on the internet and blocking each one on every device used by children, using a publicly available set of instructions that kids can get around simply by doing an incognito search.

I'm no prude but I did find some of it difficult to watch. Most of the women look so very young. Too often they were either feeling or simulating pain. Choking, rough anal sex, slapping or spitting (or a combination thereof) were in almost all the videos featured on the day I checked the site. There were many genres of porn on offer – 'amateur', 'popular with women' or 'female orgasm' tended to show more foreplay, female pleasure and realistic bodies but there were also several racial categories that featured white men degrading women of colour. And categories such as 'rough', 'old/young' and 'hardcore' were basically rape scenes.

As much as I think kids need classes on porn to make sure they see it clearly for what it is, I don't think it is reasonable or fair to expect physical education teachers to teach that class. Both teachers and kids prefer an external educator to do this – if for no other reason than that after they've explained all the issues and answered all the questions, they *leave* and take everyone's embarrassment with them.

A few years ago, I wrote about how teachers and students sometimes react when someone (in this case, it was me) explains porn to the class:[168]

> 'The teacher was listening, sitting at the back of the classroom. She was a bit red in the face but otherwise didn't react when we got to the pornography section. I was talking about how sex with someone who tried to replicate pornography sex was similar to having a professional AFL footballer turn up to your backyard game and start tackling everyone as if it were a Grand Final. One of the boys, with his chin so far down it was pressing into his chest, mumbled something I couldn't hear. I had to ask him to repeat it twice before he put his head up and bellowed 'WHAT ABOUT ANAL?' across the room. The whole class started rocking with laughter (me included).
>
> After they'd settled down, I asked Mumbling Boy if he was trying to ask why there is so much anal sex in pornography. He nodded and said, 'I don't get it, I mean it's just so... YUCK!' I explained about producers wanting to make money and, in the early days of pornography, one way to do that was by breaking taboos. I also added a bit about camera angles – missionary is still the most common sex position for heterosexual couples but there's virtually no way to get a camera in there, so it's rare in pornography. Anal sex, on the other hand, is very easy to film. The boys were all nodding, with 'Oh, I'd never thought of that, but it makes so much sense' looks on their faces.
>
> I happened to glance at the teacher. She was purple in the face and rocking in her chair. I did wonder for a minute if she was going to have a stroke, but we moved on to the next topic (where to go for advice if they need it) and she started breathing again.

When I checked in with her after the class was over, she'd mostly recovered. I thought she might be angry about the things I'd said (rare, but it happens). She wasn't. She was immensely grateful. 'It's so important that someone tells them about the… you know… the thing you were talking about, but my gosh I could never do it. I'd die. I really would. Just like that. Pouff! Dead. Right there on the ground.'

She stared mournfully at the space on the floor where talking about anal sex would lay her corpse.

I've spoken to so many parents who express the same dead-right-there-in-the-floor feelings as that teacher at the idea of talking to their own kids about porn. I get it. And I'm not convinced the 'just get over it' approach is the best one. Obviously, if you can have that discussion with your kids, that's great but don't feel bad if you can't – you are not alone.'

There are many things you can do to help kids get the information they need without confronting porn directly.

You can frame it as a media literacy issue rather than a specific porn thing – 'I'm not prying, but I just want to make sure you know how people who make porn earn money from it.' Or talk about social media algorithms (Chapter 9) and just casually mention that porn use the same tools for the same reasons (profit).

If you have specific concerns and you both just find the topic too embarrassing, try having a pre-arranged conversation with another adult while your kid is nearby and not using headphones. No matter how much you think they ignore you, I can guarantee that if they hear you talking about porn and they can pretend they're not listening, they'll have ears on elastic to hear what you're saying. Prepare the conversation with the other adult beforehand. Work out what you want to say, how you want to say it, and what you want them to know. Then start casually when your kid is around but reading or watching TV or playing a game. You want them to be close enough to you that they can hear you but far enough away that they don't have to participate in the conversation unless they want to. You could even use this book as a starting point: 'I was reading a book about consent the other day and it talked about porn. Did you know why there is so much anal sex in free porn?' Or 'I was really surprised that so much free porn is stuff most people don't usually do in bed.' Or 'it's really awful how violent some of the free porn can be, it must be a horrible shock to girls who have never seen porn if someone tries that stuff on them'. Use the sort of language you'd typically use but don't get too graphic in the first conversation. Just talk about what porn is (videos designed to shock, titillate and make money) and what it isn't (sex the way many people actually do it) and the bodies chosen for porn (most people don't look like that anymore than most men look like Chris Hemsworth in the Marvel movies).

If you want to do any follow-up, wait a few days and then when you're doing something with your kid that doesn't require eye contact (driving, gardening, etc.) casually ask if they heard the conversation and if they have any questions. Or, if you can't bring yourself to talk about the graphic stuff, you could always leave this book lying around open at the porn chapter. By the time they read this bit they'll know exactly what you're doing (hi kids!) but they'll still have the information they need to understand what they're seeing.

A Melbourne mother of a sixteen-year-old boy told me she drove around her inner city suburb until she found a billboard with an unrealistic image of a scantily clad woman (it didn't take long to find). Then she made sure she drove past it with her son and pointed it out as a way of introducing the topic of altered images and unrealistic body types. They ended up talking for hours (she told me she invented an errand on the other side of town so they could just keep driving) and she learned a huge amount about her son: how he was afraid that girls would reject him for being small and skinny, that he thought only big and confident boys could be attractive, and that girls only like sexually experienced boys. She was able to reassure him that none of those things are true and then set out to find men among her friends and family who could talk to her son about overcoming shame.

It's unreasonable to expect that every conversation will go that well, particularly if you've never had those conversations before. But most teens struggle with fears about their bodies, their sexual ability, and their attractiveness. They may not always be comfortable talking to their parents about it, or able to believe that their parents were once young and felt the same feelings, but it's always worth making the effort.

The other option, if you can't break through your mutual embarrassment, is to enlist the help of an adult you trust. Your siblings or old family friends might be able to talk to your kids about sex and porn with less embarrassment for everyone. Ask them how they feel about it, what they'd say, tell them your concerns and what you want your kids to know. If you both feel safe, send them off for a long country drive or a short city walk, and have a break while your village helps raise your child. And don't forget to pay it forward with other parents who need the same help you do.

11

The Manosphere

While image based-abuse and sexual assault are shocking, they shouldn't overshadow the exhausting effect of sexual harassment. The daily 'jokes' and constant subtle digs that both students and teachers have told me are far too common.

This is how one sixteen-year-old girl described the difference between what she called 'the serious shit and the bullshit': 'If I go to the principal and show him a screenshot of Exhausting Boy sharing a faked nude image of me, the principal is going to take it seriously whether he wants to or not. He knows I can go to the cops and he wants to stop me doing that. But if I tried to tell him that every morning Exhausting Boy finds me to ask me if I'm pregnant yet, the principal will just tell me to ignore him, then he'll ignore me.'

The 'are you pregnant yet?' question was a reference to misogyny influencer Andrew Tate's claim that a life without children is pointless for women.[169] I'll come back to Tate, but first, just to be clear on the effect of this form of harassment, Exhausting Boy was making a persistent effort to try to convince one of his classmates that her life is pointless and always will be until she gets pregnant. It's likely that part of the reason he was doing this was precisely because she is an intelligent ambitious girl who refused to feign stupidity or helplessness for the dominant boys in her class. She did her best to ignore Exhausting Boy's harassment but I don't know anyone who could remain unaffected by such deliberately demeaning torment. No one should have to start every day like that, particularly not someone who isn't yet an adult and should be able to depend on the adults around her for support and protection.

If schools are not fulfilling their responsibilities to your child, then parents can and should be advocates. If someone at your child's school is subjecting them to this kind of harassment, the school has an obligation to keep them safe. Most school leaders know this and will do their best, but if they won't work with you, don't give up. Tell the decision makers at the school that you are prepared to take the matter to the Department of Education in your state. Don't make that an empty threat. Education is a state responsibility, and all states have a department that is answerable for school management. I'd like to promise you will get the help you need from state governments, but sadly, you may get nothing more than bureaucratic nonsense. Even so, your child will see the effort you're making on their behalf, that you are serious and active in your care for their safety and feelings, and that you don't believe anyone should have to endure harassment. Seeing your actions on their behalf will have a far greater impact on them than they might be able to express at the time.

Understanding the manosphere

Online influencers who promote fear, hatred and contempt for women are known as manfluencers. Collectively with their online followers and acolytes, they're called the manosphere. Nothing about their ideas or the people they prey on are new, they've been part of the online world since its inception. The most well-known online groups in the manosphere are men's rights activists (MRAs), involuntary celibates (incels), men going their own way (MGTOW) and pick-up artists (PUAs), although there are many other subgroups and new ones spawning every day (see the Glossary for more information on these terms). While each group may have a slightly different focus, they are united in their fear and hatred of women and their belief that men are powerless victims of malevolent feminism.

The other activity they all have in common is relentlessly shaming men, boys and masculinity. I know – we're so often told (by the Manfluencers) that women and feminists are demonising men by openly discussing the evidence that it is men and boys who commit almost all violence against women and girls (as well as the violence against men, boys and non-binary people). This, along with trying to find ways to reach the men and boys who commit this violence and show them another path is according to manfluencers and their hangers-on, harming boys, vilifying men and intimidating women and girls. It serves as a distraction from the intensive shaming of boys, men and masculinity that is embedded across the entire manosphere as a means of enforcing the rigid gender roles outlined in Chapter 5. Without getting unnecessarily theoretical, this process is what famed masculinity theorist Raewyn Connell was writing about when she coined the phrase 'hegemonic masculinity' – meaning the accepted norms of manhood that legitimise men's dominance over women.[170]

That punitive shaming and dominance is best demonstrated by the standard terms for different types of men that came from the manosphere. Most of the terms originated with the incels in the early 2000s, but they are now ubiquitous across all the groups.[171]

- **Alpha males** are the leaders, the ones everyone looks up to because they are confident, dominant, 'manly' men who make money and get women.

- **Betas**, also known as 'cucks' and 'soy boys', among other such demeaning terms, are the followers. Weak, physically small, insecure, they sometimes have a mental illness or neurodivergence that makes them 'undesirable'. Betas, according to manosphere mythology, deserve and get no respect.
- **Omegas** are the weakest of men. Foolish, weaker even than the Betas, terrified of conflict, and unable to stand up for themselves, this group is despised by all.
- **Sigmas** is a relatively new category. This group are similar to alpha males but rather than dominating others, they seek self-mastery. They are attractive to women but often uninterested because their focus is 'grindset' (punishing self-improvement). Think Christian Bale's portrayal of Patrick Bateman in *American Psycho* or Tyler Durden in *Fight Club*. Sigma males are respected but only if they stay isolated and focussed.

Defining themselves and each other by terms like this is one of the many ways men and boys in the manosphere shame each other into conforming with manosphere rules about masculinity. This happens frequently in overtly misogynistic forums but it's also sadly common in places that appear to be supportive. Groups describing themselves as spaces for men and boys who want advice or companionship from other men can easily slip into bullying and shaming men who protest against misogyny or racism.[172]

incels were among the first groups that formed in the newly emerging online world of the 1990s. They started as a niche online group of young men who gathered in the deepest holes of Reddit to commiserate with each other for being, as they saw it, too weak, ugly and hopeless to find a woman willing to provide them with sex. Perhaps unsurprisingly, the incels rapidly spiralled into self-loathing and developed a deep hatred for the women they believed deprived them of sex and the men they perceived as good looking enough to get sex. It became cult-like, men who came out the other side reported being too scared to question basic tenets of the group: that women are cruel and stupid, men who get to have sex with women are the enemy, and changing themselves or their future was impossible.[173]

The apotheosis of the incel movement was Elliot Rodger, a 22-year-old American man who, in 2014, killed six people, injured fourteen others and then shot himself. Before he committed these crimes, he wrote and published an online book called *My Twisted World*, which is almost universally referred to as his 'manifesto'.

I think it's helpful to understand that *My Twisted World* was not a manifesto, in the sense that it wasn't a political document, a call to action or a proposed solution to a social or political problem. It's an autobiography vividly describing Rodger's shame, insecurity and rage about what he believed to be his inadequate masculinity and the resulting cruelty of attractive women who refused him the sex and love to which he believed he was entitled. His response to these perceived injustices was violence, but his violence was intended to be personal and retaliatory not transformative. He planned his massacre meticulously, calling it his 'Day of Retribution'. He wanted personal vengeance, not public change.

Rodger's explanation of how an insecure young man can come to believe that violence is a justifiable method of relieving the shame he feels for failing to live up to his perception of masculinity ideals is both frightening and instructive.[174] He believed that all his crushing insecurity, loneliness and shame stemmed from scorn and contempt of his physically small body and shy awkward personality. He hated the women who he believed were deliberately denying him love and sex. He equally hated the men who did get love and sex from women. He swore vengeance upon them all. Rodger inspired at least two other mass killers from the incel community, but he wasn't the first or the last man to go on a misogynistic killing spree.[175]

In his later years he claimed to view himself as immeasurably superior to the men who were favoured by women. He ascribed their rejection of him to an inherent flaw of womanhood – a brutish and cruel need for brutish and stupid men. This, in his view, was a keenly felt injustice. Underneath the grandiose picture of himself he tried to cling to, however, shame soaked his every interaction with the world.

'No one respects a man who is unable to get a woman,' he wrote in *My Twisted World*. 'A man wearing shorts and a T-shirt would be seen as superior to me if he walks into a store with a beautiful girl on his arm and I walk in all alone. A man having a beautiful girl by his side shows the world that he is worth something, because obviously that beautiful girl sees some sort of worth in him.' [176]

Elliot Rodger was the most extreme expression of gendered shame (see Chapter 6) and I'm not suggesting every vulnerable boy who consumes incel content will end up like him. But even now, more than ten years after his horrific crimes, he is still valorised in incel mythology and parents who hear their son speak positively or admiringly about him need to recognise this as a clear warning that their son is consuming extremist and dangerous content and he needs professional help. If your son's school has counsellors or well-being officers, they will be able to guide you on where to find help for him. Make sure he knows about KidsHelpLine, which is a resource for anyone under 24 years of age. If the school can't help with counselling, you could try talking to your GP or the Men's Referral Service (all the helpline details are in Appendix 1). And don't forget to lean on your village. If there are men in your family or friendship group who you trust, ask them to spend time with your son and talk to him about why he finds Rodger so appealing. Lonely teens can live very much in their online world but don't underestimate how much they are still part of the physical world. The people and relationships in that physical world can be far more important to boys and young men than even they might realise. They can also be the most effective way to bring them back to a more positive view of themselves and the world around them.

I don't want to be alarmist. Rodger was extreme; most boys will never read his book, and many would dismiss him as a loser if they did read it. Parents who hear their sons making off-colour jokes don't need to assume the worst. But we shouldn't ignore them either.

A few years ago, the 'imagine if we' meme took off on TikTok, in that inexplicable way that memes grab hold of the Zeitgeist and suddenly flood our feeds. 'Imagine if we' was mostly teenage boys posting 'joke' videos about going on dates that ended with them murdering the girl they were dating. 'Imagine we went on a gym date but instead of spotting you on bench I pushed the weight as hard as I can on your neck and you just die kinda sounds fun ngl' (not gonna lie), is a typical specimen. It's almost impossible to believe our beloved children would be laughing at, or even making, such videos, but many of them were. Many of them still are. Some are just following a trend without thinking too much about what it means. Others are joining in to demonstrate brotherhood with the original creators or to stave off shaming they think might come from boys who perceive them as weak 'cucks' for not participating. Often, they justify it with excuses such as 'but girls are sharing it too!' Which is true and not unusual. Girls who have been taught to believe in gender myths will sometimes participate in misogyny. As will girls who (like the ones in class with Maths Girl) have learned to join the game to avoid becoming its target. Their participation does not make it less harmful.

Teenage boys can be very dismissive of parents and teachers who object to this kind of content. 'As if I'm actually going to kill someone, that's just *stupid*.'

They're right of course, I don't believe for a minute that the teenage boys making what they think of as jokes are genuinely plotting murder. What they are doing, without knowing it, is desensitising themselves and each other to violence. Killing, strangling, hitting, assaulting women can become nothing more than the butt of a joke or a throwaway line. The girls and non-binary kids around them know better. Violence is not a joke to them, for far too many of them it is a terrifying reality.

A world first study released in Australia in 2025 showed that over the previous twelve years, men's self-reported violence against women has increased across all age groups. The most significant increase, however, was in men aged 18 – 24, which was about 12 per cent in 2013 and by 2022 had more than doubled to 30 per cent.[177]

The reasons for this are multilayered and complex but the influence of the online world can't be ignored. Its relentless, manipulative, escalating delivery of shame and dehumanisation of women magnifies all the beliefs and behaviours we know are contributing risk factors for violence.

Jokes and memes are typical gateways to far more extreme content. When TikTok removes these videos from the platform, boys who found them funny (or whose friends were still talking about them) followed the meme to other platforms where such things are never taken down. There are some corners of the internet so soaked in hatred and distrust of women that being there for just a short time can normalise even the most violent misogyny.

I'm guessing that most people reading this book would have seen (or at least heard about) the Netflix series, *Adolescence* and its depiction of Jamie, a thirteen-year-old boy accused of murdering his classmate,

Katie. The series explores Jamie's engagement with the darker parts of the manosphere and his parent's shocked bewilderment as they try to make sense of the inexplicable violence enacted by their young son. It's worth remembering that murder in Australia is relatively rare and murder by young children is almost unheard of in this country. *Adolescence* is a TV show – a well written, expertly filmed TV show, but still, a fictional portrayal of a very real problem. Boys from loving families can get sucked down into the mire of the manosphere. If they don't get help, they can become cruel, contemptuous and possibly even dangerous to the girls and women around them. Child murder, however, is the least likely outcome. Far more likely is that boys will learn from the manosphere to become difficult, mean, toxic influences in classrooms and social groups, or grow up to become isolated, self-hating, shame-ridden men. Most boys who have solid support at home and a reasonably robust sense of self-worth will be able to reject the worst of the online hatred of women. But we shouldn't take this for granted. We do need to take active steps to prevent our sons being preyed on by online mountebanks trying to profit from youthful male insecurity.

While there was a lot of valuable information in *Adolescence* and it sparked some very useful conversations about boys, men and masculinity, the focus on Jamie as the victim was troubling. Katie, the young girl killed by Jamie in the series was almost forgotten. Her life, her future, everything she could have been and could never be, the loneliness and pain and manipulation that lined her path, almost everything about her, including her murder, was ignored in almost every analysis I heard or read after *Adolescence* was released. Jamie was the focus, the victim, the subject of every discussion. Katie and Jamie were fictional characters and maybe it wouldn't matter so much if this wasn't so typical of public debate about the violence committed by men and boys against girls and women.

The manosphere is harming boys and men, this is undoubtedly true, but it is also training those boys and men to harm everyone. The harm is gendered, as almost everything is, but the women, girls, boys and non-binary people who are targeted by men and boys radicalised by the manosphere are not just bit players in the story of angry, insecure men.

The rise and fall of Andrew Tate

Self-described misogynist Andrew Tate is an ex-kickboxer who was booted off reality TV show *Big Brother UK* in 2016 after racist and homophobic social media posts from 2012 resurfaced, along with a video of him assaulting his ex-girlfriend. Tate said it was a joke, the ex-girlfriend said it was a misunderstanding, and no charges were laid.

Tate and his brother Tristan then started a webcam business and Hustler University (essentially a pyramid scheme for cryptocurrency), which they claim made them millions, billions, or trillions, depending on which video you watch.[178] Tate found notoriety making deliberately provocative statements in far-right-wing online platforms and rapidly built a cult-like following.

By mid 2025, despite having his account temporarily deactivated by Twitter and reactivated by Elon Musk, Tate had just under eleven million followers. Even this significantly underestimates his reach through content shared on YouTube, TikTok, Instagram and millions of group chats and private messages.

At the time of writing, Tate and his brother are on bail in Romania after being charged with rape, human trafficking and forming a criminal gang to sexually exploit women. These charges may have had some small impact on his influence over boys and young men, but Tate insists he is innocent, and his followers are devout.

His primary connection with his audience is through slickly produced videos. He frequently appears topless, puffing cigars, flexing well-maintained muscles, exhorting men and boys to stop being losers, free themselves from the matrix (his umbrella term for power structures such as politics and media) and work hard to be as rich, muscled and adored by women as he claims to be.

I watched hours and hours of Tate's videos so you don't have to and one of his constant and most powerful messages is that men have to fight for what they believe is right. He exhorts his audience to be strong, tough, fit and aggressive in pursuing their goals. Tate offers comfort and reassurance to boys and men who believe in rigid gender roles. He tells them their fear of women is real and the wounds inflicted on masculinity by increasing feminine independence are not imaginary. He identifies their enemies (strong women and weak men) and demands that they rid themselves of shame by relentless aggression against those enemies. He tells fearful, insecure men and boys that they can be rich and powerful and honourable and worthy of respect and admiration. Of course they worship him.

It might be tempting to dismiss Tate and the manosphere as a trivial online phenomenon, but his videos are as mainstream to today's teenage boys as the nightly news was to their grandparents.

He is frank, often funny, and engagingly charismatic. At times he is searingly honest to disguise the deeper lies. He tells boys and young men that the nature of a man – to be strong, brave and fierce – is their sole path to respect and success. He claims to give them a reason to feel pride, to take action, to get up off the couch and go to the gym and to work. So much so that I've even heard mothers say he has been their sons' saviour. What those mothers failed to see is the shame he piles onto boys and men with his vilification of what he says is male weakness.

He is a spiritual descendant of P. T. Barnum – the famous 19th century ringmaster and politician, credited with coining the phrase 'there's a sucker born every minute'. Tate manufactures shame in young men so he can sell them his cure. His pageant of muscle-bound misogyny and wealth is a backdrop for his contempt for men who do not or cannot display the same puffery. *Are you as arrogant as me? As muscular, as rich? Do you control women, money, power, like me? No? Then you are weak and shameful! Despise yourself and everyone you allow to stop you emulating my apex of manhood! Buy your ticket now to my magnificent spectacle or crawl away and die in your hole of womanish weakness. Roll up, roll up, roll up, for the best masculinity show in town...*

Tate is often presented as the face and cause of boys' misogyny and bad behaviour, his name appears in almost every recent research report into the manosphere. Certainly, he is a huge contributor to the current surge of toxic online content, but he is far from being the only one. The underlying issue existed long before Tate and will persist long after he has faded from view. There is a risk in perceiving him as the sole purveyor of misogyny and masculine shame. Teachers are already reporting that older teen boys are now saying they don't watch his videos anymore. This doesn't mean they're not still consuming manosphere content – they are – but if we focus only on Tate, we miss the other, less visible risks. Remember, too, that Tate is not original, he's just new.

Do you remember Milo Yiannopoulos? He was another shallow, right-wing grifter, who created a brief burst of fame in 2014 by positioning himself as the ringmaster of Gamergate[*] despite having

---

[*] Gamergate was a very loose affiliation of gamers, far right political activists, and manosphere adherents who in 2014 and 2015 conducted a sustained and dangerous campaign of harassment against feminism, diversity and progressive ideas in video game culture. Media critic Anita Sarkeesian and game developers Zoe Quinn and Brianna Wu were the primary targets, but the doxing, threats and hate speech spiralled out to include all women who spoke publicly about feminism and anyone who defended them.

earlier labelled gamers as 'pungent beta male bollock scratchers'. Yiannopoulos, like Tate, managed to eke out notoriety and profit for a few years by posturing hatred of women, diversity, and social justice. Again, like Tate, he flew too close to his own delusions and burned off most of his support when he claimed that adult men can have 'perfectly consensual' and 'life-affirming' sex with thirteen-year-old boys.[179]

Such men have always existed.[180] In the 17th century renowned jurist, executor of witches and pious misogynist, Sir Matthew Hale created legal precedence that was to haunt women until the end of the 20th century. His doctrine of corroboration *required* that judges in rape and child sexual abuse trials warn juries they could not trust the testimony of women and children unless it was corroborated by independent (male) witnesses.

Hale believed women were always 'malicious and false witnesses' against men of 'good character'.[181] He described rape as 'an accusation easily to be made and hard to be proved, and harder to be defended by the party accused, tho never so innocent'. In 1973, this statement was described by a US appellate judge (in a judgement overturning a man's conviction for raping a twelve-year-old girl) as one of the most frequently 'quoted passages in our jurisprudence.'[182]

Hale was also the source of the common law rule (later legislated) that a man could not rape his wife because, he said, 'by their mutual matrimonial consent and contract the wife has given herself up in this kind to her husband, which she cannot retract'.[183] Marital rape was not fully criminalised in Australia until the 1990s.

In 1908, Ernest Belfort Bax, known as the 'father of the men's rights movement', wrote *The Legal Subjection of Men* because he was enraged by the English suffragettes' campaign for legislative changes.[184] He advocated for 'the abolition of modern female privilege'. He was particularly incensed by 'the malice of persons, always women, who practically get up the [rape] cases or provoke them' and described a fourteen-year-old girl who reported her father's sexual abuse of her and her eleven-year-old sister as 'one of the most virulent little minxes I ever saw'.[185]

These men, and so many others like them, were the precursors to Andrew Tate. The only difference between him and all his predecessors is reach and immediacy. The online world and the Covid lockdowns created a perfect storm for boys and young men who were isolated, lonely and frightened. The MeToo movement was still very fresh in their minds and many of them saw it as a new wave of feminism that rushed women and girls ahead and away from them. The warrior myth receded even further from their reach, and they saw Tate as their saviour, giving them faith in their importance to the world. Sadly, he's no saviour, he's just another charlatan selling fool's gold, manufacturing shame in young men so he can profit by making shamelessness a virtue.

The manosphere in our algorithms

Anyone with an internet connection knows how easy it can be to lose hours following links, videos and 'related content' on Facebook, Instagram, YouTube, TikTok, or even news sites. It's not called doomscrolling for nothing. Social media algorithms know our age, gender, friends, interests and viewing habits. They will keep serving up content until our batteries die and they do the same thing for children. It's frighteningly easy for a twelve-year-old to follow a seemingly harmless meme down a Reddit rabbit hole and end up in a cesspit of racism and misogyny. If this happens only once, it probably does no harm. But if they return to that cesspit again and again, with no interruption or disruption from their physical world, a sweet, kind, considerate child can be radicalised without ever leaving their bedroom.

This can happen to boys who are not even looking for manosphere content. In a 2024 study published by Dublin City University, researchers set up accounts posing as teenage boys on YouTube and TikTok from a blank smartphone.[186] Some of the accounts actively searched for manosphere content, others looked for innocuous stuff, such as information on gym workouts, sports, and video games. A couple of accounts were completely inactive. All them were fed manosphere content within half an hour, regardless of their searches. If they clicked through or engaged with any of it, within two to three hours, that content was over 75 per cent of their recommended viewing, and between 5 and 14 per cent was right-wing hate and conspiracy theory content.

A similar study demonstrated how boys and young men on YouTube, TikTok and Instagram are targeted by algorithms that can take them from innocuous tutorials about styling their hair to frighteningly violent incel content within five hops.[187]

There are effective ways to disrupt the manosphere and its dangerous messages, and I'll come to that in a moment, but I think it's worth taking a closer look at how Tate's influence is playing out in classrooms, because the boys who follow Tate are not the only ones affected by him.

To put Tate and his ilk in context, they do not have anything close to universal support among teenage boys. The findings from the National Community Attitudes Survey I mentioned in Chapter 1 are supported by a more focused 2023 survey of Australian teenage boys. More than 90 per cent knew of Tate, 35 per cent said he was 'relatable' and 25 per cent saw him as a role model.[188] Again, in a standard co-ed class, there's probably only about three boys in every class who believe Tate's patter (average class size is 26 kids, roughly 50 per cent are boys and roughly 25 per cent of them are Tate acolytes = 26 / 2 x .25 = 3,25).

The boys who reject Tate's posturing often say they're put off by his arrogance and the way he talks about women. As one fifteen-year-old boy told me so succinctly, 'He's just a jerk'. That boy, however, shares a classroom and a playground with Tate supporters. So do the girls and non-binary kids who are so often their target. Tate weaponises his followers against those 23 other kids in the class. He demands that they fight, be 'brave' and 'show some balls'. The teenage expression of this at school looks like Exhausting Boy's daily question about getting pregnant, or telling girls to 'shut up, you're not allowed to talk' when they answer questions, or calling boys who try to stop them 'a weak pussy' or 'a failure' and even trying to fight them after class. Some teens might have the capacity, skill and power to stand up to this behaviour, but many don't. And while we can (and should) help them develop those skills, they are still children, and it is not their responsibility to teach or reprimand the boys in their school who are treating everyone so badly. We send our kids to school so they can learn knowledge and skills to help them succeed in the adult world. I can't imagine any parent wanting their kids to go to school to learn that a few aggressive, dominant, violent boys can destabilise everyone around them without hindrance or consequence.

Apart from the students, the other people deeply affected by Tate acolytes are teachers, particularly young female teachers. Boys brainwashed into toxicity can find in a young female teacher, both an oppressor (a person in a position of authority) and a victim (a woman for whom they must demonstrate contempt to win praise from their peers).

In 2021, the Queensland Teachers' Union, worried by reports they were hearing from their members, surveyed 1202 teachers. The results were disturbing. One in three female teachers said they'd experienced gender-based violence or sexual harassment at work and just over 40 per cent said it came from a student.[189]

Dr Stephanie Wescott and Professor Steven Roberts of Monash University have spent several years researching the effect of online male influencers on boys in Australian schools.[190] Their findings show that teachers, particularly young female teachers, are reporting increasingly frightening and difficult behaviour from upper primary and secondary school boys. Many of these teachers say they can hear and see Andrew Tate as the influence behind it. They report steadily increasing levels of boys being aggressive, sexual, threatening and contemptuous towards female teachers and students.

Research on Victorian public schools in 2024 also showed more than two thirds of teachers were either planning to or considering leaving the profession. While the most common reasons were excessive workloads and poor salary (83 and 71 per cent), the next two were lack of respect for the profession (68 per cent) and student behaviour (65 per cent).[191]

Some teenage boys also know, or come to learn, that the leaders at their school will give implicit support to misogynistic behaviour. Some teachers report being told they are at fault for not knowing how to 'manage a class' or deal with 'high-spirited boys' when their students are asking them for blow jobs or flashing their penis or asking what colour underwear they're wearing, as other boys in the class roar with laughter.

In co-ed schools, girls and non-binary kids watch this happening, watch the boys who do it suffer no consequences, see the female teachers as helpless, powerless and unsupported, and they learn a lesson too. One teacher told me that after a particularly nasty class, a group of girls and queer kids came to comfort her. 'We believe you,' one of them told her, 'Even if no one else does.' The teacher told me this kindness utterly crushed her. 'They're children, it's not their job to look after me, it's my job to look after them and the only lesson they learned from me is that I couldn't do anything to stop it, and no one in charge will believe me or support me. I've never been such a failure as I was right then.' She has decided to give up teaching and find another career.

Parents have a significant role to play here, and it is not giving into the reflex instinct to defend our children against a perceived attack. We do not do our sons any favours when we shield them from accountability for treating women with hostility and contempt. Not only because this behaviour makes them, at best, uncomfortable and at worst dangerous companions for women and girls, but also because the consequences for this behaviour in the adult world can be much more serious than a firm and clear discussion with his parents. Sneering and laughing at women's bodies or clothes or making sexual suggestions and gestures is sexual harassment. It's vile, degrading behaviour that can get them fired or facing criminal charges if they do it as an adult. We, as parents, have a responsibility to our sons and to our communities to make sure they know that and care about it.

Another important way to support teachers is to let the school know that you value the work they do. One letter of support is lovely, it shows much-needed appreciation and respect. One hundred letters of support for a teacher and a request for funding to give them the training and support they need shows school leaders, governments and funding bodies a collective demand for change. This does take time and effort to organise, so you could consider an online petition, which websites such as change.org or petitions.net make quite simple. It's an easy way to connect other parents to a request for funding and proves to schools, teachers and governments that parents know this work is important.

When I try to imagine the boys who follow Tate in romantic relationships, I shudder. Teenage romance is full of passion and clumsiness, but it's where they learn the beginnings of intimacy skills. Not just physical intimacy, but how to talk to the beloved other, how to think about them and build shared happiness and emotional sustenance. How can a boy do this if he is primed to exert control or display contempt and ownership rather than shared and mutual care? Does the inevitable rejection he experiences in response to boorish behaviour just reinforce Tate's message that women cannot be trusted? When and how does he learn to give and enjoy real intimacy?

Manfluencers and the kids who ignore them

Girls also talk about how often their experience of being intimidated, silenced, and undermined is ignored when schools respond to boys' problematic behaviour. A fifteen-year-old girl told me that, after an outbreak of Tate worship manifested itself at her school (one of the boys got into the teacher's laptop and replaced all her teaching videos with Tate videos), the school paid a guest speaker to spend the afternoon talking to the boys about masculinity. The girls who had been systemically victimised by the Tate acolytes were told to go to the library and study. This is not an isolated incident. I've heard about girls being sent home from school early so the boys can go to a presentation by a masculinity speaker without having to feel that the girls are distracting them. I've been told about an entire class of girls being sent off for baking lessons (seriously) and others who get 'fun' activities such as jewellery making or watching a movie while boys who have been sexually harassing and abusing them spend an afternoon soaking up sympathy for their supposed poor mental health and lack of male role models that created this violence..

I'm not suggesting that schools shouldn't get the masculinity guest speakers in, but all the evidence suggests that a single assembly-style event make little or no difference to behaviour.[192] Which makes sense. It probably took months, even years of consuming manosphere content and having it validated by online and offline friends before the behaviour escalated to the point that the school decided they needed to book a masculinity speaker. No matter how good a speaker is, they can't undo all that in one afternoon. And violence is always a choice. Sympathising with the justifications and excuses created by perpetrators of violence is not going to help them choose a different path. All it does is legitimise their choice.

Most secondary schools in Australia need some degree of support to manage the effects of escalating violence and extremist views. They can't do it alone and parents are their most valuable advocates.

You also need to know that the support your school is getting is working. If your child's school is having an assembly or a guest speaker in response to problematic behaviour, ask questions. Will the school offer support and training for teachers and parents as well? Will the school or the speaker do an evaluation of the program? Don't accept a simple 'did you like the speaker?' evaluation, because people who do this work usually know how to be engaging or amusing, but that doesn't mean they're effective. Insist the evaluation includes all students – the boys and all the other kids who were direct or indirect targets of misogyny. The evaluation should ask students about behaviour, not just attitudes: *Do you feel safer in the classroom and the school grounds? Do you feel safer to ask and answer questions in class? Do you still see or experience sexist or bullying behaviour?* Make sure the results of the evaluation are distributed to all the parents and talk to your children about them. If you or your children don't believe the behaviour has changed, ask the school to do more long-term, structural work, such as providing ongoing training and resources for parents, teachers and students, regularly checking in with all the students to find out what's going on for them and building metrics that trigger intervention as soon as problematic behaviours reach a predetermined level.

This is not cheap or easy work to do, so the school will need funding. Local councils are often a good resource for this, check their grants page for community funding opportunities. Or, as suggested above, try some collective action with the school and other parents to lobby state and federal governments for funding.

These are effective strategies, but they take time. As a parent, you probably don't want to wait for glacially slow government action. So, what can you do to interrupt manosphere messages now? I don't think it's helpful to revile people like Tate. He is many things but he's not stupid. He knows his influence depends on his followers ignoring or dismissing people who try to debunk his claims, and he pre-empts them. 'It was a joke', 'It was hyperbole', 'You're taking it out of context' and 'It was ten years ago' are his typical excuses for his worst excesses. Attempting to use those statements as evidence of his toxicity could just reinforce his claims that the only people who disagree with him are people who don't understand him or don't listen to him.

Perhaps the most effective means of disrupting his narrative is to use his own tactics against him. Ask boys who admire Tate whether they think he wants them to apply the same critical lens to his pronouncements as he tells them to apply to 'the matrix'. Ask if they think they should do what Tate thinks is right or what *they* believe to be right? Can they do what he says about looking after their body and mind and the people they love if what they're doing makes women and girls in their life afraid of them? If he is trying to help boys and men, why does he shame them so terribly? If he is telling the truth about making billions of dollars, why is he still asking troubled young men on minimum wage for money?

I'm not suggesting that it's useful to endorse Tate or his appalling claim that he is helping boys and men (he isn't), but some nuance in talking about him might help lower the defensive hackles of his most ardent supporters and provide a way into a helpful discussion.

Tate is probably on his way out. Not only because of the charges of rape and human trafficking (which may or may not ever go to court) but also by just being over-exposed and having nothing new to say, his novelty is wearing off. He has a huge following, and it will take time for them to fall away, but his eventual failure is inevitable.

The next version of Andrew Tate, however, is waiting in the wings. He's practising his patter and polishing the pitchfork he will use to pierce young men in their most vulnerable parts: their fear of masculine failure and the punitive shaming that will be inflicted upon them by other men. Whoever Tate's inevitable successor is, to successfully usurp the throne of the jester king, he will need to be even more shocking, more offensive, more extreme in his attention-grabbing gambits.

We can inoculate our sons against the grifters and con artists who want to manufacture pain for profit, but all the adults in their lives need to actively participate in helping them reject shame in favour of self worth.

How to raise our children to be safe adults

All children deserve support, kindness, empathy and help when they are in trouble. They might need support because someone else is hurting or frightening them. They might need it because they've just realised they've hurt or frightened someone else. They might need help to take responsibility for what they've done and attempt to make reparations. They might need support to ask such reparations from someone who has hurt them. Or they might just need someone to talk things over with while they try to understand a complex world.

Children and teens will get some of that support from each other, but they need the adults in their lives to be the ones providing most of the guidance and protection that will keep them safe. They have a right to expect this of us, it is after all, our job.

Most of this work happens without us thinking about it much. We teach our children values and standards by the way we live our own lives. They learn how to respect themselves and each other by watching how we respect ourselves, our children and other people. Parents and family (of blood or choice) are the people who teach children values and make those values important. They may stray or rebel, but when the foundational values are strong, even the most rebellious teen can turn around.

Many parents of teens have told me they often feel irrelevant in their kids lives. They provide useful transport, laundry and meal services but their kids are far more interested in their friends and their devices than parental advice. I know that feels true, maybe even is true, but I also know what kids say when their parents are not around. A couple of years ago when I was talking to a group of fourteen-year-old boys about role models, I asked them who their heroes were. One of them said, 'my dad' and most of the other boys agreed. 'Yeah, my dad is awesome.' I asked if they knew who their dad's heroes were. None of them did. A few days later I met their parents and told them what the boys had said about their dads. One of the dads cried openly and a few others were teary. They had no idea how their sons saw them or how crucial they were to the boy's understanding of themselves and the kind of man they could become.

The most effective way to protect our kids from harm – and to help them grow up to be the people who protect the next generation of kids from harm- is to be safe adults ourselves. Deliberately, consciously, *actively* safe and protective adults who talk to children and teens, listen to them and give them the respect they deserve from everyone for the rest of their lives.

Afterword

On Hope

While I have tried to include some positive stories, I know much of this book is difficult, even bleak. That's not surprising in a book about consent and preventing sexual violence, but I wanted to finish on a note of hope. I believe we have cause.

I have a well-practised answer to how to hold on to hope, because it's a question I get a lot. I do lots of public speaking events on all kinds of dark topics – domestic and family violence, murder, rape, child sexual abuse, toxic masculinity, and the dangers of been a girl in the world. All the fun stuff. I know how exhausting and frightening it can be. Almost every day there's a new story about another woman killed, raped or abused. Sometimes it feels like we're pushing a huge boulder up a hill and getting nothing but bruises on our hands. But that's not true.

Hope is in the long view, not in yesterday or tomorrow.

My mother can remember getting milk delivered to her house on a horse and cart. When she came to my house yesterday, she got here using a smartphone. This is how much the world has changed in a single lifetime. And she's not done yet.

Australia has seen seismic changes for women in the last 50 years. My mother got married only a couple of years after the removal of the marriage bar (which required that women in the public service give up their job when they got married). The equal pay act had not passed when she started work. The 28 per cent luxury tax on the contraceptive pill was still in place when I was born. Rape in marriage was still legal in some Australian states when I started school, being gay was still a crime in some states when I was in high school, and consent education was not on the curriculum when my daughter was at school. Now I do the work you've read about in this book.

Hope. It lives in our history and in our future. In knowing the battles already won by our mothers and grandmothers and seeing the strength in ourselves and our daughters for the battles yet to come. It's in the trans and non-binary people who fight their own battles, as they always have, but increasingly find they don't have to fight alone. It's in the men who want more for themselves and their sons than they were told they could have. It's in all the thousands of people who never give up on the work they do with children, teens and adults to prevent violence. It's in the persistence and resilience of parents and children, students and teachers, nurses and patients, activists and protesters, and all the people who change the world for the better every day, even if only the tiniest little bit.

We have come a long way in the last hundred years. We'll go even further in the next hundred because change is the only unchanging constant.

Hope lives forever in that certainty.

Appendix 1: Helplines

Support for people who are impacted by violence

In an emergency, where you or someone you know is in immediate danger, call police on 000

If you want to ask for anonymous advice for yourself or someone you know, call one of the helplines listed below, or talk to a trusted GP or nurse practitioner at your local medical centre.

1800RESPECT
24/7 support for people impacted by sexual assault, domestic and family violence and abuse.
www.1800respect.org.au
Ph: 1800 737 732

Sexual Assault Crisis Line
24/7 Support for victims of sexual assault.
Ph: 1800 806 292
www.sacl.com.au

Full Stop Australia
National violence and abuse trauma counselling and recovery service.
Ph: 1800 385 578
www.fullstop.org.au

Suicide Call Back Service
24/7 suicide prevention support.
Ph: 1300 659 467
www.suicidecallbackservice.org.au

Rainbow Sexual, Domestic and Family Violence Helpline
Support for anyone in Australia who is from LGBTIQA+ communities (or their family and friends) who has recently or in the past experienced sexual, domestic or family violence
Ph: 1800 497 212

Men's Referral Service
24/7 Support for men who use violence and abuse.
Ph: 1300 766 491
www.ntv.org.au/get-help/

Blue Knot Foundation
Phone counselling for adult survivors of childhood trauma, their friends, family and the healthcare professionals who support them.
Available between 9am and 5pm, every day.
Ph: 1300 657 380
www.blueknot.org.au

Lifeline
24/7 crisis support and suicide prevention services.
Ph: 13 11 14
www.lifeline.org.au

Children and young people

Kids Helpline
24/7 support and counselling for children and young people aged 5 to 25.
Ph: 1800 55 1800
www.kidshelpline.com.au

Reachout
14 to 25 year olds – All issues.
Parents – Resources and peer support plus phone and online counselling.
Online resources and 24 hour online peer support.
www.au.reachout.com/

Youth Law Australia
Free legal advice and information for young people under 25.
Ph: 1800 950 570
www.yla.org.au

Reporting Child Abuse

In an emergency or if you believe a child is in immediate danger, call police on 000
For non-emergency police questions call 131 444.
Each state and territory has their own service for child abuse reports. Almost all these services have websites, and many have online reporting forms. You can find the list at www.aifs.gov.au/resources/resource-sheets/reporting-child-abuse-and-neglect or search for 'AIFS Reporting child abuse and neglect'

ACT: Child and Youth Protection Services (CYPS)
Ph: 1300 556 729 (24 hours, 7 days a week).

NSW: Department of Communities and Justice, Child Protection Helpline
Ph: 13 21 11 (24 hours, 7 days a week).

NT: Department of Territory Families, Housing and Communities
Ph: 1800 700 250 (24 hours, 7 days a week).

QLD: Department of Child Safety, Seniors and Disability Services
Ph: Child Safety Services' Enquires Unit: 1800 811 810 (Business hours).
Child Safety After Hours Service Centre: 1800 177 135 (24 hours 7 days a week).

South Australia: Department for Child Protection
Ph: Child Abuse Report Line 13 14 78 (24 hours, 7 days a week).

Tasmainia: Department for Education, Children and Young People
Ph: Child Safety Service on 1800 000 123 (24 hours).

Victoria: Department of Families, Fairness and Housing
Business hours (8:45 am – 5:00 pm): Contact the service that covers the area where the child lives (search 'child protection contacts Victoria' to find the LGAs for each division).
North Division Intake – 1300 664 977
South Division Intake – 1300 655 795
East Division Intake – 1300 360 391
West Division Intake – rural and regional only – 1800 075 599
West Division Intake – metropolitan only – 1300 664 977.

After Hours Child Protection Emergency Service 13 12 78 (5:00 pm – 9:00 am Mon–Fri, 24 hours on weekends and public holidays).

Online Safety

eSafety commissioner
The eSafety Commissioner (eSafety) is Australia's independent regulator for online safety. It acts as a safety net across four reporting schemes:
- an Adult Cyber Abuse Scheme
- a Cyberbullying Scheme for Australian children
- an Image-Based Abuse Scheme
- an Online Content Scheme for illegal and restricted content.

The eSafety website provides a wide range of trustworthy and up to date information and research about online risks, current regulatory proposals and laws, as well as guidance on eSafety measures for children and contacts details for trusted eSafety training providers.
You can report online threats, bullying, abuse and illegal content via the reporting form on the eSafety website.
www.esafety.gov.au

Australian Centre to Counter Child Exploitation (ACCCE)
to report image-based abuse and online child sexual exploitation
www.accce.gov.au

Australian Cyber Security Centre (ACSC)
to report a cybercrime, incident or vulnerability
www.cyber.gov.au

Scam Watch
to report and collect resources around online scams
www.scamwatch.gov.au

Eating disorders
Butterfly Foundation
The Butterfly Foundation provides help for people experiencing eating disorders or body image issues, and those that care for them. It also provides support to professionals managing these issues with clients.
Ph: 1800 33 4673
www.butterfly.org.au

Support for First Nations people

13YARN
Confidential, culturally safe crisis support line for Aboriginal and Torres Strait Islander peoples. Available all day, every day.
Ph: 13 92 76
www.13yarn.org.au

Thirrili
Support communities in the aftermath of suicide or other fatal critical incidents
Ph: 1800 805 801
www.thirrili.com.au

WellMob
Social, emotional and cultural well-being online resources for Aboriginal and Torres Strait Islander People
www.wellmob.org.au

Djirra
Aboriginal community-run organisation providing assistance to Aboriginal and Torres Strait Islander victim survivors of family violence and sexual assault
www.djirra.org.au

Mental health support

SANE Helpline
Information, guidance, and referrals to manage mental health care and concerns. Available weekdays from 10am to 10pm AEST.
Ph: 1800 187 263
www.sane.org

Beyond Blue
24/7 support, helping Australians achieve their best possible mental health.
Ph: 1300 224 636
www.beyondblue.org.au

Mindspot
A free service helping people through stress, anxiety, worry and low mood.
Ph: 1800 61 44 34
www.mindspot.org.au

Support for parents

Counselling, information and referral service for parents and carers in each state and territory:

Parent Line TAS
Ph: 1300 808 178
https://www.health.tas.gov.au/health-topics/child-and-youth-health/child-health-and-parenting-service-chaps/parent-line

Parenting WA
Ph: (08) 9368 9368 or 1800 111 546
https://www.wa.gov.au/service/health-care/public-health-services/ngala-parenting-line

Parent Helpline SA
Ph: 1300 364 100
https://www.cafhs.sa.gov.au/services/parent-helpline

Parentline NSW
Ph: 1300 1300 52
www.parentline.org.au

Parentline NT/QLD
Ph: 1300 30 1300
www.parentline.com.au

Parentline VIC
Ph: 13 22 89
www.services.dffh.vic.gov.au/parentline

Carer Gateway
Support and advice for carers or people who support and help others.
Ph: 1800 422 737 (weekdays from 8am to 6pm)
www.carergateway.gov.au

Relationships Australia
Support for people trying to achieve positive relationships or amicable separation.
Ph: 1300 364 277
www.relationships.org.au

PANDA
Supporting families affected by anxiety and depression during pregnancy and in the first year of parenthood.
Monday to Friday, 9am - 7.30pm, Saturday, 9am – 4pm (AEST/AEDT)
Ph: 1300 726 306
www.panda.org.au

13SICK
After hours family medical care - for when your GP is closed.
Ph: 13 742
www.13sick.com.au

Red Nose Grief and Loss Helpline
24/7 bereavement support for those impacted by the death of a child through miscarriage, stillbirth and SIDS.
Ph: 1300 308 307
www.rednose.org.au

Disability services

Disability Gateway
The Disability Gateway has information and services to help people with disability, their family, friends and carers, to find the support they need in Australia.
Ph: 1800 643 787
www.disabilitygateway.gov.au

Children and Young People with Disability Australia (CYDA)
CYDA is a not-for-profit community organisation. We are the peak organisation representing the rights and interests of children and young people with disability (aged 0-25) in Australia.
Ph: 1800 222 660
wwwcyda.org.au

Support for LGBTQIA+ people
Minus18
Articles, resources and training for lesbian, gay, bi, trans, queer and/or intersex young people. As well as professional training to help support LGBTQI people.
www.minus18.org.au

QLife
Counselling and referral for people of all ages who are lesbian, gay, bisexual, trans, queer and/or intersex.
Phone counselling and online chat available every day from 3pm to 12am.
Ph: 1800 184 527
www.qlife.org.au

Rainbow Door
Specialist advice to LGBTIQA+ people and their friends and families
10am to 5pm, 7 days a week
Ph: 1800 729 367 or text 0480 017 246
www.switchboard.org.au/rainbow-door

Charlee
Suicide prevention hub made by LGBTIQA+ people who have thought about suicide, lived through suicide attempts, supported others in distress and live with the pain of loss through suicide
www.charlee.org.au

Thorne Harbour Health
Counselling, health promotion, inclusion and support for people of diverse sexualities and genders, and those with HIV in Victoria.
Ph: 1800 134 840
www.thorneharbour.org

Gambling
Gambling help online
Counselling, information and support for anyone affected by gambling.
24/7 Phone and online chat
Ph: 1800 858 858
www.gamblinghelponline.org.au

Appendix 2: Data and statistics

Until the last fifteen years or so, we didn't really know much about violence and abuse in Australia. Police and court data was the main source of information and as far back as the seventies, most informed people knew that domestic and sexual violence was rarely reported to police.[193]

The Australian Bureau of Statistics collects vast quantities of data including the Personal Safety Survey, the primary source of data on people's experience of violence. There are many other organisations and researchers that provide robust statistics, and those datasets are constantly being updated and improved. I've listed a summary of some of the most recent data below, but new and better data sources are coming out all the time and can't be updated in a print book.

I have a section on my website that lays out all these statistics with links and explainers. It's regularly updated and expanded as new research comes out and can go into much more granular detail than I can manage in a book.

You can find it on my website www.janegilmore.com For those of you who just want a brief overview, I've summarised the most well-known and robust data below.

Sexual Assault conviction rate

	2021	2022	2023
Sexual assault reported to police (a)	31,074	32,771	36,318
Estimated percent of women who report Sexual Assault to police (b)	8%	8%	8%
Estimated unreported sexual assaults	343,312	362,060	401,248
Estimated total sexual assaults	374,386	394,831	437,566
Guilty outcomes (c)	3,978	4,289	4,733
Sexual Assault Conviction Rate Australia	1%	1%	1%

Sources:
(a) Australian Bureau of Statistics, Recorded Crime - Victims (2023)
(b) Australian Bureau of Statistics, Personal Safety, Australia, (2016 & 2021/22)
(c) Australian Bureau of Statistics, Criminal Courts, Australia (2022-23)

* Data on sexual assaults and court outcomes are not an exact match for year on year comparison due to delays in investigation and trials. This data is presented as an overall indication of the ongoing national disparity between sexual assault reported to police, unreported sexual assault, and court outcomes for people accused of sexual assault.

False Allegations of sexual violence

The research on false allegations most often cited as reliable and robust (by organisations such as Victoria Police and the Australian Institute of Health and Welfare) was published in 2016 and it estimated that confirmed false allegations were about 5 per cent of all sexual assaults reported to police.[194] Other research in Australia and New Zealand estimates false allegations were around 2 per cent of all reports to police. Studies in Europe and the United States of America typically found that between 1 and 10 per cent of sexual assault reports to police are false.[195]

Gender based violence

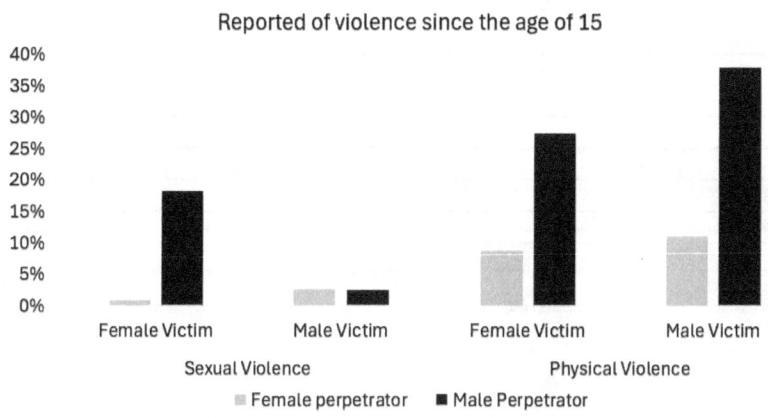

Source: Australian Bureau of Statistics, Personal Safety Survey 2016

Technology facilitated abuse

The most robust report on technology facilitated abuse in Australia was published in 2022, so it's possible, even likely that the prevalence has increased since then. However, the report does give a sound baseline to our understanding of how common it is for people to experience this form of abuse.[196]

The study analyses survey responses from just over 4500 people in 2021/22 and found:

- 74% of women and 68% of men aged 18 to 24 disclosed experiencing some form of technology facilitated abuse in their lifetime.
- 77% of women said the perpetrator was a man in their most recent experience
- 44% of men said the perpetrator was a man in their most recent experience

Child Abuse

The Australian Child Maltreatment Study (ACMS) is the most detailed and precise measurement of the many forms of violence experienced by children. The report found that: 'In total 62.2% of the people who were able to respond to the survey had experienced at least one type of child maltreatment. Exposure to domestic violence was the most common form of maltreatment, followed by physical abuse, emotional abuse, and sexual abuse. The least common type of maltreatment was neglect.' [197]

Of the people who participated in the survey,
- 32% experienced physical abuse
- 37% of girls and 19% of boys experienced child sexual abuse
- 31% experienced emotional abuse
- 40% experienced exposure to domestic violence
- 9% experienced neglect

Child Sexual Abuse	Age of survey respondent in 2021		
	Aged 16 - 24	Aged 25 - 44	Aged 45+
Adult perpetrator	12%	18%	20%
Adolescent perpetrator	18%	14%	12%

Acknowledgements

Acknowledgements

Writing a book like this is a monumental task and it would never have come together the way it did without the help and support from many people.

Living with a writer is never easy. There's no floating gently in and out of the muse's arms. It's either frozen panic or pushing madly against deadlines, both of which leave me terribly bad tempered and more than a little in need of a shower. My wonderful daughter, Bella, dealt with this with remarkable patience, cups of peppermint tea, and the occasional reminder to walk the dog or go to bed.

My agent, Jacinta di Mase believed in this book before I knew what it was about. She never lost faith in it or in me, even during the worst of the book's troubled journey to completion. I wouldn't have got through it all without her and I'll never be able to thank her enough.

Sally Heath saw the potential in an idea and was a beacon of calm integrity throughout a very difficult time. I am so grateful for her insight, patience and astute understanding of what I wanted to achieve.

I am also very lucky to be a member of The Writing Circle, where for the last seven years I have learned to be a better writer and a better person. Meg, Jen, Krati, Andy, Carolyn, Kate, Anders, and Fran, thank you for helping me build the chalice.

Huge thanks to Dr Stephanie Wescott, Carolyn Lee and Jess Hill for giving so much of their valuable time and expertise to making sure I hadn't fallen into a puddle of ridiculousness by the time I got to the end of the manuscript.

- Acknowledgements -

I was fortunate to find so many teachers, early childhood educators and school leaders who were willing to talk to me. I was surprised and touched that they put so much trust in me and were so candid about the strengths and failings of their schools and their work. I can't name them, but I would never have been able to finish the book without them. I hope they never doubt how grateful I am for their generosity and enthusiasm.

I've also been honoured by the trust parents gave me. They shared stories about being the best and the worst and the most ordinary of parents. They were hilarious and heartbreaking and inspiring, and they are the reason I wrote this book.

The children and teens whose stories are scattered through the book were so often the ones who were breaking new ground in every step of their lives. They do it with such courage, curiosity, humour and resilience.

Finally, but most importantly, I am so grateful to my mother. For everything. There's too much to list or explain, but so much of what I am and have is because of her. She'll never believe it and I'll never forget it.

Endnotes

1. Flynn, A. (2023). *Image-Based Sexual Abuse*. Oxford Research Encyclopedia of Criminology. https://oxfordre.com/criminology/view/10.1093/acrefore/9780190264079.001.0001/acrefore-9780190264079-e-534
2. Commonwealth of Australia. (2022). *National Plan to End Violence against Women and Children 2022-2032*. Department of Social Services, Canberra https://www.dss.gov.au/system/files/resources/national-plan-end-violence-against-women-and-children-2022-2032.pdf
3. Simon, J. (2014, December 12). *What's the Difference Between Activism and Journalism?* Nieman Reports. https://niemanreports.org/whats-the-difference-between-activism-and-journalism/
4. Adhikari, D. (2017, April 10). *The case against: Can journalists be activists?* Aljazeera. https://www.aljazeera.com/opinions/2017/4/10/the-case-against-can-journalists-be-activists
5. *Sex Education*. (1924, October 28). The Age (Melbourne, Vic. : 1854 - 1954) 1924 http://nla.gov.au/nla.news-article155531698
6. Mitchell, A., Smith, A., Carman, M., Schlichthorst, M., Walsh, J. & Pitts, M. (2011). *Sexuality Education in Australia in 2011*. Monograph Series No. 81, Melbourne: La Trobe University, the Australian Research Centre in Sex, Health & Society https://www.latrobe.edu.au/__data/assets/pdf_file/0019/148060/Sexual-Education-in-Australia-2011.pdf
7. Flood, M., Fergus, L. & Heenan, M. (2009). *Respectful Relationships Education: Violence prevention and Respectful Relationships Education in Victorian secondary schools*. Victorian Department of Education and Early Childhood Development, Melbourne. https://eprints.qut.edu.au/103414/
8. Ollis, D. & Dyson, S. (2017) *Respectful relationships education: a case study of working in schools*. Eliminating Gender-Based Violence https://www.researchgate.net/publication/323675900_Respectful_relationships_education_a_case_study_of_working_in_schools
9. Kearney, S., Gleeson, C., Leung, L., Ollis, D., Joyce, A. (2016). *Respectful relationships education in schools: the beginnings of change*. Deakin University. https://hdl.handle.net/10536/DRO/DU:30088089
10. Gilmore, J. (2022). *Teaching Consent: Real Voices from the Consent Classroom*
11. Laurence, W., (2022). *Boston Globe Reports on Child Sexual Abuse by Roman Catholic Priests*. EBSCO. https://www.ebsco.com/research-starters/law/boston-globe-reports-child-sexual-abuse-roman-catholic-priests
12. Davies, C. (2023). *Promoting healthy relationships: a whole-community approach. Understanding Abuse in Young People's Intimate Relationships*. Bristol University Press. https://www.researchgate.net/publication/377606553_Promoting_healthy_relationships_a_whole-community_approach
13. State of Victoria. (2016). *Royal Commission into Family Violence: Summary and recommendations*. Parl Paper No 132 (2014–16). http://rcfv.archive.royalcommission.vic.gov.au/Report-Recommendations.html
14. Ollis, D. (2018). *Building Respectful Relationships: Stepping out against gender- based violence*. State of Victoria (Department of Education and Training), Melbourne https://www.ungei.org/sites/default/files/Building-Respectful-Relationships-Stepping-Out-against-Gender-Based-Violence-2018-eng.pdf
15. Sanderson, C. (2004). *The Seduction of Children : Empowering Parents and Teachers to Protect Children from Child Sexual Abuse*. Jessica Kingsley Publishers. https://uk.jkp.com/products/the-seduction-of-children
16. Wescott, S. & Roberts, S. (2024). *Conceptualising school-level responses to sexual harassment of women teachers as institutional gaslighting*. British Journal of Sociology of Education, 46(1), 1–18. https://doi.org/10.1080/01425692.2024.2409267

17. Wescott, S. & Roberts, S. (2025). *On the utility of the concept of 'school-related gender-based violence' (SRGBV) in the context of escalating gendered violence in schools*. Critical Studies in Education, 1–19. https://doi.org/10.1080/17508487.2025.2514278

18. Potts, A. (1999). *Public and private schooling in Australia: Some historical and contemporary considerations*. The Phi Delta Kappan, Vol. 81, No. 3 pp. 242-245 https://www.jstor.org/stable/20439629

19. Patterson, M. (2021). *MP Bev McArthur says consent should be taught by parents, not teachers*. The Standard https://www.standard.net.au/story/7179450/consent-not-a-topic-for-classrooms-mp-says/

20. Weinstein, R., Walsh, J., & Ward, L. (2008). *Testing a New Measure of Sexual Health Knowledge and Its Connections to Students' Sex Education, Communication, Confidence, and Condom Use*. International Journal of Sexual Health, 20(3), 212–221. https://doi.org/10.1080/19317610802240279

21. Pacella, R., Nation, A., Mathews, B., Scott, J., Higgins, D., Haslam, D., Dunne, M., Finkelhor, D., Meinck, F., Erskine, H., Thomas, H., Malacova, E., Lawrence, D., & Monks, C. (2023) *Child maltreatment and health service utilisation: findings from the Australian Child Maltreatment Study*. Med J Aust 2023; 218 (6 Suppl): S40-S46. https://doi.org/10.5694/mja2.51892

22. Coumarelos, C., Roberts, N., Weeks, N. & Rasmussen, V. (2023). *Attitudes matter: The 2021 National Community Attitudes towards Violence against Women Survey (NCAS), Findings for young Australians*. ANROWS. https://www.ncas.au/ncas-2021-findings-for-young-australians

23. KPMG. (2016). *The cost of violence against Women and their Children in Australia*. Department of Social Services. https://www.dss.gov.au/sites/default/files/documents/08_2016/the_cost_of_violence_against_women_and_their_children_in_australia_-_summary_report_may_2016.pdf

24. Commonwealth of Australia. (2023). *Budget Papers 2023 – 2024, Federal Financial Relations Budget Paper No. 3*, Canberra https://archive.budget.gov.au/2023-24/

25. Australian Bureau of Statistics. (2024). *Schools*. ABS. https://www.abs.gov.au/statistics/people/education/schools/latest-release

26. Hendriks, J., Marson, K., Walsh, J., Lawton, T., Saltis, H. & Burns, S. (2024). *Support for school-based relationships and sexual health education: a national survey of Australian parents*. Sex Education, 2023, Vol 24 No 2, pp 208–224 https://doi.org/10.1080/14681811.2023.2169825

27. Moran, C. & Van Leent, L. (2021). *Primary school parents' perspectives on relationships and sexuality education in Queensland, Australia*. Sex Education, 22(2), 184–197. https://doi.org/10.1080/14681811.2021.1908982

28. Gilmore, J. (2022). *Teaching Consent: Real voices form the consent classroom*.

29. Cahill, H., Pretlove, R., Forster, R., Farrelly, A., Higham, L., Meakin, C., Beadle, S., Crofts, J., Smith, K. & Macrae, J. (2024). *Resilience, rights and respectful relationships*. Department of Education, Victoria, Australia. https://arc.educationapps.vic.gov.au/learning/sites/respectful-relationships/1785/Respectful-Relationships-resources

30. Wescott, S. (2020) *The child and the strict father: invoking metaphor in the Safe Schools debate*. Discourse: Studies in the Cultural Politics of Education, 41:6, 829-840, https://doi.org/10.1080/01596306.2018.1550053

31. Hamilton-Smith, L. (2024, November 11). *Premier rubbishes One Nation's claims children taught masturbation in Safe Schools program*. ABC News. www.abc.net.au/news/2017-11-11/annastacia-palaszczuk-rubbishes-one-nations-safe-schools-claim/9141520

32. Louden, W. (2016) *Review of Appropriateness and Efficacy of the Safe Schools Coalition Australia Program Resources*. Australian Government Department of Education and Training. https://www.education.gov.au/student-resilience-and-wellbeing/resources/review-appropriateness-and-efficacy-safe-schools-coalition-australia-program-resources

33. Peled, D. (2017, November 14). *One Nation MP Steve Dickson says sorry for wording about Safe Schools sex education allegations*. ABC News. https://www.abc.net.au/news/2017-11-14/one-nation-mp-steve-dickson-sorry-wording-safe-schools-claims/9147210

34. Louden, B. (2017, October 2). *FactCheck: will Safe Schools be 'mandatory' if same-sex marriage is legalised?* The Conversation. www.theconversation.com/factcheck-will-safe-schools-be-mandatory-if-same-sex-marriage-is-legalised-84437

35. Coldwater, K. (2023). *Decoding the Misinformation-Legislation Pipeline: an analysis of Florida Medicaid and the current state of transgender healthcare.* Journal of the Medical Library Association : JMLA, 111(4), 750–761. https://doi.org/10.5195/jmla.2023.1724
36. Smith, E. & Robinson, K. (2024). *'Teaching up' at school and home: young people's contemporary gender perspectives.* Aust. Educ. Res. 51, 995–1013. https://doi.org/10.1007/s13384-024-00702-z
37. Commonwealth of Australia. (2021). *National Strategy to Prevent and Respond to Child Sexual Abuse 2021–2030.* National Office for Child Safety https://www.childsafety.gov.au/resources/national-strategy-prevent-and-respond-child-sexual-abuse-2021-2030
38. Ibid
39. Quadara, A., Nagy, V., Higgins, D. & Siegel, N. (2015). *Conceptualising the prevention of child sexual abuse: Final report (Research Report No. 33).* Melbourne: Australian Institute of Family Studies. https://aifs.gov.au/research/research-reports/conceptualising-prevention-child-sexual-abuse
40. Commonwealth of Australia. (2017). Royal Commission into Institutional Responses to Child Sexual Abuse Final Report, Recommendations. https://www.childabuseroyalcommission.gov.au/final-report
41. Tucci, J. and Mitchell, J. (2021). *Still unseen and ignored: Tracking Community Knowledge and Attitudes about Child Abuse and Child Protection in Australia.* Australian Childhood Foundation, Melbourne https://www.childhood.org.au/app/uploads/2021/08/Still-unseen-and-ignored-report-FINAL-REPORT-17aug21.pdf
42. Faller, K. (1984). *Is The Child Victim Of Sexual Abuse Telling The Truth?* Child Abuse & Neglect, Vol 8. pp 473-481 https://doi.org/10.1016/0145-2134(84)90029-2
43. Bennett, N. & O'Donohue, W. (2014). *The Construct of Grooming in Child Sexual Abuse: Conceptual and Measurement Issues.* Journal of Child Sexual Abuse, 23(8), 957–976. https://doi.org/10.1080/10538712.2014.960632
44. Winters, G., Kaylor, L., & Jeglic, E. (2021). *Toward a Universal Definition of Child Sexual Grooming.* Deviant Behavior, 43(8), 926–938. https://doi.org/10.1080/01639625.2021.1941427
45. Plummer, M. (2017). *Lived Experiences of Grooming Among Australian Male Survivors of Child Sexual Abuse.* Journal of Interpersonal Violence, 33(1), 37-63. https://doi.org/10.1177/0886260517732539
46. Winters, G., & Jeglic, E. (2017). *Stages of Sexual Grooming: Recognizing Potentially Predatory Behaviors of Child Molesters.* Deviant Behavior, 38:6, 724-733, http://dx.doi.org/10.1080/01639625.2016.1197656
47. O'Donnell, K., Woldegiorgis, M., Gasser, C., Scurrah, K., Andersson, C., McKay, H., Hegarty, K., Seidler Z. & Martin, S. (2025). *Ten to Men: The use of intimate partner violence among Australian men.* Australian Institute of Family Studies https://aifs.gov.au/tentomen/insights-report/use-intimate-partner-violence-among-australian-men
48. State Government of Victoria. (2023). *Child sexual exploitation and grooming.* https://www.schools.vic.gov.au/child-sexual-exploitation-and-grooming
49. Mathews, B., Finkelhor, D., Pacella, R., Scott, J. G., Higgins, D. J., Meinck, F., Erskine, H. E., Thomas, H. J., Lawrence, D., Malacova, E., Haslam, D. M. & Collin-Vézina, D. (2024). *Child sexual abuse by different classes and types of perpetrator: Prevalence and trends from an Australian national survey.* Child Abuse & Neglect, 147, 106562. https://doi.org/10.1016/j.chiabu.2023.106562
50. Whitebread, D., Coltman, P., Jameson, H. & Lander, R. (2009). *Play, Cognition and Self-Regulation: What exactly are children learning when they learn through play?* Educational & Child Psychology Vol. 26 No. 2, 2009 http://dx.doi.org/10.53841/bpsecp.2009.26.2.40
51. Cahill, H., Pretlove, R., Forster, R., Farrelly, A., Higham, L., Meakin, C., Beadle, S., Crofts, J., Smith, K. & Macrae, J. (2024). *Resilience, rights and respectful relationships.* Department of Education, Victoria, Australia https://arc.educationapps.vic.gov.au/learning/sites/respectful-relationships/1785/Respectful-Relationships-resources
52. Ibid

53 Better Health Channel. (2022, July 4). *Trauma and children – tips for parents* https://www.betterhealth.vic.gov.au/health/healthyliving/trauma-and-children-tips-for-parents
54 Commonwealth of Australia. (2025). *National Office for Child Safety, Signs and indicators of child sexual abuse.* https://www.childsafety.gov.au/about-child-sexual-abuse/signs-and-indicators-child-sexual-abuse
55 The Royal Children's Hospital Melbourne. (2019). *How to evaluate sexualised behaviour in children.* https://www.rch.org.au/uploadedFiles/Main/Content/vfpms/Sexualised%20behaviour%20VFPMS%20seminar%202019.pdf
56 SECASA. (2025). *SECASA Current Training Programs* https://www.secasa.org.au/programs-and-services/training-education-programs/
57 eSafety Commissioner. (2025). *Track, harass, repeat: Attitudes that normalise tech-based coercive control.* Canberra: Australian Government https://www.esafety.gov.au/sites/default/files/2025-04/Track-harass-repeat-attitudes-around-tech-based-coercive-control.pdf
58 Australian Institute of Health and Welfare. (2025). *Child sexual abuse.* https://www.aihw.gov.au/family-domestic-and-sexual-violence/types-of-violence/child-sexual-abuse
59 Australian Institute of Family Studies. (2025). *Responding to children and young people's disclosures of abuse.* https://aifs.gov.au/resources/practice-guides/responding-children-and-young-peoples-disclosures-abuse#what-to-do
60 Australian Institute of Health and Welfare. (2023). *Early childhood and transition to school.* https://www.aihw.gov.au/reports/australias-welfare/childcare-and-early-childhood-education
61 Cahill, H., Pretlove, R., Forster, R., Farrelly, A., Higham, L., Meakin, C., Beadle, S., Crofts, J., Smith, K. & Macrae, J. (2024). *Resilience, rights and respectful relationships.* Department of Education, Victoria, Australia
62 Wescott, S. & Roberts, S. (2025). *On the utility of the concept of 'school-related gender-based violence' (SRGBV) in the context of escalating gendered violence in schools.* Critical Studies in Education. https://doi.org/10.1080/17508487.2025.2514278
63 Cahill, H., Pretlove, R., Forster, R., Farrelly, A., Higham, L., Meakin, C., Beadle, S., Crofts, J., Smith, K. and Macrae, J. (2024). *Resilience, rights and respectful relationships.* Department of Education, Victoria, Australia
64 Ibid
65 Ibid
66 Lumanlan, J. (2020) *12 Signs of Child Anxiety – and What to Do About Them, Your Parenting Mojo.* https://yourparentingmojo.com/12-signs-of-child-anxiety-and-what-to-do-about-them/
67 Guy-Evans, O. (2025). *Fight, Flight, Freeze, or Fawn: How We Respond to Threats.* Simply Psychology, https://www.simplypsychology.org/fight-flight-freeze-fawn.html
68 Seitz, J. (2022). *Secrecy, Sex Abuse, and the Practice of Priesthood.* The Routledge Handbook of Religion and Secrecy, (1st ed.). Routledge. https://doi.org/10.4324/9781003014751
69 Cahill, H., Pretlove, R., Forster, R., Farrelly, A., Higham, L., Meakin, C., Beadle, S., Crofts, J., Smith, K. and Macrae, J. (2024). *Resilience, rights and respectful relationships.* Department of Education, Victoria, Australia
70 Ibid
71 Turner, K. and Brown, C. (2007). *The Centrality of Gender and Ethnic Identities across Individuals and Contexts.* Social Development, 16: 700-719. https://doi.org/10.1111/j.1467-9507.2007.00403.x
72 Collard, S. (2025). *Birth alerts are meant to help children at risk of abuse. They are routinely used against Aboriginal mothers.* The Guardian. https://www.theguardian.com/australia-news/2025/jun/18/birth-alerts-are-meant-to-help-children-at-risk-of-abuse-they-are-routinely-used-against-aboriginal-mothers
73 Hill, J. (2015). *Suffer the children.* The Monthly. Schwartz Media https://www.themonthly.com.au/november-2015/essays/suffer-children
74 Allnock, D. & Miller, P. (2013). *No one noticed, no one heard: a study of disclosure of childhood abuse.* NSPCC, London https://learning.nspcc.org.uk/research-resources/2013/no-one-noticed-no-one-heard

75 Esposito, C. (2015). *Child sexual abuse and disclosure*. NSW Government Family & Community Services, Sydney https://dcj.nsw.gov.au/documents/service-providers/deliver-services-to-children-and-families/child-protection-services/child-sexual-abuse-disclosure-research.pdf

76 Wang, Z., Asokan, G., Onnela, J. (2024). *Menarche and Time to Cycle Regularity Among Individuals Born Between 1950 and 2005 in the US*. JAMA Netw Open. 2024;7(5):e2412854. https://doi.org/10.1001/jamanetworkopen.2024.12854

77 Wisbey, M. (2024) *Girls' periods starting earlier and more irregular: Study*. Royal Australian College of General Practitioners (RACGP), https://www1.racgp.org.au/newsgp/clinical/girls-periods-starting-earlier-and-more-irregular accessed June 2025

78 Department of Education and Early Childhood Development. (2011). *Catching On Early – Sexuality Education for Victorian Primary Schools*. Melbourne.

79 Ibid

80 Raising Children Network Australia. (2023). *Childhood sexual development and sexual behaviour: 7-9 years* https://raisingchildren.net.au/school-age/development/sexual-development/sexual-behaviour-7-9-years

81 Waling, A., Fisher, C., Ezer, P. et al. (2021). *"Please Teach Students that Sex is a Healthy Part of Growing Up": Australian Students' Desires for Relationships and Sexuality Education*. Sex Res Soc Policy 18, 1113–1128. https://doi.org/10.1007/s13178-020-00516-z

82 Lee RLT, Yuen Loke A, Hung TTM, Sobel H. (2018). *A systematic review on identifying risk factors associated with early sexual debut and coerced sex among adolescents and young people in communities*. J Clin Nurs. 27: 478–501. https://doi.org/10.1111/jocn.13933

83 McManus, I. (2009). *The history and geography of human handedness*. I.E.C. Sommer & R.S. Kahn (eds), Language Lateralization and Psychosis, Cambridge University Press https://jhanley.biostat.mcgill.ca/bios601/CandHchapter06/HistoryGeographyHumanHandedness.pdf

84 State Government of Victoria. (2025). *Key terms used in the LGBTIQA+ inclusive language guide*. https://www.vic.gov.au/inclusive-language-guide/key-terms-used-in-lgbtiqa-inclusive-language-guide

85 Oxford English Dictionary, s.v. 'culture (n.),' 2023. //doi.org/10.1093/OED/4985345143

86 Australian Bureau of Statistics. (2024) *Schools*. https://www.abs.gov.au/statistics/people/education/schools/latest-release

87 Department of Education and Early Childhood Development. (2011). *Catching On Early – Sexuality Education for Victorian Primary Schools*. Melbourne.

88 Cahill, H., Pretlove, R., Forster, R., Farrelly, A., Higham, L., Meakin, C., Beadle, S., Crofts, J., Smith, K. and Macrae, J. (2024). *Resilience, rights and respectful relationships*. Department of Education, Victoria, Australia.

89 Spender, D. (1979). *Language and sex differences*. In H .Andresen (Ed.), Osnabrucker Beitra̋ge zur Sprachtheorie: Sprache und Geschlecht II (pp. 38–59). Oldenburg, Germany: Red.

90 Coates, J. (2013). *Women, Men and Language : A Sociolinguistic Account of Gender Differences in Language*. Pearson Education Limited, New York https://doi.org/10.4324/9781315645612

91 Popp, D., Donovan, R., Crawford, M., Marsh, K., Peele, M. (2003). *Gender, Race, and Speech Style Stereotypes*. Sex Roles. 48. 317-325. http://dx.doi.org/10.1023/A:1022986429748

92 Cutler A, & Scott D. (1990). *Speaker sex and perceived apportionment of talk*. Applied Psycholinguistics. 1990;11(3):253-272 http://dx.doi.org/10.1017/S0142716400008882

93 Ashmore, R. & Boca, F. (2013). *The Social Psychology of Female-Male Relations: A Critical Analysis of Central Concepts*. Academic Press. https://shop.elsevier.com/books/the-social-psychology-of-female-male-relations/ashmore/978-0-12-065280-8

94 Schmader, T. Block, K. (2015). *Engendering Identity: Toward a Clearer Conceptualization of Gender as a Social Identity*. Sex Roles 73, 474–480. https://doi.org/10.1007/s11199-015-0536-3

95 Walby, S. (1989). *Theorising Patriarchy*. Sociology, 1989 Vol 23 No 2, pp 213-234. https://doi.org/10.1177/0038038589023002004

96 Department of Education and Early Childhood Development. (2011). *Catching On Early – Sexuality Education for Victorian Primary Schools*. Melbourne

97 McLemore, E. (2020). *Medieval Sexuality, Medical Misogyny, and the Makings of the Modern Witch*. University of Notre Dame, https://sites.nd.edu/manuscript-studies/2020/10/30/medieval-sexuality-medical-misogyny-and-the-makings-of-the-modern-witch/
98 Cawthorne, N. (2019). *Witches: The history of a persecution.* Arcturus. London.
99 Fulu, E. (2009). *Intimate Partner Violence In The Maldives: Globalisation And The Negotiation Of Gender And Islam.* PhD Thesis. University of Melbourne. https://search.worldcat.org/title/intimate-partner-violence-in-the-maldives-globalisation-and-the-negotiation-of-gender-and-islam/oclc/650476406
100 Gilligan, J. (1997). *Violence: Reflections on a National Epidemic.* New York, NY: Vintage Books. P 110
101 Gruber, D., Hansen, L., Soaper, K., & Kivisto, A.J. (2014). *The role of shame in general, intimate, and sexual violence perpetration.* K.G. Lockhart (Ed.), Psychology of Shame: New Research. New York: Nova Science. 2014 http://www.antoniocasella.eu/restorative/Gruber_2014.pdf
102 River, J. & Flood M. (2021) *Masculinities, emotions and men's suicide.* Sociology of Health & Illness, Vol 43, pp 910-927 7 https://doi.org/10.1111/1467-9566.13257
103 Hill, J. (2019) *See What You Made Me Do*, Black Inc., Carlton, Australia
104 The Men's Project & Flood, M. (2024). *The Man Box 2024: Re-examining what it means to be a man in Australia.* Melbourne: Jesuit Social Services https://jss.org.au/programs/research/the-man-box/
105 Raising Children Network Australia. (2023). *Self-esteem in children: 1-8 years.* https://raisingchildren.net.au/toddlers/behaviour/understanding-behaviour/about-self-esteem
106 Cahill, H., Pretlove, R., Forster, R., Farrelly, A., Higham, L., Meakin, C., Beadle, S., Crofts, J., Smith, K. and Macrae, J. (2024). *Resilience, rights and respectful relationships.* Department of Education, Victoria, Australia.
107 Sexual Health Victoria. (2024). *Level 9- 10 Sexual Continuum.* SVH Everybody Education. https://shvic.org.au/assets/resources/Grade_9and10_Sexual-continuum.pdf
108 Gilmore, J. (2022). *Teaching Consent: Real Voices from the Consent Classroom*
109 Vrankovich,S., Hamilton, G. & Powell A. (2024). *Young Adult Perspectives On Sexuality Education In Australia: Implications For Sexual Violence Primary Prevention.* Sex Education. https://doi.org/10.1080/14681811.2024.2367216
110 Ollis, D. (2018). *Building Respectful Relationships: Stepping Out Against Gender Violence,* State of Victoria. Department of Education and Training. Melbourne https://www.ungei.org/sites/default/files/Building-Respectful-Relationships-Stepping-Out-against-Gender-Based-Violence-2018-eng.pdf
111 Graziani, C., & Chivers, M. L. (2024). *Sexual Shame and Women's Sexual Functioning.* Sexes, 5(4), 739-757. https://doi.org/10.3390/sexes5040047
112 Rennie, E. (2023). *'What a lying slut': the (re)production of rape myths in online misogyny towards women disclosing their experiences of rape through the #MeToo movement.* Journal of Gender-Based Violence, 7(2), 204-219. https://doi.org/10.1332/239868021X16699044856526
113 Gilmore, J. (2022) *Teaching Consent: Real Voices from the Consent Classroom*
114 Ibid
115 Catlin, W., Dzidic, P., Phillips, M. et al. (2025) *Restricted to the "Traditional Female Role": Australian high-school graduates' perceptions of the messaging about women in relationship and sex education.* SN Soc Sci 5, 19 https://doi.org/10.1007/s43545-025-01053-5
116 Foster, T. & Callagan, R. (2025). *Encouraging Body Safety in Kids: A Guide for Parents & Caregivers.* Ability Psychological Services. https://abilitypsychologyservices.com/blog-%26-resources/f/encouraging-body-safety-in-kids-a-guide-for-parents-caregivers
117 WhatPhonePlans. 2021 *Australian Smartphone Statistics.* www.whatphone.com.au/guide/australian-smartphone-statistics
118 Fagan, B. (2019). *The bizarre social history of beds.* The Conversation. www.theconversation.com/the-bizarre-social-history-of-beds-122517
119 Lauricella, A., Cingel, D., Beaudoin-Ryan, L., Robb, M., Saphir, M. & Wartella, E. (2016). *The Common Sense census: Plugged-in parents of tweens and teens.* San Francisco, CA: Common Sense

Media. https://www.commonsensemedia.org/sites/default/files/research/report/common-sense-parent-census_whitepaper_new-for-web.pdf
120 Rideout, V., Peebles, A., Mann, S. & Robb, M. (2022). *Common Sense census: Media use by tweens and teens, 2021*. San Francisco, CA: Common Sense. https://www.commonsensemedia.org/sites/default/files/research/report/8-18-census-integrated-report-final-web_0.pdf
121 Cheung, C., & Yue, X. (2012) *Idol worship as compensation for parental absence*. International Journal of Adolescence and Youth, 17(1), 35–46. https://doi.org/10.1080/02673843.2011.649399
122 Fitzgerald. T., Bromberg, M., (2017) *Should 'pro-ana' websites be criminalised in Australia?* The Conversation https://theconversation.com/should-pro-ana-websites-be-criminalised-in-australia-79197
123 The National Eating Disorders Collaboration. *Eating Disorders in Australia*. https://nedc.com.au/eating-disorders/eating-disorders-explained/eating-disorders-in-australia viewed July 2025
124 Butterfly Foundation. (2022). *The reality of eating disorders in Australia*. The Butterfly Foundation https://butterfly.org.au/wp-content/uploads/2022/08/The-reality-of-eating-disorders-in-Australia-2022.pdf
125 Inside Out. *Eating Disorder Prevalence Among Transgender People*. https://insideoutinstitute.org.au/assets/eating-disorder-prevalence-among-transgender-people.pdf viewed July 2025
126 Volpe, U., Tortorella, A., Manchia, M., Monteleone, A., Albert, U. & Monteleone, P. (2016) *Eating disorders: What age at onset?* Psychiatry Research, Volume 238, 2016, Pages 225-227, ISSN 0165-1781, https://doi.org/10.1016/j.psychres.2016.02.048
127 Hall, R. & Keenan, R. (2025) *More than half of top 100 mental health TikToks contain misinformation, study finds*. The Guardian. https://www.theguardian.com/society/2025/may/31/more-than-half-of-top-100-mental-health-tiktoks-contain-misinformation-study-finds
128 Dodd, V. (2025). *Misogynistic content driving UK boys to hunt vulnerable girls on suicide forums*. The Guardian. https://www.theguardian.com/uk-news/2025/apr/12/uk-counter-terror-police-nca-misogyny-com-networks
129 Commonwealth of Australia. *National Plan to End Violence against Women and Children 2022-2032*
130 Flynn, A. (2023). *Image-Based Sexual Abuse*. Oxford Research Encyclopedia of Criminology. https://doi.org/10.1093/acrefore/9780190264079.013.534
131 Powell, A., Flynn, A. & Hindes, S. (2022). *Technology-facilitated abuse: National survey of Australian adults' experiences*. ANROWS. https://anrows-2019.s3.ap-southeast-2.amazonaws.com/wp-content/uploads/2022/07/27172214/4AP.3-Flynn-TFa3-Survey-of-VS.pdf
132 Bell, I., Nicholas, J., Broomhall, A., Bailey, E., Bendall, S., Boland, A., Robinson, J., Adams, S., McGorry, P. & Thompson, A. (2023). *The impact of COVID-19 on youth mental health: A mixed methods survey*. Psychiatry Research, vol. 321. https://doi.org/10.1016/j.psychres.2023.115082
133 Ringrose, J., Milne, B., Horeck, T., & Mendes, K. (2024). *Postdigital Bodies: Young People's Experiences of Algorithmic, Tech-Facilitated Body Shaming and Image-Based Sexual Abuse during and after the COVID-19 Pandemic in England*. Youth, 4(3), 1058-1075. https://doi.org/10.3390/youth4030066
134 Flynn, A., Cama, E., Powell, A. & Scott, A. J. (2022). *Victim-blaming and image-based sexual abuse*. Journal of Criminology, 56(1), 7-25. https://doi.org/10.1177/26338076221135327
135 Patchin, J., & Hinduja, S. (2020). *Sextortion Among Adolescents: Results From a National Survey of U.S. Youth*. Sexual Abuse, vol. 32, no. 1, pp. 30–54. https://doi.org/10.1177/1079063218800469
136 Internet Watch Foundation. (2023). *Sexually coerced extortion*. www.iwf.org.uk/annual-report-2023/trends-and-data/sexually-coerced-extortion
137 Liggett O'Malley, R. & Smith, K., (2024). *Suicidal Ideation Among Male Victim-Survivors of Financial Sextortion*. Victims & Offenders, 2024, pp. 1–22. http://dx.doi.org/10.1080/15564886.2024.2379818
138 McGlynn, C., Johnson, K., Rackley, E., Henry, N., Gavey, N., Flynn, A. & Powell, A., (2021). *"It's Torture for the Soul": The Harms of Image-Based Sexual Abuse*. Social & Legal Studies. Vol. 30, no. 4, pp. 541–562. https://doi.org/10.1177/0964663920947791

139 Grant, H. (2025, April 5). 'I didn't start out wanting to see kids': are porn algorithms feeding a generation of paedophiles – or creating one? The Guardian, https://www.theguardian.com/society/2025/apr/05/i-didnt-start-out-wanting-to-see-kids-are-porn-algorithms-feeding-a-generation-of-paedophiles-or-creating-one

140 Brown, R. (2023) *Prevalence of viewing online child sexual abuse material among Australian adults* Trends & Issues in Crime and Criminal Justice, No. 682. Australian Institute of Criminology. https://www.aic.gov.au/sites/default/files/2023-12/ti682_prevalence_of_viewing_online_csam_among_australian_adults.pdf

141 Australian Federal Police (2021) AFP warn about fast growing online child abuse trend. https://www.afp.gov.au/news-centre/media-release/afp-warn-about-fast-growing-online-child-abuse-trend

142 Think U Know, Parents and carers guide to online child sexual exploitation. https://www.thinkuknow.org.au/resources-tab/parents-and-carers

143 Wilkins, A. (2023). *ChatGPT AI passes test designed to show theory of mind in children.* New Scientist. https://www.newscientist.com/article/2359418-chatgpt-ai-passes-test-designed-to-show-theory-of-mind-in-children/

144 Phiddian, E. (2025, June 11) *AI companion apps such as Replika need more effective safety controls, experts say.* ABC News. https://www.abc.net.au/news/science/2025-06-11/ai-companion-apps-safety-controls-isolation-replika-loneliness/105261042

145 Brooks, R. (2023) *I tried the Replika AI companion and can see why users are falling hard. The app raises serious ethical questions.* The Conversation. https://theconversation.com/i-tried-the-replika-ai-companion-and-can-see-why-users-are-falling-hard-the-app-raises-serious-ethical-questions-200257

146 Maples, B., Cerit, M., Vishwanath, A. et al. (2024) *Loneliness and suicide mitigation for students using GPT3-enabled chatbots.* npj Mental Health Res 3, 4. https://doi.org/10.1038/s44184-023-00047-6

147 eSafety Commission. (2025). *AI chatbots and companions – risks to children and young people.* https://www.esafety.gov.au/newsroom/blogs/ai-chatbots-and-companions-risks-to-children-and-young-people

148 Bates, L. (2025, June 10). *Misogyny in the metaverse: is Mark Zuckerberg's dream world a no-go area for women?* The Guardian https://www.theguardian.com/society/2025/jun/10/the-misogyny-of-the-metaverse-is-mark-zuckerbergs-dream-world-a-no-go-area-for-women

149 Ryan, J. (2025, May 9). *Does video game monetisation harm children – and what is Australia doing about it?* The Guardian, https://www.theguardian.com/games/2025/may/10/does-video-game-monetisation-harm-children-and-what-is-australia-doing-about-it

150 Mark, N., & Wu, L. (2022). *More comprehensive sex education reduced teen births: Quasi-experimental evidence.* Proceedings of the National Academy of Sciences of the United States of America, 119(8), e2113144119. https://doi.org/10.1073/pnas.2113144119

151 Sales, J., Milhausen, R., & Diclemente, R. (2006). *A decade in review: building on the experiences of past adolescent STI/HIV interventions to optimise future prevention efforts.* Sexually transmitted infections, 82(6), 431–436. https://doi.org/10.1136/sti.2005.018002

152 Ezer, P., Kerr, L., Fisher, C. M., Heywood, W., & Lucke, J. (2019). *Australian students' experiences of sexuality education at school.* Sex Education, 19(5), 597–613. https://doi.org/10.1080/14681811.2019.1566896

153 Deri Smith, M., (2013). *Porn filters block sex education websites.* BBC News. https://www.bbc.com/news/uk-25430582

154 Edwards, C. & Vallance, C. (2025) *Porn site traffic plummets as UK age verification rules enforced.* BBC News. https://www.bbc.com/news/articles/c17n9k54qz2o

155 Andreassen, C., Billieux, J., Griffiths, M., Kuss, D., Demetrovics, Z., Mazzoni, E., & Pallesen, S. (2016). *The relationship between addictive use of social media and video games and symptoms of psychiatric disorders: A large-scale cross-sectional study.* Psychology of Addictive Behaviors, 30(2), 252–262. https://doi.org/10.1037/adb0000160

156 eSafety Commission. (2025). *Screen Time.* https://www.esafety.gov.au/parents/issues-and-advice/screen-time

157 Patil, P. (2025). *10 Oldest Porn in the World*. Oldest.org, https://www.oldest.org/people/porn/
158 Crabbe, M., Flood, M., & Adams, K. (2024). *Pornography exposure and access among young Australians: a cross-sectional study*. Australian and New Zealand journal of public health, 48(3), 100135. https://doi.org/10.1016/j.anzjph.2024.100135
159 Statista. (2024). *Market size of the online pornographic and adult content industry in the United States from 2018 to 2023*. www.statista.com/statistics/1371582/value-online-website-porn-market-us/
160 Wifitalents. (2024) *Pornography Industry Statistics: Latest Data & Summary*. www.wifitalents.com/statistic/pornography-industry/
161 Essential Research. (2024, September 23). *Responsibility for keeping children safe online*. https://essentialreport.com.au/questions/responsibility-for-keeping-children-safe-online
162 Davis, A., Wright, C., Curtis, M., Hellard, M., Lim, M., & Temple-Smith, M. (2019). *"Not my child": parenting, pornography, and views on education*. Journal of Family Studies, 2019, Vol 27, No 4, 573-588. https://researchers.cdu.edu.au/en/publications/not-my-child-parenting-pornography-and-views-on-education
163 Lim, M., Agius, P., Carrotte, E., Vella, MA, Hellard, M. (2017). *Young Australians' use of pornography and associations with sexual risk behaviours*. Australian and New Zealand Journal of Public Health. Volume 41, Issue 4 , pp 438-443. https://doi.org/10.1111/1753-6405.12678
164 Wright, P., Sun, C., Steffen, N., & Tokunaga, R. (2015). *Pornography, Alcohol, and Male Sexual Dominance*. Communication Monographs. 82:2, 252-270. http://dx.doi.org/10.1080/03637751.2014.981558
165 Pirrone, D., Zondervan-Zwijnenburg, M., Reitz, E. et al. (2022). *Pornography Use Profiles and the Emergence of Sexual Behaviors in Adolescence*. Arch Sex Behav 51, 1141–1156. https://doi.org/10.1007/s10508-021-02140-3
166 Hald, G.M. (2006). *Gender Differences in Pornography Consumption among Young Heterosexual Danish Adults*. Arch Sex Behav 35, 577–585. https://doi.org/10.1007/s10508-006-9064-0
167 Johansson, T., & Hammarén, N. (2007). *Hegemonic Masculinity and Pornography: Young People's Attitudes toward and Relations to Pornography*. The Journal of Men's Studies, 15(1), 57-70. https://doi.org/10.3149/jms.1501.57
168 Gilmore, J. (2022) *Teaching Consent: Real Voices from the Consent Classroom*
169 Brandon From ILETD *A Life Without Children Is Pointless*. Andrew Tate. YouTube. www.youtube.com/watch?v=kuk0KsXENJY
170 Connell, R., & Messerschmidt, J. (2005). *Hegemonic Masculinity: Rethinking the Concept*. Gender & Society, 19(6), 829–859. https://doi.org/10.1177/0891243205278639
171 Nelson, A. (2025). *Manosphere Glossary: 15 Toxic Terms Parents Should Know*. Bright Canary. https://www.brightcanary.io/manosphere-glossary/
172 Wakefield, S. (2025). *Jack joined a social media group to find online support. Instead he found a culture of toxic masculinity*. ABC News. https://www.abc.net.au/news/2025-04-19/better-bloke-project-blokes-advice-mental-health-toxic/104975574
173 Bates, L. (2020). *Men Who Hate Women*. Simon & Schuster. London.
174 Vito, C., Admire, A. & Hughes, E. (2018). *Masculinity, aggrieved entitlement, and violence: considering the Isla Vista mass shooting*. NORMA,13:2, 86-102. https://doi.org/10.1080/18902138.2017.1390658
175 Bosman, J., Taylor K., and Arango, T., (2019, August 10). *A Common Trait Among Mass Killers: Hatred Toward Women*. New York Times. https://www.nytimes.com/2019/08/10/us/mass-shootings-misogyny-dayton.html
176 Rodger, E. (2014). *My Twisted World: The Story of Elliot Rodger* https://www.documentcloud.org/documents/1173808-elliot-rodger-manifesto/
177 O'Donnell, K., Woldegiorgis, M., Gasser, C., Scurrah, K., Andersson, C., McKay, H., Hegarty, K., Seidler Z., & Martin, S. (2025). *Ten to Men: The use of intimate partner violence among Australian men*. Australian Institute of Family Studies. https://aifs.gov.au/tentomen/insights-report/use-intimate-partner-violence-among-australian-men
178 Purtill, J. (2022, August 22). *Booted from Facebook and Instagram, Andrew Tate is now being scrubbed from TikTok. Is this the end for his misogyny?* ABC News. www.abc.net.au/news/2022-08-22/misogynist-influencer-andrew-tate-is-being-scrubbed-from-tiktok/101356652

179 Lynskey, D. (2017). *The rise and fall of Milo Yiannopoulos – how a shallow actor played the bad guy for money*. The Guardian https://www.theguardian.com/world/2017/feb/21/milo-yiannopoulos-rise-and-fall-shallow-actor-bad-guy-hate-speech
180 Gilmore, J. (2022). *Rape is Rape*. Meanjin. https://meanjin.com.au/essays/rape-is-rape/
181 Hale, M. (1734). *Historia Placitorum Coronae* vol 1. London. Nutt & Gosling. 635-636. https://archive.org/details/historiaplacitor01hale
182 *United States of America v. David A. Wiley, Appellant*, 492 F.2d 547 (D.C. Cir. 1974) https://law.justia.com/cases/federal/appellate-courts/F2/492/547/321860/
183 Han, T. (1989). *Marital Rape – Removing The Husband's Legal Immunity*. Malaya Law Review. Vol 31 No 1, pp 112–128. https://www.jstor.org/stable/24865602
184 Bax, E. (1908). *The Legal Subjection of Men*. New Age Press. https://archive.org/details/legalsubjection00baxgoog
185 Gilmore J. (2017) *Did you forget International Men's day? Don't worry - the men's rights activists did too*. The Sydney Morning Herald https://www.smh.com.au/lifestyle/did-you-forget-about-international-mens-day-this-year-youre-not-alone-20171121-gzpsnx.html
186 Baker, C., Ging, D., & Andreasen, M. B. (2024). *Recommending Toxicity: The Role of Algorithmic Recommender Functions on YouTube Shorts and TikTok in Promoting Male Supremacist Influencers*. DCU Centre, Dublin City University, 2-33o. https://antibullyingcentre.ie/wp-content/uploads/2024/04/DCU-Toxicity-Full-Report.pdf
187 Papadamou, K., Zannettou, S., Blackburn, J., Cristofaro, E., Stringhini, G., & Sirivianos, M. (2021). *"How over is it?" Understanding the Incel Community on YouTube*. Proceedings of the ACM on Human-Computer Interaction. Vol 5. 1-25 http://dx.doi.org/10.1145/3479556
188 Defina, M., Rowland, F., Wood, K., Orr, C. (2023). *Who is Andrew Tate and why do young men relate to him?* Research Series: What's really going on with young men? (Edition 3). The Man Cave, Melbourne, Australia. https://themancave.life/wp-content/uploads/2024/10/Andrew-Tate-research-paper.pdf
189 Spalding, P. (2021). *'Expect Respect: Addressing gendered violence at work'*, Queensland Teachers Union.
190 Wescott, S., Roberts, S., & Zhao, X. (2024). *The problem of anti-feminist 'manfluencer' Andrew Tate in Australian schools: women teachers' experiences of resurgent male supremacy*. Gender and Education. Vol36, No 2, pp 167-182. https://research.monash.edu/en/publications/the-problem-of-anti-feminist-manfluencer-andrew-tate-in-australia
191 Longmuir, F., Delany, T., Lampert, J., Wilkinson J. (2024). *What The Profession Needs Now For The Future: Discussion Paper One. Work In Victoria's Public Schools*. Monash University. https://www.monash.edu/__data/assets/pdf_file/0004/3802756/WPNNF_MonashAEU_Paper2.pdf
192 Pound, P., Denford, S., Shucksmith, J. (2017). *What is best practice in sex and relationship education? A synthesis of evidence, including stakeholders' views*. BMJ Open Vol 7 https://doi.org/10.1136/bmjopen-2016-014791
193 Evatt, E., Arnott, F., Deveson, A. (1977). *Royal Commission on Human Relationships: Final Report Volume 5*. Australian Government Publishing Service. Canberra https://apo.org.au/node/34438
194 Ferguson C., Malouff J. (2016). *Assessing Police Classifications of Sexual Assault Reports: A Meta-Analysis of False Reporting Rates*. Arch Sex Behav. Vol 45 No: 5, pp 1185-93. https://doi.org/10.1007/s10508-015-0666-2
195 Orchowski, L., Bogen, K.W., Berkowitz, A. (2022). *False Reporting of Sexual Victimization: Prevalence, Definitions, and Public Perceptions*. In: Geffner, R., White, J.W., Hamberger, L.K., Rosenbaum, A., Vaughan-Eden, V., Vieth, V.I. (eds) Handbook of Interpersonal Violence and Abuse Across the Lifespan. Springer, Cham. https://psycnet.apa.org/doi/10.1007/978-3-319-89999-2_193
196 Powell, A., Flynn, A., & Hindes, S. (2022) *Technology-facilitated abuse: National survey of Australian adults' experiences*. Research report, 12/2022. ANROWS. https://www.anrows.org.au/publication/technology-facilitated-abuse-national-survey-of-australian-adults-experiences/
197 Haslam D, Mathews B, Pacella R, Scott JG, Finkelhor D, Higgins DJ, Meinck F, Erskine HE, Thomas HJ, Lawrence D, Malacova E. (2023). *The prevalence and impact of child maltreatment in Australia: Findings from the Australian Child Maltreatment Study: Brief Report*. Australian Child Maltreatment Study, Queensland University of Technology. https://doi.org/10.5694/mja2.51873

www.ingramcontent.com/pod-product-compliance
Lightning Source LLC
Chambersburg PA
CBHW022023290426
44109CB00015B/1290